The World of Small States

Volume 2

Series editors
Petra Butler
Wellington, New Zealand

Caroline Morris
London, United Kingdom

More information about this series at http://www.springer.com/series/15142

Teleiai Lalotoa Mulitalo Ropinisone Silipa Seumanutafa

Law Reform in Plural Societies

Teleiai Lalotoa Mulitalo Ropinisone Silipa Seumanutafa
TC Beirne School of Law
University of Queensland
St. Lucia, Queensland
Australia

The World of Small States
ISBN 978-3-319-65523-9   ISBN 978-3-319-65524-6 (eBook)
https://doi.org/10.1007/978-3-319-65524-6

Library of Congress Control Number: 2017956057

© Springer International Publishing AG 2018
This work is subject to copyright. All rights are reserved by the Publisher, whether the whole or part of the material is concerned, specifically the rights of translation, reprinting, reuse of illustrations, recitation, broadcasting, reproduction on microfilms or in any other physical way, and transmission or information storage and retrieval, electronic adaptation, computer software, or by similar or dissimilar methodology now known or hereafter developed.
The use of general descriptive names, registered names, trademarks, service marks, etc. in this publication does not imply, even in the absence of a specific statement, that such names are exempt from the relevant protective laws and regulations and therefore free for general use.
The publisher, the authors and the editors are safe to assume that the advice and information in this book are believed to be true and accurate at the date of publication. Neither the publisher nor the authors or the editors give a warranty, express or implied, with respect to the material contained herein or for any errors or omissions that may have been made. The publisher remains neutral with regard to jurisdictional claims in published maps and institutional affiliations.

Printed on acid-free paper

This Springer imprint is published by Springer Nature
The registered company is Springer International Publishing AG
The registered company address is: Gewerbestrasse 11, 6330 Cham, Switzerland

For my late father, our very own philosopher, Teleiai Lalotoa Mulitalo Ropinisone Silipa Seumanutafa of Apia and Saoluafata; my mother Lalotoa Mulitalo nee Asaua of Samatau and Lalomalava; my siblings Faamalu Peretiso and Rosalina Mulitalo; Mulitalo Lealali Mapuonā and Afamasaga Faauiga Mulitalo; Tupa'imatuna Fata Margaret and Tapuaī Laupu'a Fiti; Meli Kathy and Rev. Siaosi Samoa; Tupa'isiva Tamari and Emile Cheung; Sarona and Rev. Faraimo Tiitii; Manuia and Rev. Ioane Petaia; and all the 28 grandchildren and 5 great grandchildren of this family to date.

Charity begins at home
Praise the Lord for you all, always
O lau pule lea le Atua!

Foreword

In 1962, Samoa became the first Pacific Island country to gain independence. Like many of its island neighbours, Samoa gave constitutional recognition to customary laws, recognising 'any custom or usage which has acquired the force of law in Samoa or any part thereof' as part of State law. This added complexity to the existing legal pluralism in Samoa, a 'legacy' of the colonial era, which included a period as a German colony, and then as a United Nations trust territory under the administration of New Zealand. Customary laws survived this intrusion and are still widely respected. Village communities make and administer their own rules on a broad range of local matters. However, the Constitution sets up a hierarchy of laws and, as ably illustrated in this book, national legislation rarely makes any concessions for customary laws. In the case of conflict, the written law prevails in court, but in practice these positions may be reversed. This ambiguous pluralism presents formidable barriers for law reform in Samoa. As in other Pacific island countries, law reformers in Samoa have, until quite recently, tended to rely on overseas models, without taking account of local culture. Any consultation has tended to be based on an agenda heavily weighted towards transplanted ideals. It is this background which makes this book so important. Given the renewed interest in developing an autochthonous legal system, reflecting the values and aspirations of Samoans, it is also timely.

The author, Dr. Teleiai Lalotoa Mulitalo Ropinisone Silipa Seumanutafa, is a Pacific scholar and experienced legal counsel and legislative drafting consultant. Her knowledge of local culture and practices enables her to employ the *Talanoa,* a Pacific research methodology, which is explained and developed in the book. The result is rich, original empirical data, which contributes further to the value of this book. Her extensive experience in the customary and state spheres gives her insight into the issues under discussion and the possible pathways for the future.

The book commences with a vivid example of the tensions between different sources of law, telling the story of a family subjected by the village *fono* to the customary penalty of banishment for acting against village interest. This banishment order remained in effect despite a state court order setting it aside, and the family's home was subsequently burnt to the ground. This sets the scene for the book's three main propositions, which are that Samoa continues to struggle with the colonial legacy of competing legal systems. Dr. Mulitalo posits that, if Samoa continues to prioritise a western approach to law reform without taking legal pluralism into account, the result will be laws which are ill suited to the needs of the country. Effective law reform, she argues, can only be achieved if the law reform process recognises and accommodates both Samoa's legal systems.

Having explained the concept of legal pluralism and how it is employed in the book, the author draws on existing scholarship to discuss the current position regarding law reform and law reform agencies. She then moves on to discuss law reform methodologies, including *Talanoa,* which she adapts and develops to suit her field of study. Dr. Mulitalo also examines the social and cultural value of law reform and draws on her empirical work to demonstrate that Samoans require customs to be accommodated within their legal system. She identifies the challenges posed by this demand and sets out the emerging conceptual challenges. After a thorough review of existing law reform mechanisms and agents, Dr. Mulitalo sets out a pathway for more responsive law reform and strategies for dealing with the identified challenges. The book concludes with proposals for a law reform process suitable for the needs of modern Samoa.

This book makes a welcome addition to the literature on legal pluralism in the Pacific and a unique contribution to the scholarship on pluralism and law reform. Whilst the book is firmly focused on Samoa, it draws on examples from other Pacific countries and provides transferable lessons for other countries facing the challenges posed by legal pluralism. Not only does it raise awareness of the complexities and challenges of the 'legacy' of colonialism, but also it puts forward suggestions for new approaches to these dilemmas, which are of both local and global significance. It provides a vital tool for anyone undertaking law reform in a plural jurisdiction. More generally, in an environment where state law overshadows customary law, this book is a refreshing reminder of the importance of local culture and the need to move away from transplants and foreign models.

Australian Research Council Jennifer Corrin
Canberra, ACT, Australia

Comparative Law, Centre for Public
International and Comparative Law
The University of Queensland
St Lucia, QLD, Australia

Higher Degree Research (HDR)
St Lucia, QLD, Australia

TC Beirne School of Law
The University of Queensland
St Lucia, QLD, Australia
12 September 2016

Acknowledgements

I wish to express my sincerest gratitude to my mentor Prof. Jennifer Corrin for her incredible motivational capabilities, extraordinary guidance, and for showing perpetual confidence in this Samoan's efforts and thoughts. Had it not been for this belief, I would not have been fortunate to undertake the research which informs this book and receive funding to write it too.

For funding to write this book (2016), I am grateful for the financial support by the *Legitimus* Project funded by the Social Sciences and Humanities Research Council of Canada, and the TC Beirne School of Law. The award received under the Australian Leadership Award (2010) allowed me to carry out research, so thank you Australia! Faafetai tele lava!

I extend my heartfelt appreciation to the people of my beloved Samoa. Your Highness the Head of State of Samoa, Lau Susuga i le Ao Mamalu o le Malo o Samoa, Tui Atua Tupua Tamasese Efi; Honourable Prime Minister, Lau Afioga i le Alii Palemia, Tuilaepa Lupesoliai Sailele Malielegaoi; Cabinet Ministers (2011); former Hon. Speaker of the House and current Minister of Agriculture Hon. Laauli Leuatea Polataivao Fosi Schmidt; Members of Parliament (2011); the late Rev. Elder Oka Fauolo, former Chairman of the Council of Churches and church Reverends and leaders; His Honour the Chief Justice of Samoa, Afioga Patu Tiavaasu'e Falefatu Maka Sapolu and members of the Judiciary; Village Mayor Malama Tiitii and Village Council of Savaia Lefaga; Afioga Seumanutafa Tiavolo Pogai and members of the Village Council Apia; Sui o le Nuu (Village Mayors) of Savaii and Upolu; Government Women Representatives of Savaii; the Vice Chancellor and President of the National University of Samoa, Professor Fui Le'apai Tu'ua 'Ilaoa Asofou So'o; the former Attorney General Tuatagaloa Aumua Ming Leung Wai and the Office of the Attorney General; former Executive Director of the Samoa Law Reform Commission and current Justice of the Supreme Court Tafaoimalo Leilani Tuala Warren; the President of the Samoa Law Society, Savalenoa Mareva Betham-Annandale and members of the Samoa Law Society; the former President of the SUNGO Tuisafua Vaasiliifiti Moelagi Jackson; and Government Chief Executive Officers (2011); the Office of the Clerk of the

Legislative Assembly and the Samoa Bureau of Statistics. FAAFETAI TELE MO TOU TAIMI SA FA'AAVANOA MO LENEI TUSITUSIGA. Talosia ia iai se aogā o lenei taumafaiga mo Samoa. Thank you ALL for your invaluable input into this work. May it have some use to providing some resolutions to the challenges of law making in plural societies.

I am indebted to my families and friends in Brisbane, in particular Maposua Telei'ai Sila Ierome and Taulima and family; faafetai tele mo le tou agalelei.

My churches with Rev. Elder Utufua Naseri and Taiaopo of EFKS Apia; and Rev. Makisua Reupena and Nima of EFKS Centenary, Sherwood Brisbane; my immediate family, relatives and friends in Samoa and Brisbane—your prayers have been invaluable support and I shall be eternally grateful. I acknowledge my late father Teleiai Lalotoa Mulitalo Ropinisone Silipa Seumanutafa of Apia and Saoluafata and my mother Lalotoa Mulitalo nee Asaua of Samatau and Lalomalava. I thank you for the gift of education.

It is sincerely hoped this book will in some way assist my country Samoa, the Pacific Islands, the indigenous post colonial societies and societies facing the challenges of legal pluralism, find ways of developing relevant and suitable laws that benefit their populations. I look forward to future dialogue and research taking the challenges and possible responses in this book further.

Faafetai i le alofa o le Atua! ALL Glory to God! O lau pule lea le Atua!

Contents

1	**Introduction**		1
	1.1 Divergent Currents		1
	1.2 Geographical Context		2
	1.3 Legal Pluralism and Law Reform		5
	1.4 Overview		7
	References		8
2	**Law Reform and Legal Pluralism Developments**		11
	2.1 Law Reform		11
		2.1.1 Development of Law Reform Institutions and Agents	11
		2.1.2 More Recent Developments	13
		2.1.3 Legal Transplantation	15
		2.1.4 Attempts to Recognise Customary Laws in State Laws	17
		2.1.4.1 Codification of Customary Laws	17
		2.1.4.2 Restatement of Customary Laws	18
		2.1.4.3 Incorporation of Customary Laws by Reference	19
	2.2 Law Reform Commissions (LRCS) and Legal Professions of the Pacific Islands		21
		2.2.1 Proposal for a Regional Law Reform Commission	21
		2.2.2 The Legal Profession	22
	2.3 Legal Pluralism		23
		2.3.1 Old Legal Pluralism, Colonial and Postcolonial Pluralism	23
		2.3.2 New and Postmodern Pluralism	24
		2.3.3 Other Categories of Legal Pluralism	25
	2.4 Legal Pluralism in the Pacific Islands		26
		2.4.1 Legal Pluralism in the Pacific Islands	26
		2.4.2 Regional and Local Jurisprudence	26
		2.4.3 A New Approach To Examining The Customary Law and State Law Divide	27

	2.5	Overview		28
	References			29
3	**A Research Methodology for the Pacific**			**35**
	3.1	Indigenous and Pacific Research Methodologies		35
		3.1.1	Postcolonial Research Methodologies	36
		3.1.2	Pacific Specific Methodologies	37
		3.1.3	*'Talanoa'* Research Methodology	38
	3.2	Utilising Pacific Research Methodologies to Resolve Indigenous and Pacific Issues		39
		3.2.1	*'Talanoa'* and Ethical Interview Principles	39
		3.2.2	Analysing *'Talanoa'* Interviews	42
		3.2.3	Pacific Islands Legislative Drafters Survey	43
	3.3	Primary Material and Documentary Data		43
		3.3.1	Court Judgments and Hansard Reports	43
		3.3.2	Commission of Inquiry Reports	44
		3.3.3	National Reports	44
		3.3.4	Local Newspaper Research: The Samoa Observer	45
	3.4	Overview		46
	References			46
4	**The Value of Law Reform: Social and Cultural**			**49**
	4.1	The Ideological Principles Behind Law Making: Customary Laws and State Laws		50
		4.1.1	Social Views on Law Reform	51
		4.1.2	Limited Understanding of State Laws	51
		4.1.3	Lack of Formal Education	52
		4.1.4	Relevance to Village Life	53
		4.1.5	Cultural Factors	54
		4.1.6	Language Barriers	55
		4.1.7	Support from Secondary Data: Local Newspaper Research	55
		4.1.8	Challenges to Address	57
	4.2	Demand for Customs and Respect for the Constitution		58
		4.2.1	Customary Laws as the Basis of the Legal System	59
		4.2.2	Laws in the Samoan Context	59
		4.2.3	Respect for the Constitution	60
		4.2.4	Challenges to Address	61
	4.3	Should Customs be Codified in Samoa's Laws?		62
		4.3.1	Opposition to Codification	62
			4.3.1.1 Conflicting Values	62
			4.3.1.2 Flexibility	62
			4.3.1.3 Ascertainment and Uniformity	63
			4.3.1.4 Serving the Interests of Non-Locals Only	63

		4.3.1.5	Absence of Customary Structures to Support Customs in Legislation	63

		4.3.1.6	Difficulties for Legislative Drafters	64
		4.3.1.7	Secondary Data: Pacific Legislative Drafters Survey	64
	4.3.2	Benefits of Codification		66
		4.3.2.1	Certainty and Constitutional Compliance	66
4.4	Emerging Conceptual Challenges			66
	4.4.1	Understanding the Dichotomy		66
	4.4.2	Need to Promote Understanding of State Laws		67
	4.4.3	Customs to be Recognised in State Laws		67
	4.4.4	Emerging Acceptance of Modern Laws		67
	4.4.5	Interdependency		68
References				68

5 State Focused Law Reform: Constitutional Offices, Institutions and Agents 69

5.1	The Courts		70
	5.1.1	Jurisdiction on Customs	70
	5.1.2	Judicial Training	72
	5.1.3	Role of the Judiciary in Law Reform	73
	5.1.4	Expatriate Judges	74

		5.1.4.1	General Pacific Experiences	74
		5.1.4.2	Interpretive Function of the Court	74
		5.1.4.3	Village Agreement Unenforceable Under Contract Law	76
		5.1.4.4	Obiter Unsupported by Local Realities	77
	5.1.5	Overview: The Courts		78
5.2	The Parliament			78
	5.2.1	Lack of Systems in Place to Support Assembly of *Matai*		79
		5.2.1.1	Language in Parliamentary Proceedings	80
		5.2.1.2	Law Making Procedures: Assembly Process and Private Members Bills	80
	5.2.2	Unsuccessful Legal Transplants		82
	5.2.3	Acts of Parliament with Custom References 1962–2015 (Samoa)		84
		5.2.3.1	Acts 1962 (Independence) to 1989	85
		5.2.3.2	Acts from 1990 to 2000	90
		5.2.3.3	Acts After 2000	93
		5.2.3.4	Overview	96
	5.2.4	Analysis: Acts of Parliament and Acts with Customs References (2008–2016)		97
	5.2.5	Overview: The Parliament		99

	5.3	The Executive		99
		5.3.1 Executive Law Making Process		99
			5.3.1.1 Cabinet Handbook	99
			5.3.1.2 Legislative Drafting Handbook	100
		5.3.2 Overview: The Executive		101
	5.4	The Samoa Law Reform Commission (SLRC)		101
		5.4.1 Establishment and Personnel		102
			5.4.1.1 What Model of Law Reform Institution?	102
			5.4.1.2 The Initial Years	103
			5.4.1.3 Western Educated Personnel	103
			5.4.1.4 The SLRC Advisory Board	104
		5.4.2 Law Reform Process		105
		5.4.3 Public Consultation		107
			5.4.3.1 Costly Cultural Protocols	107
			5.4.3.2 Law Reform Consultation	108
		5.4.4 Overview: The SLRC		110
	5.5	Other Law Reform Agents		110
		5.5.1 Commissions of Inquiry (COI)		111
			5.5.1.1 COIs for Customary Reforms	111
			5.5.1.2 COI Investigations and Reforms to Date	112
			5.5.1.3 COI Strengths	112
			5.5.1.4 COI Challenges	113
			5.5.1.5 Law Reform Driven by Both Matais (Customary) and Lawyers (Modern)	114
		5.5.2 The Samoa Law Society (SLS)		115
			5.5.2.1 Law Reform Functions	115
			5.5.2.2 Challenges	116
		5.5.3 Office of the Ombudsman		117
			5.5.3.1 Law Reform Functions	117
			5.5.3.2 Challenges	118
		5.5.4 Non-Government Organisations (NGOs)		119
			5.5.4.1 Law Reform Influence	119
			5.5.4.2 Challenges	120
	5.6	Emerging Conceptual Challenges		121
		5.6.1 Law Reform Framework Not Embedded in Customs		121
			5.6.1.1 Laws Authorising Law Making	121
			5.6.1.2 Procedures Guiding Law Making	121
		5.6.2 Limited Professional Training Opportunities		122
		5.6.3 Involving the Village Structures in the Law Reform Process		122
		5.6.4 Funding Constraints		122
References				123

6	**Towards Responsive Law Reform**		129
	6.1 Public Awareness of State Laws		130
		6.1.1 Develop Community Awareness	130
		6.1.2 Facilitate Public Access to Acts and Court Decisions	131
	6.2 Professional Training: Judiciary, Parliament, Legal Profession		133
		6.2.1 The Judiciary	133
		6.2.1.1 Judicial Training	133
		6.2.1.2 Judicial Guidance Clause	134
		6.2.1.3 Code of Judicial Conduct	135
		6.2.1.4 Court Benchbooks	136
		6.2.1.5 New Developments in the Courts of Samoa	137
		6.2.2 Parliament	137
		6.2.2.1 Professional Training	137
		6.2.2.2 Customary Duties to Village Communities	139
		6.2.2.3 Private Members Bill (PMB)	140
		6.2.2.4 Recent Developments for Parliament	141
		6.2.3 Legal Profession	142
		6.2.3.1 Professional Training on the Rule of Law and Samoan Customs	142
		6.2.3.2 Training on Samoan Language and Cultural Protocols	142
		6.2.3.3 Engaging in Academic Conferences and Quality Research	144
	6.3 State Responsibilities in Law Reform		145
		6.3.1 Constitutional and Legislative Review, Drafting Handbooks	145
		6.3.1.1 Reference Guide to Customary Practices	147
		6.3.1.2 Village Fono Act (1990) Review	148
		6.3.1.3 Cabinet and Drafting Handbooks	149
		6.3.2 Promote Formal Education	149
		6.3.3 National Plans	151
		6.3.3.1 Samoa's National Plan 2012–2016	151
		6.3.3.2 Law and Justice Sector Plan	152
	6.4 Village Responsibilities in Law Reform		152
		6.4.1 Change of Village Mayor Criteria	153
		6.4.2 Develop Constitutionally Compliant Village Rules	154
	6.5 Managing Funding Constraints		155
		6.5.1 Involving Customary Structures in Law Reform Consultation	155
		6.5.2 Prioritising and Justifying Costs for Customary Reforms	156
	6.6 Local Jurisprudence: Customary Law as the Basis of Common Law		157

	6.7	Legislative Drafters and Draft Laws	159
	6.7.1	Pacific Specific Drafting and Law Reform Training	159
	6.7.2	Drafting in the Samoan Language, Legislative References, Context	160
	6.7.3	Review of Draft Laws for Customary Compliance	162
	6.8	Summary of Responses to Legal Pluralism	164
	References		165
7	**A Suitable Law Reform Framework for Pluralist Countries**		169
	7.1	Introduction	170
	7.2	A Suitable Law Reform Process for Samoa	171
		7.2.1 Before the Terms of Reference (TOR)	171
		7.2.1.1 Step 1	171
		7.2.2 After a TOR Is Received by the SLRC	171
		7.2.2.1 Step 2: Research and Consultation	171
		7.2.2.1.1 Doctrinal Research	171
		7.2.2.1.2 Socio-Legal Research	172
		7.2.2.2 Step 3: Issues Paper	173
		7.2.2.3 Step 4: Research and Consultation	173
		7.2.2.4 Step 5: Final Report with Recommendations	174
		7.2.2.5 Step 6: Report Tabled in Parliament	174
		7.2.3 The Draft Bill Process	175
		7.2.3.1 Legislative Drafting	175
		7.2.3.2 Vetting for Customary Compliance	175
		7.2.3.3 Passage Through Parliament	175
		7.2.4 Law Reform Process of Law Reform Agents	176
		7.2.4.1 Commissions of Inquiry, Ombudsman, NGOs	176
	7.3	Legislative Reforms and Guides	176
		7.3.1 Local Jurisprudence	177
		7.3.2 Judicial Clause and Guides	177
		7.3.2.1 Constitutional Amendment	177
		7.3.2.2 Code of Judicial Conduct	178
		7.3.2.3 Court Benchbooks	178
		7.3.3 Reference Guide to Customary Practices	178
		7.3.4 Parliament Guides and Procedures	179
		7.3.4.1 Guide for Members of Parliament	179
		7.3.4.2 Standing Orders of Parliament	179
		7.3.4.3 State Handbooks	179
		7.3.4.3.1 Cabinet Handbook	179
		7.3.4.3.2 Legislative Drafting Handbook of Samoa	180
		7.3.5 Statutory Obligation to Consider Customs	180
	7.4	Conclusions	181
		7.4.1 Systematic Studies on Law Reform	181
		7.4.2 The Challenges of Legal Pluralism for Law Reform in Samoa	181

	7.4.3	Taking Advantage of Pluralism	182
	7.4.4	Emerging Trends	183
		7.4.4.1 A Winning Model?	183
		7.4.4.2 Incorporation by Reference	183
		7.4.4.3 State Initiatives that Accommodate Pluralism...	184
7.5	Future Research		184
	7.5.1	Constitutional Review	184
	7.5.2	Local Jurisprudence	185
	7.5.3	Pacific Island Specific Research	185
	7.5.4	Samoa's Constitutional Compliant Village Rules	185
	7.5.5	Follow up Research on Legal Pluralism and Law Reform in Samoa	186
	7.5.6	Pacific Research Methodologies	187
	7.5.7	Professional Training that Addresses Customs	187
References			188

Appendices 191

Appendix A: List of Interview Participants 191

Appendix B: Commissions of Inquiry and Legislative Reforms 193

Appendix C: Law Reform Commissions Statutory Functions 194

Appendix D: Samoa Law Reform Commission: Law Reform Process ... 196

Appendix E: Respondents: Pacific Islands Legislative Drafters Survey ... 196

Samoan Terminology

aiga	family unit, refers to the immediate and the extended family
agaifanua	rules which specifically apply to a family or a village
aganuu	rules that apply nationally to all Samoans
Alii ma Faipule	village council
aumaga	sons of matai, all male organisation of the village
faalupega	honorifics and salutation
faamatai	Samoan traditional chiefly system
fale	traditional Samoan meeting house or dwelling
faletua ma tausi	wives of matai
fa'a Samoa	the Samoan way
fautasi	long boat or to build together
fono	meeting, council
fono o Aso Gafua	Monday meetings of the village council
gafa	genealogy
lauga Samoa	Samoan oratory
malae	open village field for village activities
matai	Samoan traditional chief
monotaga	village services, assistance or contribution
puletasi	contemporary Samoan traditional wear for a female
sene	cent
sui o le malo	government representative
sui o le nuu	village representative, formerly known as '*Pulenuu*'
soalaupule	making decisions on a consultative basis
talanoa	to talk freely, in the absence of a strict agenda
tamaitai	daughter/s of *matai*
tofa faatupu, tofa loloto	long view, deep wisdom
tulafono	law or rules

Chapter 1
Introduction

Contents

1.1 Divergent Currents 1
1.2 Geographical Context 2
1.3 Legal Pluralism and Law Reform 5
1.4 Overview 7
References 8

1.1 Divergent Currents

On 10 December 2011, following several unsuccessful attempts to reach agreement, and convinced that the village *matai* (traditional Samoan chief) Leota Ituau Ale (Ale) was acting against the interests of the village, the village council of Solosolo banished Ale and his family from the village of Solosolo.[1] On 9 February 2012, Ale petitioned the Land and Titles Court of Samoa (LTC) to overturn the decision of the village council. A week later, in a decision handed down on 17 February 2012, the LTC ruled in favour of Ale and revoked the banishment order of the village council.[2] On 20 February 2012, a family home belonging to Ale at Solosolo was scorched to the ground.[3] Despite the LTC decision, the village council continued to enforce its banishment order over Ale and his descendants.

> On 24 February 2012, deeply affected by the destruction of Ale's residence, Satoa a village youth wrote to the editor of the local newspaper the Samoa Observer,[4] expressing profound disappointment, and questioned the *tofa faatupu* (customary deep wisdom) and

---

[1] Ripine (2012), *Samoa Observer*.

[2] *Leota Leuluaialii Ituau Ale et al v Alii & Faipule Solosolo* (Unreported, Land and Titles Court of Samoa, LC.11469 P2, 17 February *2012*). Solosolo is a Samoan village on the eastern coast of Apia.

[3] Ilalio (2012), Samoa Observer.

[4] Pseudonym, 2012, Samoa Observer. The writer wrote under a pseudonym, and was later identified by the local newspaper as Satoa. Since the banishment order, Satoa has lived in another village, while his wife and two children continue to live at Solosolo.

© Springer International Publishing AG 2018
T.L. Mulitalo Ropinisone Silipa Seumanutafa, *Law Reform in Plural Societies*,
The World of Small States 2, https://doi.org/10.1007/978-3-319-65524-6_1

the Christian morals of the village council. He challenged Solosolo villagers around the globe to fight against 'village corruption', to prevent future destruction to property and families resulting from village council decisions in Samoa.

On 28 February 2012, Satoa's family was banished from Solosolo.[5] Satoa's parents paid ST $2,000 and two sows, following which the banishment order was partially lifted and only Satoa's family members were allowed to remain and participate in village activities. The banishment order against Satoa remained. From the village council's perspective, Satoa was banished because he had shamed the village by publicising Solosolo village matters in the local newspaper. It was also to remind the youth to respect the institution of the village council, which is the highest traditional authority responsible for the welfare of the village.

Satoa later published a public apology to the Solosolo village council in the local newspaper.[6] He accepted the banishment order against him, but also posed a challenge, 'if the village council can prohibit the freedom of speech, there is no point in government preaching the importance of individual rights'.

This case scenario illustrates the conflicts between the state legal system and the customary legal system in Samoa and in many other post-colonial plural societies, to which no adequate response has yet been found. This book examines how this tension may be addressed through a law reform process which is appropriate for societies experiencing legal pluralism.

The central argument in this book is comprised of three propositions. Samoa, like other Pacific Islands, continues to struggle with the colonial legacy of plural legal systems: both the western legal system and customary legal systems are recognised. Where Samoa continues to adopt a western approach to law reform without taking account of legal pluralism, this may result in laws which are unsuitable and irrelevant to Samoa. Against this paradigm, effective law reform in Samoa can only be achieved where the law reform process recognises the validity of the two primary legal systems existing in Samoa.

1.2 Geographical Context

Samoa is the main focus of this book. Examples to support or demonstrate a point will be drawn from other Pacific Islands. Conducting in-depth research in one society, Samoa, allows for investigations to be carried out in a comprehensive manner effectively resulting in stronger, authentic and relevant recommendations.[7] Although these recommendations are directed to Samoa, some of them are transferrable to other Pacific Islands with commonalities in colonial histories and socio-political environments. To shed light on the social and cultural challenges for law

---

[5]Tupufia (2012), The Samoa Observer.
[6]Ibid.
[7]McLachlan (1988), p. 336. In a study on state recognition of customary laws in the South Pacific, McLachlan finds that due to the complexities of the relationship between state law and customs, studies of each separate jurisdiction are realistic.

1.2 Geographical Context

reform discussed in later chapters, some background information on Samoa is helpful.

From 1830 to 1900, Germany, Britain and the United States of America were increasingly involved in Samoa's power struggles. In 1900 when the German flag was first raised in Apia, Samoa became a German protectorate and the German administration played a significant part in shaping the events of that period in Samoa. From 1914, Samoa was under the control of the British (New Zealand) Army Forces until 1920 when New Zealand governed Samoa firstly as a League of Nations Mandate and later as a United Nations Trust Territory.[8]

Since 1908, Samoan traditional leaders (*matais*) sought to assert claims to independence through the *Mau* Movement (Opinion Movement). This was a non-violent movement led by the chiefly elite, the customary *matai* leaders entrenched in Samoan tradition and the *fa'a Samoa*. The movement culminated in 1929 when New Zealand military opened fire on a procession attempting to prevent the arrest of one of their members. Up to 11 Samoans were killed including the high chief Tupua Tamasese Lealofi II and many others wounded. The Mau Movement efforts ultimately resulted in Samoa's political independence from colonial powers in 1962, the first of the Pacific Islands to reach this milestone. Thereafter, the rest of the Pacific Islands followed suit, gaining political independence or self-governance.[9] The Samoan population is made up largely of indigenous Samoans. Of the combined land area of 2800 square kilometeres, 4% is freehold land, 15% is government land and 81% is customary land[10] which cannot be alienated.[11] By 2011, the total population of Samoa reached 187,820 of which 96% were indigenous full Samoan citizens.[12] Samoa's customary law system and state law system are operated by indigenous Samoans.

The majority of the families are agriculturally active and rely heavily on subsistence farming for everyday consumption, and cultivation for sale or commercial trade is uncommon.[13] The bulk of the population are more dependent on the customary legal system for economic development as opposed to the state system.[14]

---

[8]Meleisea (1987).

[9]Ibid; Field (1984), Campbell (1990).

[10]Taule'alo et al. (2002), p. 2.

[11]*Constitution of the Independent State of Samoa 1962* (Samoa) art 102.

[12]Samoa Bureau of Statistics (2011), p. 27. Other inhabited islands Manono and Apolima account for less than 3% of the population and are counted in the Upolu population.

[13]Samoa Bureau of Statistics (2009a, b), p. 25, 31. A majority of 68% of households surveyed were classified as agriculturally active, 34% were involved in subsistence farming largely for home consumption.

[14]Samoa Bureau of Statistics, above n 12, 27–28. This 2011 census found that of the working age group of Samoa aged 15 and above (115,871), 59% were non-economically active, while 41% were economically active. Of the non-economically active, 71.4% were involved in domestic duties and 23% attended school. Of the 41% economically active, 35.6% were involved in subsistence employment such as agriculture, farming and fishing while 57% were employed in non-subsistence employment.

In terms of education, Samoa continues to work towards achieving a more qualified workforce to lead and sustain its social and economic developments in the future.[15] Formal education is a modern feature in Samoa. Informal education received from the village elders and the *matai* system was generally more vital to village life. This impacts on the level of understanding and interest in the state system and presents a challenge in developing law reform in Samoa. Modern communication technology has yet to reach most parts of Samoa.[16] Accessibility to state laws and law reform initiatives through modern means of communication such as the internet is significantly limited.

The communal system of Samoa operates on a traditional chiefly system known as the *faamatai* dating back some 3000 years and traceable to the ancient gods.[17] The underlying principle of communal living in Samoa is that one is not an individual, but part of the cosmos, sharing inheritance with family, village and nation.[18] This is the basis of the conflict with individual rights. Genealogies (*gafa*) and honorific salutations (*faalupega*) connect the village chiefly system to 81% of the total land area which is customary land, record oral history, ascertain boundaries and connect blood links of families, villages and districts.[19]

The village council derives authority from established practices and conventions[20] with executive, judicial and enforcement functions, collectively as the *Fono* or as its individual members.[21] In many villages, the village councils meet in the first Monday of each month, a practise commonly referred to in Samoa as '*Fono o Aso Gafua*' (Monday Meetings) for general business, or meet on any other day or night for urgent matters.[22] The unit of the native political structure is the village (*nuu*) which is autonomous[23] and in which most individual family groups are related. There are over 300 villages[24] in Samoa of which a recorded 189[25] (in the government records) are traditional villages with village councils. The majority of

---

[15] Ibid, 68. About 46% of the population 5 years and above only reached secondary education and 22% attained tertiary education. Although about 87% of the population aged 15 and over reached secondary school or achieved the Pacific Senior Secondary Certificate (PSSC), only 6% completed a Post-Secondary Certificate, 4% gained diplomas, and 3% completed a first degree or higher qualification.

[16] Ibid. Of 26,205 Samoan households surveyed, only 2611 had access to a computer of which 1905 can access internet, the majority of this number were located in the urban area Apia.

[17] The origins of Samoa's indigenous institutions are complex. A simplified account of it in this book could unfortunately diminish its importance. The brief account here is to put this study into context.

[18] Suaalii-Sauni et al. (2009), p. 157.

[19] Vaai (1999), p. 37.

[20] Ibid, 41.

[21] Le Tagaloa (1992), p. 121.

[22] Interview with VC1 Focus Group (Samoa, 1 March 2011).

[23] Meleisea (1987), pp. 1–2.

[24] Samoa Bureau of Statistics (2001), p. 1.

[25] Officer of Internal Affairs (MWSCD) to Lalotoa Mulitalo (2012).

the population are village based and are largely dependent on village governance for their livelihood.

The village council is assisted by three village organisations, the *tamatai* (daughters of *matai*), *aumaga* (sons of *matai*), and *faletua* ma *tausi* (wives of *matai*)[26] each having specific roles to promote village welfare.[27] *Tamaiti* refers to the young children who are not required to play a specific role in the development of the village until they are of age to join the three main organisations. The most important unit in Samoa is the family, headed by the *matai* who is responsible for the welfare and is the spokesperson for the family at formal gatherings such as the village council meetings or any public congregation. As with developing societies, most of the formally educated and employed population reside in the urban area and are less familiar with village protocols, genealogical addresses and village governance. The prominent socio-economic characteristics of the villages attribute to the respect given to village councils to date.

1.3 Legal Pluralism and Law Reform

Legal pluralism in this study is the co-existence of two or more legal systems in one society, at times conflicting with each other and on other occasions complementary. It is on this premise that legal pluralism is the legal framework upon which this book is based. In Samoa, legal pluralism manifests itself in the co-existence of the customary legal system (decentralised village councils with law making, judicial and enforcement powers) and the state legal system formally adopted at independence in 1962. Legal pluralism is experienced not only in the operation of two overall legal systems (customary and state) but also at the village level through the existence of more than 300[28] villages. All villages practise unique, separate legal orders operating under firstly the overriding general custom rules (*aganuu*) applying across all villages, and secondly village specific customary rules (*agaifanua*). Customs are therefore not uniform in Samoa. It is not the purpose of this book to explore all village legal orders against the state or each other. This may be for another study. The focus is on the two main overriding legal systems, the customary legal system and the state legal system.

'Custom' has recently been defined by statute to mean,

> the customs, usages and traditional practices of the Samoan people existing in relation to the matter in question at the time when the matter arises, regardless of whether or not the custom, usage or practice has existed from time immemorial.[29]

---

[26]Le Tagaloa, above n 21, 118–119.
[27]Keesing (1934), p. 52.
[28]Samoa Bureau of Statistics, above, n24.
[29]*Acts Interpretation Act 2015* (Samoa) s 3.

In this study, customs and usages are referred to interchangeably as 'customs', 'customary laws' or the 'customary practices' of Samoa.

This book does not specifically discuss the impact of legal pluralism on human rights, although some examples may be used to elaborate on the issues of legal pluralism. Religion is now successfully merged with customs in Samoa.[30] It plays a major role in shaping opinion and behaviour in Samoa. However, save for some references to the church where mentioned by interviewed respondents for this book, the church is not a traditional 'village organisation' in this book and is not part of the substantive discussions following.

This book focuses on law reform of state laws. 'Law reform' here refers to the reform of state laws through Acts of Parliament, and through subsidiary legislation made by the Head of State on the advice of the executive[31] and judicial precedents of the courts. The law reform process refers to the process by which changes to state laws are initiated and developed by the constitutional offices (Parliament, judiciary, executive); the Samoa Law Reform Commission, the Office of the Attorney-General and its legislative drafters, and other agents having a law reform function by virtue of empowering or enabling legislation or through the nature of their official functions.

This study treats customary law as 'law' as observed under the Constitution and the relevant literature.[32] Arguably a law reform study of the customary legal system is also possible given its traditional law making,[33] executive and enforcement functions.[34] However, the state as a central authority has responsibilities to make available a justice system including a law making process that meets the demands of a plural society. In a modern environment, the customary legal system cannot meet this. Further, state law reform can be studied more effectively through the central public infrastructure that supports it as compared to a study of flexible law making procedures of multiple and decentralised traditional authorities of the customary legal system. The onus of implementing the recommendations put forward in this study is on the state. It is realistic therefore for the study to focus on law reform of state laws.

---

[30]Interview with SOH Respondent 4 (Samoa, 11 July 2011).

[31]*Regulations Ordinance 1953* (Samoa).

[32]*Constitution of the Independent State of Samoa* (1962) art 111; Narokobi (1989), p. 4; Aleck (1995), p. 3.

[33]For the procedure of law making of the village councils, see Suaalii-Sauni et al. (eds), above, n 18, 165.

[34]Le Tagaloa (1992), pp. 117, 121. Le Tagaloa argues that the *faamatai* is the most appropriate social organisation for the Samoan people on the basis that the *faamatai* gives everyone the right to be an heir, the insistence of culture on unity or holistic view of life, the inclusive decision-making process of *soalaupule*, and the ability of the Samoan culture to adapt to change and new ideas.

1.4 Overview

The next chapter reviews the available work on the overlapping concepts used in this book: the development of law reform machineries, and the expansion of legal pluralism as a legal framework. The discussion then shifts to the writings on law reform and legal pluralism in the Pacific Islands.

Owing to the significant relevance of the use of suitable research methodologies for this study, Chap. 3 provides an insight into the importance of the use of research methods fitting for indigenous research. A review of existing writing on indigenous and Pacific research methodologies is provided. This is followed by discussions of how this book employed *Talanoa*, a methodology specifically developed by the author for the purposes of the empirical research interviews for this book. The use of *Talanoa* here builds upon the emerging Pacific research methodologies developed in New Zealand and the United States, in areas with growing Pacific populations. Other conventional research methods were employed as will be seen in this chapter. These include doctrinal analyses (of local court decisions and legislation), local national reports and other documentary data.

One of the limitations of the current law reform process in many Pacific Islands is its disregard of customary laws consideration in favour of state laws. Chapter 4 explores the 'socio-cultural challenges' of legal pluralism that impact on law reform as informed by the interview data. It reflects on people's aspirations for customary laws to be the basis of Samoa's legal system, as well as the overwhelming support for customs to be incorporated in parliamentary laws. It also discusses an emerging respect for the Constitution and the rule of law. The codification of customary laws to give legal effect to customs is not supported for reasons discussed in this chapter. The chapter concludes with a summary of conceptual socio-cultural challenges to be addressed in Chap. 6.

Chapter 5 investigates the second broad set of challenges referred to as the 'institutional challenges'. The chapter highlights different ways in which customs are not embedded in the law making processes of the State, the judiciary, Parliament and the institutional law reform commission, the Samoa Law Reform Commission (SLRC). It identifies the compositions that contribute to the lack of regard for customs such as the lack of systems and professional training in place to accommodate customary laws in state laws. The chapter also examines the challenges for other agents of law reform such as the Samoa Law Society (SLS), the Office of the Ombudsman and the non-government organisations (NGOs) in developing effective law reform. This chapter concludes with a summary of conceptual institutional challenges for law reform, for which responses are suggested in Chap. 6.

Chapter 6 explores suggested responses to the challenges raised in Chaps. 4 and 5. These include closing the gap between the customary legal system and the state legal system, through public awareness programmes and professional training across all institutions and agents performing a law reform function. Possible legislative amendments empowering the village structures within the ambit of the

Constitution are explored. An analysis of the feasibility of those approaches in light of the current political and social environment of Samoa is provided. Chapter 7 concludes the book with a suggested law reform framework that better suits Samoa, many of the Pacific Islands and similar post-colonial societies. It also provides the recommendations and conclusions to this book, and proposes area for further research.

References

Aleck J (1995) Introduction: custom is law in Papua New Guinea. In: Aleck J, Rannelles J (eds) Custom at the crossroads. University of Papua New Guinea, p 3
Campbell IC (1990) A history of the Pacific Islands. University of Queensland Press
Email from an Officer of Internal Affairs (MWSCD) to Lalotoa Mulitalo (2012)
Field MH (1984) MAU – Samoa's struggle against New Zealand oppression. A.H. & A.W. Reed Ltd
Ilalio MH (2012) Family home gutted after court case. Samoa Observer Samoa
Keesing FM (1934) Modern Samoa, its government and changing life. George Allen & Unwin Ltd, London, p 52
Le Tagaloa AF (1992) The Samoan culture and governance. In: Crocombe R et al (eds) Culture and democracy in the South Pacific. University of the South Pacific, pp 117, 121
McLachlan C (1988) State recognition of customary law in the South Pacific. PhD Thesis, University of London, p 336
Meleisea M (1987) The making of modern Samoa: traditional authority and colonial administration in the history of Western Samoa. University of the South Pacific Fiji, pp 1–2
Narokobi B (1989) Lo Bilong Yumi Yet: Law and Custom in Melanesia. Melanesian Institute for Pastoral and Socio-Economic Service and the University of the South Pacific, Fiji, p 4
Ripine S (2012) Solosolo banishes former Speaker Leota Itu'au Ale again. Samoa Observer Samoa
Sad Solosolo blood [sic] (2012) Shame on you Solosolo! Samoa Observer Samoa
Samoa Bureau of Statistics (2001) Population and Housing Census
Samoa Bureau of Statistics (2009a) Agriculture Census Analytical Report, p 25
Samoa Bureau of Statistics (2009b) Agriculture Census Tabulation Report, p 31
Samoa Bureau of Statistics (2011) Population and Housing Census Analytical Report, p 27
Suaalii-Sauni T et al (eds) (2009) Su'esu'e Manogi: In Search of Fragrance, Tui Atua Tupua Tamasese Ta'isi and the Samoan Indigenous Reference. National University of Samoa, p 157
Taule'alo TI, Fong SD, Setefano PM (2002) Samoan customary lands at the crossroads - options for sustainable management. In: Proceedings of the National Environment Forum, Department of Lands, Surveys and Environment
Tupufia LT (2012) Banned forever. Samoa Observer Samoa
Vaai S (1999) Samoa Faamatai and the Rule of Law. National University of Samoa, p 37

Court Decision

Leota Leuluaialii Ituau Ale et al v Alii & Faipule Solosolo (Unreported, Land and Titles Court of Samoa, LC.11469 P2, 17 February 2012)

Legislation

Constitution of the Independent State of Samoa 1962 (Samoa)
Acts Interpretation Act 2015 (Samoa)
Regulations Ordinance 1953 (Samoa)

Chapter 2
Law Reform and Legal Pluralism Developments

Contents

2.1	Law Reform	11
	2.1.1 Development of Law Reform Institutions and Agents	11
	2.1.2 More Recent Developments	13
	2.1.3 Legal Transplantation	15
	2.1.4 Attempts to Recognise Customary Laws in State Laws	17
	2.1.4.1 Codification of Customary Laws	17
	2.1.4.2 Restatement of Customary Laws	18
	2.1.4.3 Incorporation of Customary Laws by Reference	19
2.2	Law Reform Commissions (LRCS) and Legal Professions of the Pacific Islands	21
	2.2.1 Proposal for a Regional Law Reform Commission	21
	2.2.2 The Legal Profession	22
2.3	Legal Pluralism	23
	2.3.1 Old Legal Pluralism, Colonial and Postcolonial Pluralism	23
	2.3.2 New and Postmodern Pluralism	24
	2.3.3 Other Categories of Legal Pluralism	25
2.4	Legal Pluralism in the Pacific Islands	26
	2.4.1 Legal Pluralism in the Pacific Islands	26
	2.4.2 Regional and Local Jurisprudence	26
	2.4.3 A New Approach To Examining The Customary Law and State Law Divide ...	27
2.5	Overview	28
References		29

2.1 Law Reform

2.1.1 Development of Law Reform Institutions and Agents

In England, Australia and Canada, there are records of early attempts to establish law reform machinery dating as far back as the fifteenth century.[1] The systematic process of law reform achieved in the nineteenth century was in the form of temporary and part time law reform commissions. The first formal body established to carry out law reform was the 1934 Law Revision Committee in England

---

[1]Hurlburt (1986), p 15; Sutton (1970), p. 19; Kirby (1983).

appointed by Lord Chancellor Sankey. The institutional Law Commission was established under the Law Commission Act of 1975[2] to be an independent and permanent office staffed by lawyers and support staff. The early literature on law reform offers useful insights for this book on how the forces of government, the bureaucracy and civil society transform law reform machineries and agencies at a given place and time.[3]

Contemporary law reform institutions became more modern when institutions were resourced with more relevant law reform expertise, having a specific focus of reforms and a commitment to full consultation and public participation.[4] These requirements have since been regulated by legislation.[5] However, law reform was not always carried out by formal institutions; reforms were also developed by advisory groups, ad hoc bodies, law faculties and prominent individuals.[6] The common trend in the Commonwealth was for law reform to be initially driven through law reform agents prior to the establishment of formal institutions specialising in law reform. The convenience of ad hoc law reform agents has crowded the law reform field and thus questions the value of full time independent institutions. There are however significant features of the institutional commissions that render them more effective and preferable to other agents of law reform.[7] These include permanence, independence and authoritativeness to name a few. Further, despite the rise and fall of institutional law reform institutions in Canada and Australia in the 1990s, an overview of the development of law reform institutions reveal that law reform institutions have had a special role in bringing about significant change and therefore must be retained.[8] The most recent argument for the retention of commissions is that institutional law reform is better suited for the post-modern environment than when it first emerged.[9]

In the latter half of the twentieth century, the commonwealth developing countries of India[10] and Sri Lanka,[11] and the Pacific island states[12] followed the

---

[2]Law Commission Act 1965 (UK) ch 22; Geoffrey Sawer (1970), p. 183.

[3]Neave (2001).

[4]Commonwealth Secretariat (2005); Sutton, above n 1.

[5]For example, the Australian Law Reform Commission Act 1996 (Cth) which repealed the Australian Law Reform Commission Act 1973 (Cth), and the Law Reform Commission Act 1970 (Canada) which was later repealed and the Commission was re-established under the Law Commission Act 1996 (Canada).

[6]Ross (1982), King (1969), pp. 403–410.

[7]Weisbrot (2002).

[8]Handford (1999), p. 519.

[9]Weisbrot (2005), p. 38.

[10]Law Commission of India, Government of India, Early Beginnings http://www.lawcommissionofindia.

[11]Law Commission Act 1969 (Sri Lanka).

[12]Constitutional and Law Reform Commission Act 2004 (Papua New Guinea); Law Reform Commission Act (Fiji) ch 26; Law Commission Act (Vanuatu) ch 115; Law Reform Commission Act 1994 (Solomon Islands); Law Commission Act 2007 (Tonga); Law Reform Commission Act 2008 (Samoa).

considerable development of law reform institutions around Australia.[13] By the 1990s, about 60 law reform agencies had been established around the world varying according to scope and capacity and resources.[14]

The development of law reform machineries is not entirely relevant to the context of the small Pacific Island societies. The Pacific Islands law reform institutions developed much later, and in contrasting environments. However, this literature is valuable where it gives insight into the environment in which today's modern law reform institutions were developed. It sheds light on the main influences behind the choice of law reform machinery in different situations and environments. The early literature is a useful record for the Pacific Islands institutions as they join their more modern counterparts in driving progress through law reform.

2.1.2 More Recent Developments

Recent literature highlights the challenges of law reform faced by developing and transitional states.[15] Two collections published in 2005 and 2007 respectively are worth specific mention where they are relevant to this study.

In 2005, the Australian Law Reform Commission (ALRC) celebrated its 30th anniversary. This was marked by the publication of the 'The Promise of Law Reform', a compilation of writings by academics, law reformers, practising solicitors and the judiciary of Australia. This book provides invaluable guidance on how the consultation process and community participation can be made more effective through actual consultation and the use of the media and websites.[16] It offers doctrinal and socio-legal research strategies on primary, library and web based resources.[17] It discusses the values and differences in other existing law reform bodies such as the statutory Royal Commissions and law reform agents in terms of procedures, independence and authority.[18] It offers insight into the law reform of the executive, in developing and managing executive policies.[19] Some vital elements in the law reform process of Parliament is the effectiveness of Select Committee inquiries; obtaining the tacit approval of the executive in private members Bills and ensuring that Bills use plain drafting.[20] There are also helpful discussions on the occasions the courts are called upon to make law on novel

---

[13]Kirby (1983), p. 51.
[14]Sayers (2009), p. 70.
[15]Lindsey (2007).
[16]Atkinson (2005), p. 160; Davis (2005), p. 148.
[17]Partington (2005), p. 134.
[18]Sackville (2005), p. 274.
[19]Glenfield (2005), p. 288.
[20]Payne (2005), p. 302.

questions.[21] A fitting overview by Michael Kirby, the first Chairperson of the ALRC encapsulates the contributions and highlights some significant achievements in Australia since the establishment of the ALRC.[22] Such progress includes the judiciary's increasing reliance on law reform commission (LRC) reports in judicial decisions, a strengthened commitment to quality academic research and networking and utilising the benefits of modern cyberspace in influencing law and public policy. In a chapter entitled 'The Challenges of Law Reform in the Pacific Island States', Guy Powles gives an account of the law reform agencies and reform processes of the Pacific Islands states up to the mid-2000s.[23] He reflected that the Pacific Islands lack the requisite resources and expertise for institutional setups; this hinders full consideration being given to law reform techniques and processes.[24] In the absence of law reform institutions, there is heavy dependence on the central government offices such as the offices of the Attorney-General for law reform.[25]

The contributions from the 'Promise of Law Reform' are in the context of Australia. They provide useful models for Pacific Islands for future adoption although with a deference to the customary basis and environment of the Pacific Islands. The writings on the law reform role of each of the constitutional offices, the executive, Parliament and the judiciary add value to an analysis of the challenges for those institutions discussed in the context of Samoa.

The second collection of writing relevant to this study as reflected in the title is 'Law Reform in Developing and Transitional States' published in 2007.[26] This text identifies similar challenges for law reform in Asian countries which are comparable to those found in the Pacific Islands. These include an unresponsive society, an inactive judiciary and a passive legal profession. The book suggests various ways in which law reform and the legal system can be more effectively enhanced other than by legal reforms, such as by changing the structures of expectation in society.[27] It reveals that hasty and ill-conceived reforms cannot remove corruption[28] and introducing new laws does not necessarily strengthen market forces reform.[29] However, it does not fully explore the law reform process or the impact of reforms that are state based, on society's traditional structures. Other contributions in this text that are more relevant to this book discuss the legal transplantation theory as a method of law reform.[30] This is relevant to the Pacific Islands where legal systems and laws were either voluntarily or involuntarily imposed on traditional systems. The

---

[21]Mason (2005), p. 314.
[22]Kirby (2005), p. 433.
[23]Powles (2005), pp. 404–421.
[24]Ibid, 414.
[25]Slade (2004).
[26]Lindsey (2007).
[27]Goodpaster (2007), p. 134.
[28]Dick (2007), p. 42.
[29]Neilson (2007), p. 313.
[30]Lindsey, above n 26.

transplantation theory is discussed at more length below in so far as it is relevant to the Pacific Islands.

2.1.3 Legal Transplantation

'Legal transplant' is the movement of a system of law or a rule from one country to another.[31] In the Pacific region, there was substantial involuntary transplantation involving not only the promulgation of new laws, but also massive transformation of legal and political institutions. Perhaps the most influential are the supreme laws (the constitutions) of the South Pacific Islands which derive from the Westminster system.[32]

There is a vast amount of literature on legal transplantation which contains arguments for and against the practice.[33] The main problem with a legal transplant is the uncertainty of the form it would take in the host country.[34] The transition involves painful evolutionary adjustments,[35] and demonstrates that a foreign framework is never a perfect fit.[36] At the receiving end, legal transplants require time and resources to take root in the customary environment. It is difficult to restore and sustain the primacy of traditional law once transplantation is introduced, and westernisation becomes an irreversible change.[37] Watson proposes three categories of voluntary legal transplants, one of which is applicable to the Pacific Islands, when 'a people voluntarily accept a large part of the system of another people or peoples.'[38] In adopting a Constitution that establishes a Westminster system of government, Samoa voluntarily accepted the modern setups of a Parliament, an Executive and a Judiciary to regulate the affairs of Samoa.

Transplantation may be successful where it is adopted with caution, or if it was developed under similar legal, economic, social and political frameworks as the receiving country, or if the population is already familiar with the basic principles of those laws.[39] Despite these positives, home grown legal rules are more relevant to the host country than transplants.[40]

---

[31] Watson (1974).

[32] Dale (1993), p. 80.

[33] Legal transplantation has its origins in Montesquieu C *The Spirit of Laws* [Thomas Nugent trans] Available online http://www.thefederalistpapers.org/wp-content/uploads/2013/01/The-Spirit-of-The-Laws.pdf; Teubner (1998), p. 12; Lindsey, above n 26.

[34] Grajzl and Dimitrova-Grajzl (2009), p. 615.

[35] Ojwang (1986), p. 115.

[36] Lindsey, above n 26, 3–41.

[37] Ojwang, above n 35, 99–123.

[38] Watson, above n 31.

[39] Watson (1976), p. 79; Berkowitz et al. (2003), p. 168.

[40] Grajzl and Grajzl, above n 34.

At independence, the Pacific Islands adopted the common law legal systems facilitated by their constitutions.[41] There is some attempt to include the customary systems in the constitutions to localise the foreign system of government.[42] Following independence, the challenges of accommodating both the introduced legal system and the customary legal systems fell on the indigenous populations, particularly those taking over state functions. For instance, for Samoa, those involved in law reform must be formally educated to continue the adopted system and be sufficiently traditional to develop laws that are relevant to the traditional *faamatai*.

The increasing demand for laws and the lack of local drafting expertise makes the transplantation of laws convenient. Transplants are now readily adopted particularly where they have the features that can be taken advantage of. Transplants are a significant issue to Samoa but their implications are not given adequate consideration. All too often it is convenient to accept model laws offered by international organisations so as 'not to reinvent the wheel'. Although transplantation is now an acceptable practice, there are still some concerns in the case of Samoa. How can the success of transplants be measured?

Success is measured in the way the legal idea or framework has embedded in legal culture, as part of the local culture, or as an instrument for particular purposes.[43] Accomplishments depend largely on the recipient country's desire for the foreign rule to apply[44] although the desire may be severely hampered by other national priorities. Success is linked to how the transferred law fits into the new environment, but whether a transplant 'fits' is subjective[45] especially if there are conflicting interests of those affected by the law. Success can also be a mixed experience; it may be partial where the receiving state chooses to use only the part that is suitable for their environment.[46] Such success measures are useful considerations for policy makers in the executive and Parliament.

Transplantation may also be processed through institutional and policy transfers.[47] Peter Lamour discussed how a foreign framework to be adopted for customary land registration in a Pacific Island failed.[48] The concept of 'land' in the Pacific region was not accommodated by the transplanted framework resulting in the failure. Land is life in the indigenous communities and is not the object of the law but the source of law.[49] Lamour's experiences add value to this study in providing insight into bigger scale transplantation.

---

[41]For example, the *Constitution of Samoa* (Samoa) art 111; *Constitution of Solomon Islands* (Solomon Islands) sch 2.
[42]*Constitution of Samoa 1962* (Samoa) art 103; *Constitution of Vanuatu* (Vanuatu) arts 51, 52.
[43]Cotterell (2001), p. 79.
[44]Watson, above n 39, 83.
[45]Nelken (2001), p. 47.
[46]Ibid.
[47]Lamour (2005).
[48]Ibid 189.
[49]Black (2011), p. 184.

2.1.4 Attempts to Recognise Customary Laws in State Laws

There are various approaches to the incorporation and the recognition of customs in formal laws. Two of those approaches are through the codification and the restatement of customary laws, processes which have been employed outside of the Pacific region. These are explored next in terms of the benefits and disadvantages in those approaches. The discussions extend to specific ways in which customary laws may be incorporated in legislation.

2.1.4.1 Codification of Customary Laws

Codification is where 'much of the customary laws of a society are collected, collated and reduced into writing in the form of a statute or code having the stamp of law.'[50]

There are some benefits in codification. The codification of customary law into formal law weeds out irrelevant areas and uncertainties in the law.[51] It has also been argued that codification is essential for a reliable legal system; it addresses loopholes, inconsistencies, inadequacies, and the harsh consequences of some customary legal applications.[52] To prevent customs from being frozen in time, any such code must include a clear proviso that the description of the law is a snap shot of a moving object and that the description does not freeze the law.[53] This would allow customary laws to continue to evolve naturally with the changing values of the communities subject to them.

There are however many arguments against codification.[54] Customary laws were passed through oral culture and are not easy to draft into a written code. By reason simply of their sources in that a code is an introduced practice while customary rules originate from the local customs, a code is necessarily in opposition to customary law.[55] Whether the legislators share the attitudes and values of the people to whom the code will be applied is an important consideration for enforceability.[56]

---

[50]Salman (2006) p. 13. Codification has received many definitions and has been fully studied in many areas such as in the United States, France, England and African states.

[51]Field (1866), Onuoha (2008).

[52]Narebo (1991), p. 55. For the benefits of codification in certain American states, see Miller (1886), pp. 315–322.

[53]Danino (2005), p. 5.

[54]For example, on the experiences of some African states, see Fenrich et al. (2001). The difficulties of the application of the Natal Code of Native Law in 1878 (Welsh 1971) are further discussed in McClendon (1996).

[55]Bennett and Vermeulen (1980).

[56]Ali (1994).

The experience of codification in many countries suggests that the previous genitors of the law, the people, no longer have a direct role to play in the change and adaptation of the law; the changes and adaptation now fall on a professional elite or political authority.[57] For example, in Australia, the principal objection to codification is that it takes the question of the interpretation and content of their customary laws and traditions out of the hands of the Aboriginal people concerned.[58]

The language to be used in such a code of customary law is another important consideration. Although law does serve to coordinate social interaction, it does so through specific conceptual language and grammar, the product of customary experiences over time.[59] A code of law implies the existence of uniformity, whether geographical or cultural, in relation to the laws. It is a difficult task to decide which system of tribal law is to be elevated to the favoured position of a proposed code and expressed with the sensitivity necessary to reflect accurately the manner in which they function.[60]

Codification freezes custom to the extent it loses flexibility. Customary norms and standards are too flexible and uncertain to be encompassed in precise phraseology.[61] It is the flexibility of customary norms that gives them life and endurance; to deprive them of this is to deprive them of life.[62] Customary law cannot be reformed by Parliament without losing its customary character.[63]

The drafters of a code may be unfamiliar with the social context within which the customary law evolves. Customary law reduced to writing and then applied in court necessarily undergoes change; and this change may result in the disregard for the codified customary law. Based on the nature of customary law, codification would run the risk of being misapplied and disregarded.[64] The customary practises and procedures, the judicial personnel, their attitudes, the ways and techniques by which they arrive at a settlement that contributes towards social harmony, are no less part of the customary law than abstract rules of substance.[65]

2.1.4.2 Restatement of Customary Laws

Restatement 'brings together, clarifies, connects, re-arranges in a more logical comprehensive way, previous expressions of the law on a particular topic.'[66] It is

---

[57]Danino (2005).
[58]Australian Law Reform Commission, *Recognition of Aboriginal Customary Laws*, Report 31 (1986) 122.
[59]Webber (2009), p. 624.
[60]Bennett and Vermuelen, above n 55, 216.
[61]Ali, above n 56.
[62]Ibid.
[63]Powles, above n 23, 410.
[64]Bennett and Vermuelen, above n 55, 209.
[65]Danino, above n 57.
[66]Allot and Cotran (1971), p. 18.

an alternative to the harsh consequences of codification.[67] A restatement of customary laws has the same objectives as those of codification; that of uniformity and certainty. However, in contrast to codification, a restatement of laws may take the form of guidelines and manuals containing recordings of customary laws without customary laws being reduced into codes and having the force of law.[68] It may be a recording of customary laws to be used by the courts as an authoritative guide and legislators as a starting point for reform.'[69] When a restatement of customary laws is combined with legal textbooks, it may achieve better certainty, objectivity and flexibility than codification.[70]

There are various complexities in restating customary laws. One of the objections to the restatement of Kenya's customary laws was the failure to identify that 'an essential part of customary law is that it cannot be divorced from its social context and still purport to give a complete picture of tribal law.'[71] It is difficult to find suitable methods of restatement,[72] and disagreements on what exactly was sought and how best to find it was still widespread after decades of recording Kenya's customary laws.[73] Restatement prevents the progressive development of customary law. Rules of customary law may become obsolete and judges may make reference to out of date rules.[74] With reference to the recording of the customary laws of France, it was noted that to attribute the force of law into the rules of the restatement may eventually tie it with legislative action which is equivalent to freezing customary laws.[75]

2.1.4.3 Incorporation of Customary Laws by Reference

Incorporation by reference occurs where the state law incorporates customary laws without specifying the precise terms or meaning of concepts of customary law.[76] Following extensive public consultation by the Australian Law Reform Commission (ALRC) on the recognition of Aboriginal customary laws in Australian laws, the ALRC put forth some recommendations for recognition.

---

[67]Salman (2006), p. 15.
[68]Vanderlinden, 3 *Journal of African Customary Law* 165, 168.
[69]Twining (1963), p. 221.
[70]Epiphany (1991), p. 289.
[71]Ali, above n 56, 359.
[72]Roberts (1971), pp. 12–21. Roberts argues that one of the problems in recording the customary laws of Africa was the method employed. He opposes interviews as an interview respondent's opinion cannot reflect a true account of customary laws. He proposes 3 methods of investigation consisting of interviews, investigating related court decisions and observations.
[73]Ali, above n 56, noted that Kenya's lengthy attempts to ascertain and restate the customary law of various tribes in Kenya produced more uncertainties than anticipated.
[74]Oyebanji (1991), p. 270.
[75]Vanderlinden, above n 68.
[76]Morse and Woodman (1988), p. 13.

One of the ALRC's recommendations is the incorporation of customary laws by reference. The ALRC prefers recognition that avoids the need for precise definitions of Aboriginal customary laws, and specific, particular forms of recognition to general ones.[77] The lack of specificity is to preserve the flexibility of Aboriginal customary laws. There is recent example in Samoa with the recognition of 'village service requirements'[78] a term not specifically defined, to take account of the variety of village requirements unique to each village. Other more general and detailed examples of incorporation of customary laws by references are found in the Constitutions of some Pacific Islands.[79] Other approaches recommended by the ALRC include the translation of customary rules into formal laws to give them equivalent effect, for example for rules relating to marriage or adoption, and accommodating traditional or customary ways, for example the recognition of customary penalties in legislation.[80] Where customary laws are relevant they should be included and recognised in legislation but formal laws should not be altogether excluded.[81]

The ALRC's Report is a study of the recognition of the customary laws of a minority population as opposed to a majority indigenous population such as those found in Samoa and other Pacific Islands. However, as indigenous populations face similar struggles in incorporating customs in state laws, the ALRC's recommendations are valuable considerations for other law reform agencies searching for approaches to address these struggles. Incorporation by reference is applicable to the Pacific Islands where there is a restricted scope of recognition of customs if they are not repugnant to the constitutions and written laws.[82]

---

[77] Australian Law Reform Commission, *Recognition of Aboriginal Customary Laws*, ALRC Report 31 (1986) 122.

[78] *Electoral Amendment Act 2009 No 21* (Samoa) s 5.

[79] *Constitution of Papua New Guinea* (Papua New Guinea) sch 2.1; *Constitution of Solomon Islands* (Solomon Islands) sch 3(2); *Constitution of the Republic of Vanuatu* (Vanuatu) s 95(3), *Constitution of the Federated States of Micronesia* (Federated States of Micronesia) art V.1.

[80] *Village Fono Act 1990* (Samoa) s 8.

[81] Australian Law Reform Commission, above n 77.

[82] For example, the *Constitution of Papua New Guinea* (Papua New Guinea) sch 2.1; *Constitution of Solomon Islands* (Solomon Islands) sch 3(2); *Constitution of the Independent State of Samoa* (Samoa) art 111; *Underlying Law Act 2000* (Papua New Guinea); *Customs Recognition Act* (Papua New Guinea) ch 19; *Customs Recognition Act 2000* (Solomon Islands). There is useful literature that discusses the difficulties in implementing some of these legislation for example, see Care and Zorn (2001), p. 49.

2.2 Law Reform Commissions (LRCS) and Legal Professions of the Pacific Islands

2.2.1 Proposal for a Regional Law Reform Commission

The research on Pacific Law Reform Commissions shows that law reform institutions were for many years either non-existent or inactive.[83] This led to proposals for a regional law reform commission.[84] Most Pacific Islands have similar concerns and few resources. A regional agenda such as examining the imperial laws for appropriateness in the modern environment, investigating the relationship between the written law and customary law, and reprinting and revising statutes encompass common concerns.[85] Resources may be pooled together to share the limited expertise, to deal with common issues and preventing reinventing the wheel, to strengthen the region's capacity for security and cooperation,[86] and promote economic and cultural relationships.[87]

However, there are obstacles to the establishment of law reform commissions in the Pacific Islands.[88] In contrast to the influential legislative frameworks in the Australian states and Canada, the Pacific LRCs are expressly obligated by statute to develop law reform proposals that reflect the cultural and moral will of the Pacific Islands.[89] Appendix C illustrates this with an overview of the different functions of LRCs of several Australian states, Canada and New Zealand, as well as the Pacific Islands. Although law reform institutions were recognised as an important setup at the attainment of political independence, the progress has been delayed due to the lack of resources and uncertainty as to the kind of institution required.[90] Due to the lack of resources and expertise, some Pacific Islands law reform commissions were established when those Pacific societies were not ready to embrace the features typical of an institutional setup.[91] Adequate public consultations on law reform projects are hindered by geographical distances between the islands, and the various languages of the different tribes and villages of the Pacific Islands.[92]

Today the proposals for a regional law reform commission have not come to fruition for various reasons. All Pacific Islands experience diverse competing

---

[83]Conte (2005), Boister (2005).
[84]MacFarlane and Lakshman (2005).
[85]Slade, above n 25, 74.
[86]Sayers, above n 14.
[87]MacFarlane and Lakshman, above n 84.
[88]Six law reform institutions established under legislation in the Pacific Islands, see above, n 12.
[89]Appendix C Section 2 presents a summary of the statutory functions of the law reform commissions of the Pacific Islands.
[90]Leung-Wai (2008).
[91]Kabui and Guthleben (2008).
[92]Ishmael (2008).

priorities, are supported by different economic growth and make independent decisions on progress strategies. A regional LRC is not part of the near future strategies of development. It is perhaps more realistic to focus first on developing effective local law reform institutions before considering the feasibility of a regional law reform institution.

2.2.2 The Legal Profession

To address legal pluralism challenges, Pacific law societies must be active in developing a vibrant and more relevant local legal system that takes account of customary realities. Proper legal training with a focus on Pacific local contexts is necessary to address this. Research shows that a committed law society may exert great influence on law reform[93] and this is another avenue through which customs may be promoted. Training in the common law is necessary with the adoption of the western legal culture, but there must also be due regard to the local customs and traditions.[94] Efforts to develop Pacific law in the context of local customary development however are often hampered by the lack of resources and commitment,[95] and the cultural diversity amongst Pacific Islands.[96]

In relation to the work of the legislative drafters of the legal profession, in the absence of qualified, skilful and experienced policy makers in the Pacific Islands, legislative drafters have significant influence on draft laws developed.[97] The government, through legislative drafters, has substantial influence on law making[98] and there is heavy reliance on the offices of the Attorney-General to develop laws.[99] There are also reasons for avoiding the use of common law terms in customary matters as they do not fully capture the spirit of the customary principles.[100] These are the challenges to the codification of customs more fully discussed above.

---

[93]Narokobi (1986), p. 227.
[94]Corrin (2006), p. 185.
[95]For example, see Weisbrot (1988), pp. 1–5.
[96]Care (2005).
[97]Slade, above n 25.
[98]Nand (2008).
[99]Powles, above n 23, 414.
[100]Corrin (2008), p. 305.

2.3 Legal Pluralism

2.3.1 Old Legal Pluralism, Colonial and Postcolonial Pluralism

A brief background on the development of 'legal pluralism' as a concept is helpful to appreciate the proposition that it must be taken into account in the law reform processes of the Pacific Islands. It is particularly useful where the features of colonial and post-colonial legal pluralism reflect some realities of the Pacific Islands. The study of legal pluralism became prevalent in the 1970s and 1980s in the wake of growing awareness of the need to understand the complexities in societies with two or more legal systems.[101] The leading scholars on legal pluralism to name a few include Galanter,[102] Griffiths,[103] Baxi Upendra,[104] Boaventura de Sousa Santos,[105] Tamanaha,[106] Merry,[107] Chiba[108] and Moore.[109]

The experiences of Samoa and the Pacific Islands as former colonial societies currently struggling with two or more legal systems are not unique. Legal pluralism is experienced by many other distant developing countries, particularly those with similar historical backgrounds. Legal pluralism originally developed as a means of understanding the effect of the imposition of European law on the 'indigenous law' of the colonised societies.[110] There is a wealth of legal pluralism studies, for example, relating to imperial impositions on colonial societies governed by customary legal systems with traditional powers to judge or punish.[111]

The autonomous villages and tribes and customary structures in the Pacific Islands are good examples of 'semi-autonomous social fields' in the legal pluralism model offered by Sally Folk Moore.[112] As such, villages generate their own rules and customs internally through their village councils. These rules are vulnerable to decisions and other forces emanating from the state. Legal pluralism recognises the existence of customary laws alongside state laws and it opposes the European positivistic legal philosophy of state domination.[113] However dominant and

---

[101] Sharafi (2008), p. 139.
[102] Galanter (1981), p. 36.
[103] Griffiths (1986).
[104] Baxi (1986), 51–61.
[105] Santos (2002), pp. 85–98.
[106] Tamanaha (2008), p. 378.
[107] Merry (1988), pp. 869–896.
[108] Chiba (1986).
[109] Moore (1973), p. 720.
[110] Tamanaha (2008), p. 390.
[111] Merry, above n 107, 874; Chiba, 1986; and others discussed in this review. For contributions on legal pluralism in family law see for example Wardle (1998), pp. 381–396.
[112] Moore, above n 109, 719; Santos, above n 105, 85–98.
[113] Baxi, above n 104; Griffiths, above n 103; Galanter, above n 102.

imperious the state is, it is one among many social 'groupings' or 'orderings'.[114] In the same way that the state needs an apparatus of social control such as laws and institutions for the institutionalisation of conflicts and resolution, similar needs are required by social orderings other than the state. Villages, districts and provinces of customary communities operate alongside the state, and at times the customary laws and the state laws may overlap, but they do not suppress each other to the point of destruction. The different legal systems may even supplement each other on issues particular to a social order and in which that social order provides the best resolutions.[115]

2.3.2 New and Postmodern Pluralism

Legal pluralism is not solely a colonial and postcolonial phenomenon[116]; there is a third paradigm which exists largely in the western developed jurisdictions. This new legal pluralism extends the concepts outside of developing societies to western civilization and the interplay between the official and unofficial law and to describe legal relations in advanced industrial countries.

At a national sphere not all dispute resolutions take place in the courts. Other forms of social regulation draw on the symbols of the law but operate in the shadows of the law for example, parking lots and mediation offices.[117] These social regulations need to be recorded. On the global front, new legal pluralism is characterised by inter-legality in the transnational sphere, beyond the individual localised state or community whether colonial or western.[118] This third phase is where suprastate, global legal orders coexist in the world system with both state and infrastate legal orders.[119] New legal pluralism shifts legal analysis away from legal centralism ideologies to a recognition of decentralised legal sources that also have capacity to impose and resist laws, in the form of corporations, national and international.[120] It has a broader focus beyond the individual localised state or community and towards the transnational sphere[121] in the modern era.

Although this new legal pluralism phase is not directly relevant to the discussion of the position in the Pacific Islands, it is worth mentioning for two reasons. Firstly, new legal pluralism confirms the universalism of the theories of legal pluralism,

---

[114]Sack (1986).

[115]Tamanaha, above n 110.

[116]Sack, above n 114, 1.

[117]Merry, above n 107.

[118]Michaels (2009).

[119]Santos, above n 105, 92. In chapter 5 of this text, Santos provides a useful overview of postmodern pluralism.

[120]Griffiths (2002), pp. 289, 298.

[121]Michaels, above n 118, 243–262.

where legal pluralism has the potential for growth and taking various forms and shapes. Secondly, it provides insights into what may be expected in the future by Pacific Islands, such as where legal states create through recognition, other legal systems, and how the mutual recognition among legal systems in turn creates stability.[122] This branch of study may be more relevant to the Pacific Islands at a later more advanced stage of their social, political and economic development, but it is not the main focus here.

2.3.3 Other Categories of Legal Pluralism

The concept of legal pluralism has been grouped into three categories by Wardle.[123] Liberal pluralism occurs where differences are transferred to the area of private matters, but there is harmony as to the main public core ideals. Radical pluralism is the belief in universal principles such as basic human rights which cannot apply to all societies with different legal philosophies and practices, as the case in legal pluralistic societies. Extreme pluralism values all differences equally, and does not differentiate between social orderings, it fosters the pluralism and is accommodating to differences. In applying Wardle's principles to Samoa, these three categories are valuable in fostering legal pluralism, to instigate more understanding of legal pluralism and to reform state law to give adequate recognition of pluralism within state law.

Griffith classifies pluralism into weak and strong pluralism.[124] The definition of 'weak juristic or classical' pluralism is a reflection of the constitutions and the current laws of the Pacific Islands in that they offer a limited scope for the recognition of customs and usages. Customary law is kept separate and distinct from state laws which define the parameters and independence of customary law from state law. 'Strong, deep and new pluralism' believes that legal pluralism exists in all societies. This reflects the realities of the Pacific Islands although mostly in areas outside of the state premises. State law has not penetrated the foundation of customary legal frameworks existing independently of the state and not requiring state law for validity. The practice of strong pluralism is required for effective law reform, where both customary laws and the state laws are respected.

The literature reviewed in above examined the development of legal pluralism as a legal framework, through the concepts of 'old legal pluralism' and 'new legal pluralism'. The old legal pluralism literature developed from the colonial and postcolonial perspectives are all too familiar and relevant to the Pacific Islands, whereas the third new pluralism paradigm belongs to the future. Weak legal pluralism refers to other legal systems being weakened by the supremacy of the

---

[122]Ibid.
[123]Wardle, above n 111, 381–396.
[124]Griffiths, above n 120.

Constitution discouraging pluralism. Strong legal pluralism is more commonly practised amongst the villages, where the villagers respect their differences in customary practices and village governance. The discussions now turn to an analysis of the literature on legal pluralism and law reform.

2.4 Legal Pluralism in the Pacific Islands

2.4.1 Legal Pluralism in the Pacific Islands

There is some research on legal pluralism that highlights the aspirations of Pacific societies to have their customary rules recognised in state laws. It is acknowledged that one must define 'custom' and determine how it fits with the state legal system[125]; that the customary legal systems be recognised in the state formal system[126]; and for the customary laws to be reconciled with state laws.[127] There are valuable findings from research on harmonising custom and human rights from a human rights perspective,[128] in which religion was used as an example of how a foreign concept can be successfully integrated into and become part of the way of life of the Pacific Islanders.[129] There are also propositions for traditional systems to be strengthened and given more recognition within the western styled systems.[130] One scholar is unenthusiastic about changes being brought about by law reform in the Pacific Islands[131] where narrow techniques of law reform may not move law reform projects forward. However, arguably those narrow techniques are promoted by a state based law reform process lacking a consideration of customs in customary based societies.

2.4.2 Regional and Local Jurisprudence

In some Pacific Islands it is observed that law reform occurs on a piecemeal basis and is largely left to the judges.[132] For this reason, the development of a national legal jurisprudence to promote and acknowledge customs in the legal systems of the Pacific societies has been proposed.[133]

---

[125]Narokobi (1989), Corrin (2001), pp. 277–305.

[126]Weisbrot (1984), pp. 51–59; Care (2006), pp. 27–60.

[127]Weisbrot (1981), pp. 717–731; Corrin (2008), pp. 305–333.

[128]The International Council on Human Rights (2009).

[129]New Zealand Law Commission (2006).

[130]Techera (2009).

[131]Ntumy (1995), p. 17.

[132]Farran (2009), 181–195.

[133]Weisbrot, above n 95; Narokobi, above n 93, 227; Efi (2009), pp. 153–172.

2.4 Legal Pluralism in the Pacific Islands

It has been suggested that judges could consider how the values underlying customs might align with constitutional principles.[134] The judiciary may have regard to the development of the autochthonous nature of supreme laws with sensitivity and awareness of indigenous laws.[135] Developing a local jurisprudence however requires committed judges. The judiciaries of some Pacific Islands have yet to reach this level of confidence.[136] In the context of Melanesia, Narokobi posited that whether or not a Melanesian jurisprudence emerges in Melanesia depends significantly on the social values of the judges of the Supreme Court.[137]

Candidates for Pacific judiciaries will always be those with western training[138] with little to no appreciation of how this training may be placed in the customary context, and the highest courts are often constituted by expatriate judges who are not necessarily well placed to adjudicate on matters involving customs.[139] A local jurisprudence requires a systematic approach that is backed by doctrine and philosophy.[140] Unless the above realities are addressed, there is little chance of the development of a national or regional jurisprudence.[141] With specific regard to the Samoan context, the customary practices in conflict resolution, such as traditional conciliation must be recognised and applied by the formal courts.[142] The Land and Titles Court decisions must be periodically reviewed, and access to lawyers, to the Land and Title Court records, Samoan law reports and legal studies particular to the Samoan legal system must be facilitated by the state.

2.4.3 A New Approach To Examining The Customary Law and State Law Divide

The challenges of legal pluralism may be better addressed through a more suitable process for law reform. This needs to be developed by those with firsthand knowledge of the Pacific Islands, and ideally have experienced the communal and customary way of living in the Pacific Islands. This will remove any monistic approach lacking a customary perspective. The challenges and responses to those challenges must be developed in the Pacific context i.e. with regard to the local traditional structures, the historical links to ancestral gods and strong genealogical links Research methodologies which are more relevant to Pacific Islands must be

---

[134]New Zealand Law Commission, above n 129, 242.
[135]Vaai (1999), p. 265.
[136]Lunabek (2008).
[137]Narokobi, above 93, 226.
[138]Vaai (1997), pp. 225, 242.
[139]Hassall and Saunders (2013), p. 186.
[140]Ntumy, above n 131, 16.
[141]Corrin and Paterson (2011), p. 9.
[142]Efi, above n 133, 17.

employed. Data collected from the local offices and authorities also allows for a more contextual investigation and relevant possible resolutions.

2.5 Overview

In investigating a law reform process suitable for Samoa, the following issues must be kept in mind. Other jurisdictions have attempted to incorporate customs into state laws through codification or restatement (in the form of manuals and guides), or with the use of legal transplants. These experiences are valuable in consideration of any similar attempts being carried out in the Pacific Islands.

In the chapters that follow, codification and restatement will be explored in the context of Samoa. Caution must be applied in enacting legal transplants, as will be demonstrated by the discussions of an unsuccessful legal transplant of more than 50 years in Samoa. Law reform through judicial precedents is relevant to this study, and a few examples will be discussed of how law reform through the exercise of judicial discretion of expatriate judges' impacts negatively on customary laws and positively for individual rights and state laws. The possibility of a local Samoan jurisprudence facilitating a law reform process that is relevant to Samoa will be discussed.

This book proposes a law reform process that is more appropriate for the purposes of accommodating Samoan customs in state laws. Although Samoa is the focus of the study, the discussions are also applicable to other Pacific Islands with similar issues arising from their social and customary structures. The book promotes the involvement of customary structures, the use customary references and reliance on customary institutions in law reform initiatives. The factors that attribute to the courts, Parliament, executive, legal profession and the legislative drafters having little regard to customary laws which have not been investigated elsewhere will also be discussed.

Unlike other state based research, this book draws on a local perspective, with the study on Samoa being undertaken by a Samoan living and experiencing the realities of legal pluralism in Samoa. In addition, this research relies on empirical data from qualitative research interviews carried out with Samoan respondents living and experiencing being governed by both the customary legal system and the state legal system. Empirical documentary research relied upon are the analysis of local commission and Hansard reports, national plans of government and local newspaper data. A survey on Pacific legislative drafters adds a regional dimension on the challenges of legislative drafting in plurals societies. The empirical data places the study findings and resolutions in context.

In summary, the two overlapping legal frameworks 'legal pluralism' and 'law reform' have largely been investigated separately. The crucial issue in the Pacific Islands is how to accommodate two or more legal systems in one society. An effective strategy towards accommodation is to identify how legal pluralism is taken into account in the law making process of the Pacific Islands (if at all). It argues that legal pluralism must be taken into account in the law reform process for effective laws. In other words, as law reform is an apparatus of change, and change is more often state based, it is at this stage in the process that customary perspectives (and therefore legal pluralism) can be filtered in. Laws are thus developed having considered the impacts on both the state and prevalent customs. There are no easy or correct solutions to the conflicts arising from the customary law and state law relationship. The aim of this study is to offer another way of addressing the conflicts, and continue the dialogue on this significant issue, which continues to impact on the lives of Pacific Islanders. The next chapter discusses the research methods employed in this study.

References

Ali OH (1994) The conversion of customary law to written law. In: Alison D, Rentlen AD (eds) Folk law: essays in the theory and practice of lex non scripta. University of Wisconsin Press, p 1
Allot AN, Cotran E (1971) A background paper on restatement of laws in Africa: the need, value and methods of such restatement. In: Allot AN (ed) Integration of customary and modern legal system in Africa. Africana Publishers Corporation, New York, p 18
Atkinson R (2005) Law reform and community participation. In: Opeskin B, Weisbrot D (eds) The promise of law reform. Federation Press, p 160
Australian Law Reform Commission (1986) Recognition of aboriginal customary laws. ALRC Report 31(1986)
Baxi U (1986) Disciplines, repression and legal pluralism. In: Sack P, Minchin E (eds) Legal pluralism, proceedings of the Canberra law workshop, vol VII. Pink Panther, ANU Canberra, pp 51–61
Bennett TW, Vermeulen T (1980) Codification of customary law. J Afr Law 24(2):206
Berkowitz D, Pistor K, Richard JF (2003) The transplant effect. Am J Comp Law 51(1):163, 168
Black CF (2011) The land is the source of the law – A dialogic encounter with the indigenous jurisprudence. Routledge UK
Boister N (2005) Regional cooperation in the suppression of transnational crime in the South Pacific. In: Geoff L, von Tigerstrom B (eds) International law issues in the South Pacific. Ashgate, England
Care JC (2005) Legal representation, training and legislative drafting in smaller jurisdictions. Paper presented at the Commonwealth Law Conference, United Kingdom, 11–15 September 2005
Care JC (2006) A green stick or a fresh stick? Locating customary penalties in the post-colonial era. Oxford Univ Commonw Law J 6(1):27–60
Care JC, Zorn JG (2001) Legislating pluralism: statutory developments in Melanesian customary law. J Leg Pluralism 46:49
Chiba M (ed) (1986) Asian indigenous law: in interaction with received law. KPI, New York
Commonwealth Secretariat (2005) Law reform agencies: their role and effectiveness. Paper presented at the meeting of commonwealth law ministers and senior officials, Accra, Ghana, 17–20 October 2005
Conte A (2005) International terrorism and the South Pacific. In: Geoff L, von Tigerstrom B (eds) International law issues in the South Pacific. Ashgate, England
Corrin J (2001) Customary land in Solomon Islands: a victim of legal pluralism. Revue Juridique Polynesienne 12:277–305

Corrin J (2006) Finding the right balance in plural systems: training lawyers in the South Pacific. J Commonw Law Leg Educ 4(2):171, 185
Corrin J (2008) Customary law and the language of common law. Commonw Law World Rev 37
Corrin J, Paterson D (2011) Introduction to South Pacific law. Palgrave Macmillan
Cotterell R (2001) Is there a logic for legal transplants? In: Nelken D, Feest J (eds) Adapting legal cultures. Hart, Oxford, p 79
Dale W (1993) The making and remaking of commonwealth constitutions. Int Comp Law Q 42:67, 80
Danino R (2005) Customary law systems as vehicles for providing equitable access to justice for the poor and local governance, the Peruvian experience. In: Leadership dialogue with traditional authorities, Kumani, Ghana, December 5, 2005
Davis I (2005) Targeted consultations. In: Opeskin B, Weisbrot D (eds) The promise of law reform. Federation Press, p 148
Dick H (2007) Why law reform fails, Indonesia's anti-corruption reforms. In Lindsey T (ed) Law reform in developing and transitional states. Routledge, New York, p 42
Efi TATT (2009) Samoa jurisprudence and the Samoan lands and titles court: the perspective of a litigant. In: Suaalii-Sauni et al (eds) Su'esu'e manogi: in search of fragrance: Tui Atua Tupua Tamasese Ta'isi and the Samoan indigenous reference. National University of Samoa, pp 153–172
Epiphany A (1991) Codification of customary law: a mission impossible? In: Osinbajo Y, Kalu AU (eds) Towards a restatement of customary law. Federal Ministry of Justice Lagos, p 289
Farran S (2009) Palm tree justice? The role of comparative law in the South Pacific. Int Comp Law Q 58:181–195
Fenrich J, Galizzi P, Higgins T (eds) (2001) The future of African customary law. Cambridge University Press
Field D (1866) Codification. Am Law Rev 20:1
Galanter M (1981) Justice in many rooms: courts private ordering and indigenous Law. J Leg Pluralism Unofficial Law 19(25):36
Grajzl P, Dimitrova-Grajzl V (2009) The choice in the lawmaking process: Legal transplants vs. Indigenous law. Review of Law & Economics 5(1):615
Glenfield L (2005) Law reform through the executive. In: Opeskin B, Weisbrot D (eds) The promise of law reform. Federation Press, p 288
Goodpaster G (2007) Law reform in developing countries. In: Lindsey T (ed) Law reform in developing and transitional states. Routledge, New York, p 134
Griffiths J (1986) What is legal pluralism? J Leg Pluralism 24:1
Griffiths A (2002) Legal pluralism. In: Banaka R, Travers M (eds) An introduction to law and social theory. Hart, p 298
Handford P (1999) The changing face of law reform. Aust Law J 37:519
Hassall G, Saunders C (2013) Asia-Pacific constitutional systems. Cambridge University Press
Hurlburt WH (1986) Law reform commissions in the United Kingdom, Australia and Canada. Juriliber Limited, Canada
Ishmael KA (2008) The birth and rebirth of law reform agencies: the establishment of Vanuatu's Law Reform Commission. Paper presented to the Australasian Law Reform Agencies Conference, Vanuatu, 10–12 Sept 2008
Kabui F, Guthleben A (2008) The establishment of a Commission in Solomon Islands. Paper presented to the Australasian Law Reform Agencies Conference, Vanuatu, 10–12 Sept 2008
King DB (1969) The law reform challenge. Saint Louis Univ Law J 13:403–410
Kirby M (1983) Reform the law. Oxford University Press
Kirby M (2005) Are we there yet? In: Opeskin B, Weisbrot D (eds) The promise of law reform. Federation Press, p 433
Lamour P (2005) Foreign flowers. University of Hawaii Press

Leung-Wai MC (2008) Samoa's experience with the establishment of a law reform commission. Paper presented to the Australasian Law Reform Agencies Conference, Vanuatu, 10–12 Sept 2008

Lindsey T (ed) (2007) Law reform in developing and transitional states. Routledge, New York

Lunabek V (2008) Judicial activism. Paper presented at the Australasian Law Reform Agencies Conference, Vanuatu, 10–12 Sept 2008

MacFarlane P, Lakshman C (2005) Law reform in the South Pacific. J S Pac Law 9(1)

Mason A (2005) Law reform and the courts. In: Opeskin B, Weisbrot D (eds) The promise of law reform. Federation Press, p 314

McClendon TV (1996) A dangerous doctrine - twins, ethnography and the Natal code. Presented as a paper at the Stanford-Berkeley and UCLA Symposium on law, colonialism, and inheritance in Africa, 10 May 1996

Merry SE (1988) Legal pluralism. Law Soc Rev 22(5):869–896

Michaels R (2009) Global legal pluralism. Annu Rev Law Soc Sci, 5 Available via http://ssm.com/abstract=1430395. Accessed 10 May 2010

Miller SF (1886) Codification. Am Law Rev 20:315–322

Moore SF (1973) Law and social change: the semi-autonomous field as an appropriate subject of study. Law Soc Rev 7(4):720

Morse BW, Woodman GR (1988) Introductory essay: the state's options. In: Morse BW, Woodman GR (eds) Indigenous law and the state. Foris Publications, Dordrecht, p 13

Nand N (2008) Legislative drafting, distance education and its contribution to good governance in the Pacific. Paper for the 5th Pan-Commonwealth forum on open learning, July London, 13–17 July 2008

Narebo D (1991) Codification of customary law. In: Osinbajo Y, Kalu AW (eds) Towards a restatement of customary law in Nigeria. Nigeria Federal Ministry of Justice, p 55

Narokobi B (1986) In search of a Melanesian jurisprudence. In: Sack P, Minchin E (eds) Legal pluralism, proceedings of the Canberra law workshop VII. Pink Panther, ANU Canberra 227

Narokobi B (1989) Lo bilong yumi yet, law and custom in Melanesia. The Melanesian institute for pastoral and socio-economic service and the University of the South Pacific

Neave M (2001) Law reform in the 21st century – some challenges for the future. Commissioners' Speeches with the Victorian Law Reform Commission, Victoria Australia, 11 October 2001

Neilson WA (2007) Competition laws for Asian transnational economies: adaption to local legal cultures in Vietnam. In: Lindsey T (ed) Law reform in developing and transitional states. Routledge, New York, p 313

Nelken D (2001) Towards a sociology of legal adaptation. In: Nelken D, Feest J (eds) Adapting legal cultures. Hart, Oxford, p 47

New Zealand Law Commission (2006) Converging Currents: Custom and Human Rights in the Pacific. Study Paper 17

Ntumy M (1995) The dream of a Melanesian jurisprudence. In Aleck J, Jackson R (eds) Customs at the Crossroads, UPNG Law Faculty, p 17

Ojwang J (1986) Legal transplantation: rethinking the role and significance of Western Law in Africa. In: Sack P, Minchin E (eds) Legal pluralism, proceedings of the Canberra law workshop VII. Pink Panther, ANU Canberra 115

Onuoha RA (2008) Discriminatory property inheritance under customary law in Nigeria: NGOs to the rescue. Int J Not-for-Profit Law 10:2

Oyebanji MB (1991) Codification of customary law: prospect and problems. In: Osinbajo Y, Kalu AU (eds) Towards a restatement of customary law. Federal Ministry of Justice Lagos, p 270

Partington M (2005) Research. In: Opeskin B, Weisbrot D (eds) The promise of law reform. Federation Press, p 134

Payne M (2005) Law reform and the legislature. In: Opeskin B, Weisbrot D (eds) The promise of law reform. Federation Press, p 302

Powles G (2005) The challenge of law reform in Pacific Island states. In: Opeskin B, Weisbrot D (eds) The promise of law reform. Federation Press, pp 404–421

Roberts S (ed) (1971) The recording of customary law: some problems of method, folk law: essays in the theory and practice of Lex Non Scripta. University of Wisconsin Press, p 1994

Ross S (1982) Politics of law reform. Penguin Books, Melbourne

Sack PG (1986) Legal pluralism: introductory comments. In: Sack P, Minchin E (eds) Legal pluralism, proceedings of the Canberra law workshop VII. Pink Panther, ANU Canberra

Sackville R (2005) Law reform agencies and royal commissions: tolling in the same field? In: Opeskin B, Weisbrot D (eds) The promise of law reform. Federation Press, p 274

Salman RK (2006) Codification and restatement of customary law in Africa: the journey so far. In: Borokini AA (ed) Kogi Reading in law. Stebak Books & Publishers, Akure

Santos BdeS (2002) Toward a new legal common sense, 2nd edn. Thompson Litho Ltd, Scotland, pp 85–98

Sawer SG (1970) The legal theory of law reform. Univ Toronto Law J 20:183

Sayers M (2009) Law reform in the commonwealth, in small states and in the Caribbean. Commonw Law Bull 35(1):69, 70

Sharafi M (2008) Justice in many rooms since Galanter. Law Contemp Probl 71:139

Slade TN (2004) Law reform potential in the Pacific area. Paper presented at the Australasian Law Reform Agencies Conference, Wellington New Zealand, 13–16 April 2004

Sutton TC (1970) The pattern of law reform in Australia. University of Queensland Press

Tamanaha BZ (2008) Understanding legal pluralism: past and present, local to global. Sydn Law Rev 30:378

Techera EJ (2009) Law, customs and conservation, the role of customary law in community-based marine management in the South Pacific. Dissertation, Macquarie University

Teubner G (1998) Legal irritants: good faith in British law or how unifying law ends up in new divergences. Mod Law Rev 61(1):12

The International Council on Human Rights (2009) When legal worlds overlap, human rights, state, and non-state law. ATAR Roto Press SA, Vernier, Switzerland

Twining W (1963) The restatement of African customary law: a comment. J Mod Am Stud 1(2):221

Vaai S (1997) The idea of law, a Pacific perspective. J Pac Stud 21:225

Vaai S (1999) Samoa faamatai and the rule of law. The National University of Samoa

Vanderlinden J, The recording of customary law in France during the fifteenth and sixteenth centuries and in recording of African customary law. J Afr Customary Law 3:165, 168

Wardle LD (1998) Same-sex marriage and the limits of legal pluralism. In: Eekelaar J, Nhlapo T (eds) The changing family, family forms and family law. Hart, Oxford, pp 381–396

Watson A (1974) Legal transplants: an approach to comparative law. Edinburgh

Watson A (1976) Legal transplants and law reform. Law Q Rev 92:79

Webber J (2009) The grammar of customary law. McGill Law J 41(579):624

Weisbrot D (1981) Customizing the Common Law: The True Papua New Guinea Experience. Am Bar Association J 67:717–731

Weisbrot D (1984) The recognition of custom in Papua New Guinea and the Pacific. Ch 16 in the report of working seminar on the aboriginal customary law reference, Australian Law Reform Commission and Australian Institute of Aboriginal Studies 51-59

Weisbrot D (1988) Papua New Guinea's indigenous jurisprudence and the legacy of colonialism. Univ Hawaii Law Rev 10(1):1–5

Weisbrot D (2002) What is the value of a full time standing law reform commission? Paper presented at the Australasian Law Reform Agencies Conference. Darwin, 20 June 2002

Weisbrot D (2005) The future for institutional law reform. In: Opeskin B, Weisbrot D (eds) The promise of law reform. Federation Press

Legislation

Australian Law Reform Commission Act 1996 (Cth)
Australian Law Reform Commission Act 1973 (Cth)
Constitutional and Law Reform Commission Act 2004 (Papua New Guinea)
Constitution of Solomon Islands
Constitution of Papua New Guinea (Papua New Guinea)
Constitution of Solomon Islands (Solomon Islands)
Constitution of Vanuatu (Vanuatu)
Constitution of the Federated States of Micronesia (Federated States of Micronesia)
Constitution of the Independent State of Samoa (Samoa)
Constitution of the Republic of Vanuatu (Vanuatu)
Customs Recognition Act 1963 (Papua New Guinea)
Customs Recognition Act 2000 (Solomon Islands)
Electoral Amendment Act 2009 No 21 (Samoa)
Law Commission Act 1965 (UK)
Law Commission Act 1996 (Canada)
Law Commission Act 1969 (Sri Lanka)
Law Commission Act 2007 (Tonga)
Law Commission Act 2011 (Vanuatu)
Law Reform Commission Act 1970 (Canada)
Law Reform Commission Act 1979 Cap 26 (Fiji)
Law Reform Commission Act 1994 (Solomon Islands)
Law Reform Commission Act 2008 (Samoa)
Underlying Law Act 2000 (Papua New Guinea)
Village Fono Act 1990 (Samoa)

Online Databases

Law Commission of India, Government of India, Early beginnings. http://www.lawcommissionofindia
Montesquieu C (2012) The spirit of laws. [Thomas Nugent trans] Available via http://www.thefederalistpapers.org/wp-content/uploads/2013/01/The-Spirit-of-The-Laws.pdf. Accessed 10 May 2012

Chapter 3
A Research Methodology for the Pacific

Contents

3.1 Indigenous and Pacific Research Methodologies 35
    3.1.1 Postcolonial Research Methodologies 36
    3.1.2 Pacific Specific Methodologies 37
    3.1.3 'Talanoa' Research Methodology 38
3.2 Utilising Pacific Research Methodologies to Resolve Indigenous and Pacific Issues ... 39
    3.2.1 'Talanoa' and Ethical Interview Principles 39
    3.2.2 Analysing 'Talanoa' Interviews 42
    3.2.3 Pacific Islands Legislative Drafters Survey 43
3.3 Primary Material and Documentary Data 43
    3.3.1 Court Judgments and Hansard Reports 43
    3.3.2 Commission of Inquiry Reports 44
    3.3.3 National Reports 44
    3.3.4 Local Newspaper Research: The Samoa Observer 45
3.4 Overview 46
References 46

3.1 Indigenous and Pacific Research Methodologies

The debate on the appropriate research methods to be employed in research on and for indigenous people by both indigenous and non-indigenous researchers is a recent phenomenon. Pacific islands researchers are developing Pacific specific research methodologies for research on, by and for Pacific Islanders. This involves the use of research methodologies that are appropriate to the cultural environment of the Pacific Islands. *Talanoa*, a Pacific specific interview method fitting for Pacific research was developed to collect empirical interview data. The deliberate choice of research interview method adopted is to highlight that pluralism exists everywhere in Samoa. This is shown by the differences in which *'Talanoa'* was employed to accommodate the variances between the village and state interviewees. For the purposes of this book, the interviewees are referred to as 'respondents'. To promote the position that research methods must be relevant for Pacific societies the subject of studies, recent scholarly work on postcolonial and Pacific methodologies is worth mention.

3.1.1 Postcolonial Research Methodologies

The study of postcolonial indigenous research methodologies became the focus of indigenous studies in the 2000s.[1] Research methodologies studies put emphasis on the concerns and worldviews of the colonised to understand themselves through their own assumptions and perspectives. In the 'Indigenous Research Methodologies', Chilisa advocates that postcolonial methodologies must be employed for all research carried out on indigenous communities.[2] She argues that current dominant methodologies should be decolonised to legitimise and allow knowledge production processes that accommodate shared knowledge and wisdoms of those suffering from the oppressive colonial research tradition.[3] A postcolonial indigenous research paradigm is developed as an alternative to undertaking research, indigenising approaches and Western research paradigms. The indigenous methods are informed by a relational ontology (philosophies of the social realities of the indigenous peoples), epistemology (indigenous ways of knowing) and axiology (ethics and values systems of the indigenous peoples).

The 'Handbook of Critical and Indigenous Methodologies',[4] highlights similar challenges to developing indigenous research methodologies in India,[5] the United States,[6] South Africa[7] and New Zealand.[8] These contributions focus on critical and indigenous pedagogies,[9] critical and indigenous methodologies[10] and research ethics.[11] The crux of the contributions is that research by and on the indigenous peoples must adopt techniques and methods drawn from the traditions and knowledge of the indigenous peoples.[12] This work promotes 'research design strategies that respect indigenous ways and wrest social science away from a dominant and domineering western model'.[13] It offers a road map and a bridge into a new decade of critical indigenous inquiry.

There texts are relevant to Pacific research as they explore research methods applicable to countries which have a history of colonisation. In studies of postcolonial societies, research methods from within those areas are more applicable as opposed to the domineering colonial perspective. Indigenous research

---

[1]Mutua and Swadener (2004), Bishop (2008a), pp. 145–183.
[2]Chilisa (2012).
[3]Ibid, 39.
[4]Denzin et al. (2008).
[5]Cook-Lynn (2008), pp. 329–346.
[6]Begaye (2008), pp. 459–469.
[7]Krog et al. (2008), pp. 531–546.
[8]Bishop (2008b), pp. 439–458.
[9]Meyer (2008), pp. 217–232.
[10]Cook-Lynn, above n 5.
[11]Battiste (2008), pp. 511–530.
[12]Gonzalez and Lincoln (2006), p. 1.
[13]Lincoln and Denzin (2008), p. 563.

methods are influenced by the social realities, indigenous ways of knowing and value systems. Samoa and other Pacific Islands feature colonial backgrounds; thus the dominating western research methods must be replaced by more relevant Pacific methods defined by the Pacific way of knowing.

3.1.2 Pacific Specific Methodologies

Pacific-specific research methodologies have been the subject of debate since the 1990s.[14]

This took place in New Zealand, influenced largely by generations of multicultural Pacific communities that have made New Zealand home. This new approach to undertaking Pacific research is employed here, using appropriate Pacific research methodologies to obtain material to inform the book. The employment of a Pacific interview method supports the development of Pacific-specific research methodologies on research carried out in the Pacific Islands.

Relevant methodologies must be employed to inform any form of research on the Pacific Islands. Research methods must be culturally appropriate and must support the ethical principles which define those Pacific Islands. This proposition is supported by some scholarly work.

Initial publication on indigenous Pacific methodologies in the Pacific region is 'Decolonizing Methodologies – Research and Indigenous Peoples'.[15] In it, Smith questions the applicability of colonial imposed methodologies[16] on research on Maori people. She advocates Kaupapa Maori, a research process based on a methodological strategy where research is conceived, developed, and carried out by Maori and where the outcomes benefit Maori people.[17] Seven ethical principles appropriate for research on Maori people are emphasized. These include respecting people, presenting yourself and being seen, listening and speaking according to custom, sharing and hosting people, being generous, being cautious, not trampling over the *mana* (pervasive power) of the people and not flaunting one's own knowledge.[18]

Research on Pacific education systems in New Zealand[19] echoed similar sentiments on research on Pacific societies in general. Owing to the existence of Pacific communal practices, it found that the familial and collective roles, patterns of individual and group behaviour, responsibilities and relationships, all have a substantial effect on the research process that makes it possible to argue for the

---

[14]Tupuola (1993), p. 175–189; Anae (1998), pp. 273–279; Tamasese et al. (1997).
[15]Smith (1999).
[16]Ibid 23.
[17]Ibid 185.
[18]Ibid 120.
[19]Anae et al. (2001).

existence of a specific Pacific research methodology. The 'Researching Pacific and indigenous peoples: Issues and Perspectives'[20] was the first collection of writings by Pacific researchers that focussed on research methods relevant to the Pacific societies. Contributors shared the same views on the development of research methods for Pacific research expressed by Smith in 1999 and the New Zealand education research in 2001. The gist of the contributions was that culturally appropriate methodologies were relevant and must be applied in carrying out research in Pacific societies. They address methodological issues in research on indigenous societies,[21] language and cultural aspects of research[22] and Pacific specific features of research.[23] In 2005 the Health Research Council of New Zealand published guidelines on appropriate methods for such research[24] which promoted eight ethical research principles along the same lines as those proposed by Smith. These include respect, cultural competency, meaningful engagement, reciprocity, utility, rights, balance and protection. These ethical codes are not separate from the cultural protocols that govern Pacific peoples' relationship with each other.

Relevant Pacific methodologies have recently been developed by Pacific Islanders. For example, the 'hui and Talanoa' or the Pacific way of talking,[25] the Kakala framework sourced from Tongan valued contexts of thinking,[26] and the Samoan *teu le va* applied in education research on Pacific schooling.[27] These provide an alternative non-western way of research. *Talanoa* is a unique method specifically for one on one interview or focus group interviews. This study draws upon and further develops this method in the empirical interviews undertaken to inform the study.

3.1.3 'Talanoa' *Research Methodology*

Talanoa allows for a more 'free' gathering of information with less structured social and linguistic rules of exchange.[28] *It* is literally translated as *'tala'* meaning 'to tell' and *'noa'* meaning 'nil or without boundary' indicating the absence of a fixed agenda. It signifies freedom of conversation and 'telling' without restriction. It

---

[20]Baba et al. (2004).
[21]Smith (2004), pp. 4–16; Nabobo-Baba (2004), pp. 17–32.
[22]Mutu (2004), pp. 54–62; Taumoefolau (2004), pp. 68–76.
[23]Baba et al. above n 20, 95–104; Mahina (2004), pp. 186–201.
[24]Health Research Council of New Zealand (2005).
[25]Robinson and Robinson (2005).
[26]Thaman (2003), p. 10.
[27]Melani (2010), p. 1.
[28]Faafetai (2009), p. 96.

is through *Talanoa* that meanings and interpretations in Samoa are commonly shared and disclosed, and to interrupt a person speaking is culturally inappropriate. It demands notions of respect in approach, in deferring to village time schedules, in dress, in voice, in cultural addresses, in familiarity with genealogies, in building good relationships, in respecting boundaries, and in reciprocity. Respecting protocols before, during and after interviews helps develop a good relationship and rapport between the interviewer and the person interviewed. The author was accepted and viewed as a friend rather than an outsider. The respondent is more inclined to give information freely where good relationships and trust are established at the outset. *Talanoa* can be employed wherever there is a Pacific population[29] and has been employed to create dialogue for peaceful resolutions.[30] It is a culturally appropriate methodology in carrying out interviews with Pacific island interview respondents. In essence, the '*Talanoa*' process influences data collected in volume and authenticity. For this book, six ethical principles relevant to research undertaken in Samoa were applied. These are respecting people; building good relationships; presenting yourself and being seen; meaningful engagement; listening and speaking according to customs and reciprocity.

3.2 Utilising Pacific Research Methodologies to Resolve Indigenous and Pacific Issues

3.2.1 'Talanoa' and Ethical Interview Principles

Respecting people is an underlying ethical principle that applies from preliminary steps, in choosing the interview sample, through all interview steps and beyond the research. In the context of Samoa, a purposive sample targeted individuals who are leaders within the community. These included the *matai* of the village councils, the village mayors (*Sui o le Nuu*) and government women representatives (*Sui o le Malo*), government leaders and important office holders, lawyers and State leaders having capacity to influence law reform. As stated earlier, *matais* are the spokespersons of families and villages; they are believed to have the status of those knowledgeable in society due to their long term village services and leadership. In this book, a reference to 'village respondents' is a reference to the respondents who are village mayors, village council members and government women representatives while 'state respondents' are the significant office holders, members of Parliament, judiciary, government chief executives and lawyers. A full list of respondents in abbreviated form to respect anonymity is attached as Appendix A.

---

[29]Ibid. Chapter 5 of Faafetai's thesis discusses how *Talanoa* was successfully employed on a study of the Samoan community in Hawaii.
[30]Halapua (2003).

Table 3.1 Interview respondents

Categories	Nos
Village respondents	
Village council 1	Focus group (x5 *matai*)
Village council 2	x 5
Village mayors	x 9
Government women representatives	x 2
State respondents	
Significant office holders	x 9
Members of parliament	x 6
Members of the judiciary	x 7
Government chief executives	x 7
Legal profession	x 6
Total	1 Focus group and 51 individuals

Table 3.1 provides a summary of the categories of respondents, defined earlier as 'respondents'.

Virtually all interview respondents are Samoan *matai*, some residing in their respective villages influencing village governance. Others are responsible for state law reform initiatives in an official capacity but return to *matai* duties at the end of a working day.

After determining the sample, the first contact with the respondents should be carried out in a culturally appropriate manner to establish good relationships. It is disrespectful and culturally inappropriate to seek an interview over the telephone. The involvement of a 'broker' who understands the status of each interview respondent in the village is sometimes necessary. In building good relationships with the government of Samoa, an Information Paper was submitted to the Ministry of the Prime Minister and Cabinet (MPMC) indicating the purpose of the research, the methodology to be adopted and the potential benefits of the research for Samoa. The MPMC advised that the purpose for these government requirements was to keep the government informed of all research being undertaken in Samoa.[31] The author visited each state respondent to seek an interview and to confirm interview times.

Proper presentation of oneself requires culturally appropriate wear e.g. the Samoan *puletasi* for female. Face to face discussions establishes trust, closed the uncomfortable gap of unfamiliarity with the presence of the other and created meaningful relationships with respondents. The interview venue and schedule were consciously designed to allow the interviews to be carried out in areas comfortable and familiar to the respondents. For interviews carried out in the

---

[31]Discussions between a representative of the Ministry of the Prime Minister and Cabinet, Samoa and Lalotoa Mulitalo (Samoa, 15 December 2010).

village, cultural addresses[32] were exchanged. Each party acknowledges the historical and genealogical links of the other and exchange respectful addresses before moving on to the formal introductions. If a researcher's genealogical linkages are not directly connected to most of the village respondents, a short introduction with genealogical addresses is required. This is important to build good relationships. A 'broker' was employed for some interviews and in those cases; the broker introduced the author first by traditional status and second by professional status. The professional background[33] is of lesser importance at this forum, and important only in so far as indicating some authenticity on the purposes and intentions of the interviews.

As in other developing countries, Samoans in the village sector have a high regard for formal professions including lawyers. To settle everyone involved into the *Talanoa* interviews, the author respectfully requested to be seen as merely a researcher who was interested in the views of the respondents on the questions to be posed, and not a lawyer. This 'broke the ice' and allowed for the author to be 'de-roled' from her professional capacity to fit into the surroundings of the respondent and the *Talanoa* conversation. The conversations were comfortable, unrushed and relaxed. The distance between the author and the respondents before *Talanoa* was undertaken was removed as both the author and respondent participated in a conversation.[34] The exercise becomes not one of researcher and researched but where both become part of a story unfolding, where the respondent provides answers but was also enriched by other information from the author relevant to the respondent's world.

The informal setting allowed for the '*Talanoa*' process to be applied freely, where the respondent speaks without hindrance, unless interruptions are necessary to return the discussions to the interview issues. In many occasions, generosity was freely given and refreshments and meals were provided by the families. It is culturally appropriate to close a *Talanoa* by a short prayer administered by either the respondent or the researcher. In many cases, the respondent offered to conduct the prayer. *Talanoa* interview sessions are concluded by speeches exchanging expressions of appreciation from both sides.

In comparison with the interviews with the State respondents, employing *Talanoa* with the State respondents was at a limited level due to their busy schedules. The capacities in which these respondents were interviewed were not

---

[32] After taking a seat at the appropriate side of the Samoan *fale* (dwelling) the author and broker were greeted by the host family by utterances of genealogical names and families and ancestral gods to which the visitors are linked. The visitors do the same in turn. Where the visitors are from overseas, they are generally addressed according to their occupational statuses or utterances of references to their home country. People are linked to spaces and places which are uttered at the outset, respectfully giving identity to each present before addressing the purpose of the meeting. This is important to create good relationships.

[33] The author is a member of the Samoa Law Society and a former Parliamentary Counsel of the Office of the Attorney-General, Samoa.

[34] Vaioleti (2006), pp. 25–26.

traditional. Despite this, as all State respondents are Samoan *matai*, the ethical principles of *Talanoa* interviews employed with the village respondents were still employed. Save for some interviews with particular state respondents in which the English and the Samoan languages were used interchangeably, the Samoan language was the means of communication in virtually all interviews.

Reciprocity is one of the fundamental principles in Samoan culture where, 'If you have received from another, then you have an obligation to return the favour.'[35] The practice is also entrenched in Samoan proverbial sayings such as '*Avatu ni lo ae aumai ni lo*' meaning where something is given, the deed of giving must be returned. This practice is not mandatory and is based on free will. The amount or quantity of the 'return' to a respondent is unimportant; that something is offered is central to the norm. The author offered a small token of appreciation (monetary gift) to each village respondent either 'to buy sugar for a cup of tea' or 'for transport costs' to attach a different purpose or name to the gift, in an attempt to convince the respondent it is not a form of payment. In almost all cases the gift was first refused; while most accepted out of respect and appreciation of the giver. Reciprocity in research also requires that knowledge gained through research will be used to benefit research respondents and the society which is the subject of the research.[36] This is one of the main objectives of this research. With government sector interviews, there was (an unspoken) mutual understanding that the reciprocity practice (such as the monetary gifts offered to village respondents) is unnecessary. A handshake symbolises the end of the interviews with the state respondents.

3.2.2 Analysing 'Talanoa' Interviews

As *Talanoa* belongs to the phenomenological research family (along with the grounded theory method of research),[37] a phenomenological scrutiny was applied in constructing analysis. This analysis requires the 'viewpoint of eliciting essences and review the responses in acknowledgement of existential and individual differences'.[38] Phenomenological validation was also practised during the interviews. This involves the respondent and the researcher continuously providing a challenge or legitimatizing one another's stories and shared information,[39] in a respectful and reciprocating manner. Three approaches to 'testing and confirming findings'[40] were applied to validate interviews further. This includes' checking for representativeness,' 'checking for researcher effects' and 'weighing the evidence' on which

---

[35]Suaalii-Sauni et al. (2009), p. 205.
[36]González and Lincoln, above n 12, 785.
[37]Vaioleti, above n 34, 25.
[38]Hycner (1985), pp. 279, 292.
[39]Vaioleti, above n 34, 25.
[40]Miles and Huberman (1994), pp. 248, 265, 267.

responses were more trustworthy. In the analysis process, effort was also made to examine any sources of invalidity.[41] The same process of analysis was applied to focus group interviews with emphasis on 'content analysis' particular to focus group interviews.[42]

3.2.3 Pacific Islands Legislative Drafters Survey

In the Pacific Islands, the work of a legislative drafter impacts heavily on the laws passed by Parliament. Firsthand information on their views on the challenges of drafting in the Pacific Islands offers a regional perspective on those challenges. When the opportunity presented itself, a brief survey was carried out on the senior legislative drafters of the Pacific Islands at a regional forum of legislative drafters.[43] The sample consists of 11 senior legislative drafters from 11 Pacific Islands.[44] Appendix E lists the respondents in abbreviated names in respect of anonymity. The main purpose of the survey was to obtain the views from Pacific legislative drafters on the challenges of legal pluralism on the work of a Pacific Island legislative drafter. This is one of the two 'triangulation of methods' exercises employed in this book, the second being the newspaper data discussed further below. In this exercise, the insights drawn from this survey was compared against the interview data to confirm the findings relating to the difficulties faced by drafters in the plural societies of the Pacific. In brief the survey generally confirms the empirical interview findings.

3.3 Primary Material and Documentary Data

3.3.1 Court Judgments and Hansard Reports

Another useful source of information for the book is the analyses of Samoan court judgments and the Acts of the Parliament of Samoa and other Pacific Islands. Several parliamentary reports were reviewed for this study from which three will be referred to.[45] These materials are relied on mainly in discussions on the

---

[41]Kvale and Brinkmann (2009), pp. 248–253.

[42]Wilkinson (2011), p. 170.

[43]The Pacific Islands Legislative Drafters Forum held at the Pacific Islands Forum Secretariat (PIFS), Suva, 23–25 July 2012. The PIFS is acknowledged for allowing the author to undertake this survey at this forum.

[44]Vanuatu, Kiribati, Solomon Islands, Papua New Guinea, Samoa, Marshall Islands, Nauru, Palau, Cook Islands, Federated State of Micronesia, Niue.

[45]Samoa Parliamentary Debates (1990a, b), pp. 22–23, 2–4; Samoa, Parliamentary Debates (2010), p. 703. At the time of data collection for this thesis, the library of the Legislative Assembly of Samoa did not hold English versions of the parliamentary debates on the Village Fono Bill 1990

challenges of legal pluralism in Chap. 5. The Hansard reports on the Village Fono Bill 1990 (Samoa) provide some valuable background to the original policies behind the *Village Fono Act 1990* (Samoa). Those debates also portray the complexities of merging two equally important legal systems in Samoa.

3.3.2 Commission of Inquiry Reports

Another excellent source of information is the Commissions of Inquiry (COI) Reports. Five such COIs reports in Samoa[46] set up for specific objectives to meet in the years 2001 to 2011.[47] Creating ad hoc commissions to investigate and recommend on law reform is not a recent phenomenon in Samoa. The first ad hoc body in the form of a committee was established in 1975 to review the law, carry out public consultation, and make recommendations for reform on the customary land and titles.[48] COIs established for specific law reform projects have been relatively successful in Samoa, even after the establishment of the Samoa Law Reform Commission (SLRC) in 2008.

Although resulting legislation does not fully measure the success of a law reform project, it provides an indication of whether such commissions may be successfully utilised. Later in Chap. 5, the reasons COIs have been a success in influencing reforms in Samoa as compared with the SLRC will be explained. To supplement those discussions, an overview of the outcomes of the law reform work of COIs in Samoa from 2001 to date is attached as Appendix B.

3.3.3 National Reports

National or country reports also provide a useful source for this study. In developing policy, Samoa is influenced by the global United Nations Millennium

---

(Samoa). All references to parliamentary debates on this Bill are made to the Samoan version. The relevant debates were translated by the author for the purposes of this study. Effort was made for the translations to reflect the content of the reports as accurately as possible. The third Hansard report, which records parliamentary debates on the Casino Control and Gambling Bill 2010 (Samoa) is in the English language.

[46]Samoa Commission of Inquiry into the Electoral Act Report 2001; Samoa Commission of Inquiry into the Electoral Act Report 2006; Samoa Commission of Inquiry into Matters relating to the Divergence Between the Decision Making Authority of the Alii and Faipule and the Formal Courts Report 2007; Samoa Commission of Inquiry into Matai Titles Report 2010; Samoa Commission of Inquiry into the Freedom of Religion Report 2010.

[47]These Commissions were set up by Cabinet under the provisions of the Commission of Inquiries Act 1964 (Samoa).

[48]Epati (1988), p. 169.

Development Goals and the regional Pacific Plan.[49] These goals and plans are filtered into Samoa's national plans, sector plans and government corporate plans. The Strategy for the Development of Samoa is Samoa's National Plan for the period 2012–2016.[50] The corporate and sector plans are designed to meet the objectives of the national plan which emphasises strengthening traditional structures and community development. The national plans are used to evaluate the feasibility of the suggested proposals (responding to legal pluralism challenges) discussed in Chap. 6.

3.3.4 Local Newspaper Research: The Samoa Observer

Samoa's local newspaper the Samoa Observer actively encourages public opinion. It is pivotal in challenging state accountability. On this basis, the local newspaper is a useful source of information for this study. Public opinion and analysis of those opinions was used for triangulation purposes.[51] Research was carried out on the local newspaper to reaffirm the level of public interest in Samoa on law reform, from a different dimension. This is through a 'residential count' of public views on State reforms, expressed by those residing in Samoa and outside of Samoa. The study counted public opinions expressed through letters to the editor (LTE) of the Samoa Observer in the years 2008 to 2010, on three of the most controversial parliamentary reforms according to public opinion.[52] These are namely the Act that changed the side of the road to drive on from the right to the left (*Road Transport Reform Act 2008* (Samoa) (RTR Act)), the Act that was feared to facilitate the alienation of customary land (*Land Titles Registration Act 2008* (Samoa) (LTR Act)), and a law that many cautioned would threaten the most important institution in Samoa, the family (the *Casino and Gambling Control Act 2010* (Samoa) (CGC Act)).

In the 3 years of the study (2008–2010), of the 248 LTEs to the Samoa Observer relating to the RTR Act, 215 opposed this reform, 23 were in favour of it and 10 were neutral. All 55 LTEs written on the LTR Act were against it. Of the 31 LTEs relating to the CGC Act, 25 opposed this reform, four were in support and 2 took no position. This shows overwhelming opposition to the three reforms. The significant public interest received by these reforms made them an ideal sample to inform a comparative study of the level of interest from within Samoa and overseas.

This study recorded the number of LTE published in the newspaper under each of the three reforms in 2008, 2009 and 2010 respectively, and the residence or

---

[49]Pacific Islands Forum Secretariat (2012). Pursuant to the Pacific Plan, the Pacific leaders met and identified agreed priorities to strengthen regional cooperation and integration.

[50]Report of the Ministry of Finance Samoa (2012).

[51]Patton (1990), p. 464.

[52]Protestors demonstrated opposition through public marches and court proceedings challenging the RTR Act. These are discussed briefly in a review of the law reform work of the Samoa non-government organisations in Chap. 5.

location of the LTE authors. Of the LTE writers living in Samoa, their local residence (whether urban or rural) and employment (where indicated) were recorded and analysed for this study. The LTEs written in the Samoan language did not form part of the data as they were mainly translations of the English versions.

From a total number of around 1095 daily Samoa Observer editions published in the years 2008 to 2010, 885 editions were reviewed for this study (about 80%). From 885 editions, around 550 (about 62%) LTEs relate to law reform in general in Samoa, and some 335 (about 38%) related specifically to the three contentious reforms referred to above. In sum, these findings confirm that there is little interest and value placed by the local public on law reform, which verifies a main finding of the interview data. The newspaper findings are referred to further in Chap. 4.

3.4 Overview

In developing upon the *Talanoa* interview method, this book strongly supports Pacific specific research methodologies. This method complies with the philosophies of the social realities of the Samoan people, the indigenous ways of knowing and the ethics and values systems of the Samoan people. The ethical principles of the Pacific peoples are respected in research. Perhaps the most valuable form of reciprocity is that the findings from this study are useful for Samoa and other Pacific Islands. The legislative drafters' survey which provided a collective regional view supported the findings from the interview data, on the divergence between the enacted laws and the general public which the laws are intended to govern. This book also drew from various other helpful methods of documentary analysis. These are namely the doctrinal analyses of court judgments and Samoan Acts of Parliament, the Hansard records and commission of inquiry reports, national reports and an appraisal of the local newspaper collection. The next chapter discusses the broad category of challenges which this book refers to as the social and cultural challenges for law reform.

References

Anae MS (1998) Inside out: methodological issues on being a 'native' researcher'. Pac Health Dialog 5(2):273–279

Anae M et al (2001) Pasifika education research guidelines. Auckland Uniservices Limited, University of Auckland

Baba TL et al (eds) (2004) Researching Pacific and indigenous peoples: issues and perspectives. University of Auckland

Battiste M (2008) Research ethics for protecting indigenous knowledge and heritage: institutional and researcher responsibilities. In: Denzin NK, Lincoln YS, Smith LT (eds) Handbook of critical and indigenous methodologies. Sage Publications, pp 511–530

References

Begaye T (2008) Modern democracy – The complexities behind appropriating indigenous models of governance and implementation. In: Denzin NK, Lincoln YS, Smith LT (eds) Handbook of critical and indigenous methodologies. Sage Publications, pp 459–469

Bishop R (2008a) Freeing ourselves from neo-colonial domination in research: A Kaupapa Maori approach to creating knowledge. In: Denzin NK, Lincoln YS (eds) The landscape of qualitative research, 3rd edn. Sage Publications, Thousand Oaks, pp 145–183

Bishop R (2008b) Te Kotahitanga – Kaupapa Maori in mainstream classrooms. In: Denzin NK, Lincoln YS, Smith LT (eds) Handbook of critical and indigenous methodologies. Sage Publications, pp 439–458

Chilisa B (2012) Indigenous research methodologies. Sage Publications

Cook-Lynn E (2008) 'History, myth and identity in the New India story. In: Denzin NK, Lincoln YS, Smith LT (eds) Handbook of critical and indigenous methodologies. Sage Publications, pp 329–346

Denzin NK, Lincoln YS, Smith LT (2008) Handbook of critical and indigenous methodologies. Sage Publications

Epati AS (1988) Lawyers and the customary law court. In: Powles CG, Pulea M (eds) Pacific courts and legal systems. University of the South Pacific, Fiji, p 169

Faafetai L (2009) The impact of Samoan christian churches on Samoan language competency and cultural identity. PhD Thesis, University of Hawaii, p 96

Gonzalez y Gonzalez EM, Lincoln YS (2006) Decolonizing qualitative research: non-traditional reporting forms in the Academy. Forum Qual Soc Res 7(4):1

Hycner RH (1985) Some guidelines for the phenomenological analysis of interview data. Hum Stud 8(279):292

Krog A, Mpolweni-Zantasi N, Ratele K (2008) The South African truth and reconciliation commission (TRC): ways of knowing Mrs Konile. In: Denzin NK, Lincoln YS, Smith LT (eds) Handbook of critical and indigenous methodologies. Sage Publications, pp 531–546

Kvale S, Svend Brinkmann S (2009) Interviews - learning the craft of qualitative research interviewing, 2nd edn. Sage Publications, pp 248–253

Lincoln YS, Denzin NK (2008) The lions speak. In: Denzin NK, Lincoln YS, Smith LT (eds) Handbook of critical and indigenous methodologies. Sage Publications, p 563

Mahina O (2004) Issues and challenges in Pacific research: some critical comments. In: Baba TL et al (eds) Researching Pacific and indigenous peoples: issues and perspectives. University of Auckland, pp 186–201

Meyer MA (2008) Indigenous and authentic: Hawaiian epistemology and triangulation of meaning. In: Denzin NK, Lincoln YS, Smith LT (eds) Handbook of critical and indigenous methodologies. Sage Publications, pp 217–232

Miles MB, Huberman AM (1994) Qualitative data analysis: an expanded sourcebook. Sage Publications, Thousand Oaks, pp 248, 265, 267

Mutu M (2004) Researching the Pacific. In: Baba TL et al (eds) Researching Pacific and indigenous peoples: issues and perspectives. University of Auckland, pp 54–62

Mutua K, Swadener B (2004) Decolonising research in cross-cultural contexts. State University of New York Press, Albany

Nabobo-Baba U (2004) Research and Pacific indigenous peoples: silenced pasts and challenges futures. In: Baba TL et al (eds) Researching Pacific and indigenous peoples: issues and perspectives. University of Auckland, pp 17–32

Patton MQ (1990) Qualitative evaluation and research methods, 2nd edn. Sage Publications, Newbury Park, p 464

Samoa Commission of Inquiry into the Electoral Act Report (2001)

Samoa Commission of Inquiry into the Electoral Act Report (2006)

Samoa Commission of Inquiry into matters relating to the divergence between the decision making authority of the Alii and Faipule and the formal courts Report (2007)

Samoa Commission of Inquiry into matai titles Report (2010)

Samoa Commission of Inquiry into the freedom of religion Report (2010)

Samoa Parliamentary Debates (1990a) 22–23 January
Samoa Parliamentary Debates (1990b) 2–4 July
Samoa Parliamentary Debates (2010) 12 October, 703
Smith LT (1999) Decolonizing methodologies, research and indigenous peoples. University of Otago
Smith LT (2004) Building research capability in the Pacific, for the Pacific and by Pacific peoples. In: Baba TL et al (eds) Researching Pacific and indigenous peoples: issues and perspectives. University of Auckland, pp 4–16
Suaalii-Sauni et al (eds) (2009) Su'esu'e Manogi, in search of fragrance, Tui Atua Tupua Tamasese Ta'isi and the Samoan indigenous reference. National University of Samoa, p 205
Tamasese K et al (1997) O le taeao afua, the new morning: A qualitative investigation into Samoan perspectives on mental health and culturally appropriate services. Health Research Council of New Zealand
Taumoefolau M (2004) A place to stand. In: Baba TL et al (eds) Researching Pacific and indigenous peoples: issues and perspectives. University of Auckland, pp 68–76
Tupuola AM (1993) Raising research consciousness the Fa'asamoa Way. NZ Annu Rev Edu 3:175–189
Thaman KH (2003) Decolonising Pacific studies: indigenous perspectives, knowledge and wisdom in higher education. Contemp Pac 15(1):10
Vaioleti TM (2006) Talanoa research methodology: a developing position on Pacific research. Waikato J Edu 12:25–26
Wilkinson S (2011) Analysing focus group data. In: Silverman D (ed) Qualitative research, 3rd edn. Sage Publications, p 170

Legislation

Commission of Inquiries Act 1964 (Samoa)

Online Databases

Government of Samoa, Ministry of Finance (2012) Strategy for the development of Samoa (SDS) 2012-2016 http://www.mof.gov.ws/Services/Economy/EconomicPlanning/tabid/5618/Default.aspx
Halapua S (2003) Walking the knife-edged pathways to peace. Pacific Islands Report http://166.122.164.43/archive/2003/July/07-08-halapua.htm
Health Research Council of New Zealand (2005) Guidelines on Pacific health research 3rd ed. Health Research Council of New Zealand http://www.hrc.govt.nz
Melani A (2010) Research for better Pacific schooling in New Zealand: Teu le va – a Samoan perspective. MAI Review 1 http://www.review.mai.aci.nz
Pacific Islands Forum Secretariat, Pacific Plan (2012) Annual Progress Report http://www.pacificplanreview.org/index.cfm
Robinson D, Robinson K (2005) Pacific ways of talk – hui and talanoa. Community Research, New Zealand http://www.communityresearch.org.nz/wp-content/uploads/formidable/robinson4.pdf

Chapter 4
The Value of Law Reform: Social and Cultural

Contents

4.1	The Ideological Principles Behind Law Making: Customary Laws and State Laws	50
	4.1.1 Social Views on Law Reform	51
	4.1.2 Limited Understanding of State Laws	51
	4.1.3 Lack of Formal Education	52
	4.1.4 Relevance to Village Life	53
	4.1.5 Cultural Factors	54
	4.1.6 Language Barriers	55
	4.1.7 Support from Secondary Data: Local Newspaper Research	55
	4.1.8 Challenges to Address	57
4.2	Demand for Customs and Respect for the Constitution	58
	4.2.1 Customary Laws as the Basis of the Legal System	59
	4.2.2 Laws in the Samoan Context	59
	4.2.3 Respect for the Constitution	60
	4.2.4 Challenges to Address	61
4.3	Should Customs be Codified in Samoa's Laws?	62
	4.3.1 Opposition to Codification	62
	4.3.1.1 Conflicting Values	62
	4.3.1.2 Flexibility	62
	4.3.1.3 Ascertainment and Uniformity	63
	4.3.1.4 Serving the Interests of Non-Locals Only	63
	4.3.1.5 Absence of Customary Structures to Support Customs in Legislation	63
	4.3.1.6 Difficulties for Legislative Drafters	64
	4.3.1.7 Secondary Data: Pacific Legislative Drafters Survey	64
	4.3.2 Benefits of Codification	66
	4.3.2.1 Certainty and Constitutional Compliance	66
4.4	Emerging Conceptual Challenges	66
	4.4.1 Understanding the Dichotomy	66
	4.4.2 Need to Promote Understanding of State Laws	67
	4.4.3 Customs to be Recognised in State Laws	67
	4.4.4 Emerging Acceptance of Modern Laws	67
	4.4.5 Interdependency	68
References		68

© Springer International Publishing AG 2018
T.L. Mulitalo Ropinisone Silipa Seumanutafa, *Law Reform in Plural Societies*,
The World of Small States 2, https://doi.org/10.1007/978-3-319-65524-6_4

4.1 The Ideological Principles Behind Law Making: Customary Laws and State Laws

This chapter presents a grass roots perspective on state laws and their relevance to everyday life based on customary practices. In order for the respondents to be heard, quotes are used in this chapter to give respondents a voice in this book.

In the course of the interviews, it became apparent that the majority of respondents believed that Samoa practises two unique ideologies. There is overwhelming consensus from all respondents that there are unique differences in the underlying principles on which the state and customary systems are founded, and that this poses a challenge to developing law reform.[1] Members of the judiciary interviewed pointed out that customs and formal laws are founded on two different philosophies[2] while village respondents in particular were of the view that individual rights promoted by the state do not go hand in hand with village philosophies of communal living.[3] The different philosophical principles were observed to exist in the following ways.

Customs promote communal rights whereas parliamentary laws protect individual rights.[4] Second, the emphasis of customs is to keep the peace and harmony in the village whereas state laws are to punish the wrongdoer.[5] Third, there is a customary system of hierarchy practised in the village in all village practises whereas the state advocates equality before the law and protection from the state.[6] In terms of penalty, although the offender is the target of a customary penalty, the extended family is affected, for example banishment of a whole family from the village.[7] State penalties on the other hand are individual based. Finally, customs are based on Christian values whereas formal laws are based on secular beliefs.[8] State laws are founded on foreign values rather than on respect, humbleness and love which are the principles of village rules.[9] In terms of the hierarchy of laws, customs regulated by the village councils are more authoritative and

---

[1] Interviews in Samoa with: VM Respondent 3 (8 March 2011); VM Respondent 4 (16 March 2011); VM Respondent 5 (16 March 2011); VM Respondent 6 (9 March 2011); VM Respondent 8 (16 March 2011).

[2] Interviews in Samoa with MOJ Respondent 1 (28 March 2011); MOJ Respondent 3 (7 March 2011); MOJ Respondent 5 (1 April 2011); MOJ Respondent 6 (4 April 2011).

[3] Interviews with: VM Respondent 8 (16 March 2011); VM Respondent 3 (8 March 2011); VM Respondent 4 (16 March 2011); VM Respondent 5 (16 March 2011); VM Respondent 6 (9 March 2011).

[4] Interview with VC1 Focus Group (Samoa, 1 March 2011).

[5] Interview with SOH Respondent 6 (Samoa, 12 April 2011).

[6] Interviews in Samoa with: VM Respondent 2 (9 March 2011); VM Respondent 3 (8 March 2011).

[7] Interview with SOH Respondent 6 (Samoa, 12 April 2011).

[8] Interviews in Samoa with: VC2 Respondent 5 (15 March 2011); MOP Respondent 2 (4 January 2011); SOH Respondent 4 (11 July 2011); VM Respondent 2 (9 March 2011).

[9] Interview with VC1 Focus Group (Samoa, 1 March 2011).

4.1 The Ideological Principles Behind Law Making: Customary Laws and State Laws

effective[10] compared to state laws. The traditional structures give validity to the existence of the state systems.[11] Parliamentary laws however marginalise the importance of customary laws and the traditional village structures from which the traditional authorities derive, and this threatens the existence of Samoan customs and identity.[12]

The empirical data echoes the conflicts of the underlying values of state laws and customary laws experienced by many post-colonial societies. This is discussed in a vast range of scholarly work including those discussed earlier in Chap. 2. Customary laws regulate the relationship between private individuals (private law) whereas state laws regulate the relationship with the state (public law).[13] By nature of their origins, purposes, procedures and dynamics, the two ideologies are contradictory. Efforts by the state to promote state law reform are hindered by the existence of strong customary practices. In many cases, the conflicting differences are not highlighted and properly acknowledged and explored by law reformers. This heightens misunderstanding and mistrust of State laws. There must be genuine efforts to identify the complexities and find strategies to take advantage of the differences to develop resolutions from both legal systems.

4.1.1 Social Views on Law Reform

Except for those involved in law making, there is little value placed on law reform. The public needs to be informed of the state legal system, the objectives and future benefits of reforms, for any appreciation of what state advocates. To create ownership and appreciation of laws, the input from the public is important. Participation in law making will result in respect for the law and therefore the legitimacy of laws.

4.1.2 Limited Understanding of State Laws

In relation to an understanding of laws and law reform, the interview data revealed the following observations from a village council.

> The public cannot identify themselves with laws; they are unaware of the law reform process and do not understand the state system. People do not see laws as important; they leave laws to lawyers and government; and would rather spend time with daily chores than attend consultations. Also, people do not understand the language of consultation; they are

---

[10]Ibid.
[11]Interview with MOP Respondent 2 (Samoa, 4 January 2011).
[12]Interview with VC1 Focus Group (Samoa, 1 March 2011).
[13]Ntumy (1995), p. 11.

afraid and are discouraged to say anything in case they are reprimanded. Only the town people know of those laws.[14]

There were also individual comments as follows. 'An understanding of human rights and the constitution is lacking.'[15] 'The public do not concern themselves with state laws as they have their own laws'[16] and 'state laws are largely irrelevant to the village activities like operating a plantation'.[17] 'Laws are of a different language with different interpretations and perceptions.'[18] 'Sometimes the public do not understand why they should be consulted on law reform where they see this as a prerogative of government.'[19] *The Village Fono Act 1990* (Samoa) is good law which gives some recognition to customary practices but it is not understood by all, especially the elderly in Samoa.'[20] A non-government respondent observed 'I believe more than 70% of persons in Samoa have no knowledge of their rights under the formal laws. There is so much people do not understand, I feel sorry for the people.'[21]

4.1.3 Lack of Formal Education

The limited appreciation of laws and law reform is believed by some respondents to be a result of a lack of formal education.[22] Immersed in village activities, it was essential to be knowledgeable and fluent in genealogies and village honorifics. Formal education was unimportant[23] and not entirely appropriate for Samoa.[24] One of the respondents expressed a view common of the majority of the respondents interviewed.

> In Samoa, most of the people in the rural areas have not attended formal education. So, an understanding of the government laws should be encouraged in the next generation. The younger generation would understand the laws of government. It is difficult to explain deeds to the villagers or financial accounts of money received and expenses. Most of the older generation are confused and this may create suspicion and complaints. These all result

---

[14] Interview with VC1 Focus Group (Samoa, 1 March 2011).
[15] Interviews in Samoa with: SOH Respondent 9 (21 March 2011); MOJ Respondent 3 (7 March 2011); MOJ Respondent 5 (1 April 2011).
[16] Interview with MOP Respondent 3 (Samoa, 11 January 2011).
[17] Interview with SOH Respondent 6 (Samoa, 12 April 2011).
[18] Interview with LP Respondent 5 (Samoa, 14 March 2011).
[19] Interview with GCE Respondent 2 (Samoa, 11 March 2011).
[20] Interview with MOJ Respondent 6 (Samoa, 4 April 2011).
[21] Interview with SOH Respondent 9 (Samoa, 21 March 2011).
[22] Interviews in Samoa with: MOP Respondent 7 (4 April 2011); VM Respondent 1 (11 March 2011); VM Respondent 2 (9 March 2011); VC2 Respondent 4 (8 March 2011); VC2 Respondent 2 (10 March 2011); VC2 Respondent 3 (7 March 2011).
[23] Interview with MOJ Respondent 5 (Samoa, 1 April 2011).
[24] Interview with MOP Respondent 5 (Samoa, 11 January 2011).

4.1 The Ideological Principles Behind Law Making: Customary Laws and State Laws

from the fact that there is a lack of formal education. Our people's minds are uninformed on these matters.[25]

The respondents acknowledge that to keep up with modern developments, formal education is necessary. Samoa must have an educated population as this is important for development and integrity in decision making.[26] There is a competing interest between the rule of law and customs and usages and in some villages people believe their village laws are superior to the Constitution.[27] There is lack of formal education on human rights and formal laws.[28]

4.1.4 Relevance to Village Life

If the laws are not relevant to the people's daily activities in the village, this would present difficulties in encouraging public input in reforms. A number of interview respondents point to the lack of interest in laws as a challenge to law reform.[29] Although there are law reform public notices inviting the public to public consultations, members of the public do not make use of the available forums.[30] The following observations were noted from the respondents.

People simply do not show up at law reform public consultations particularly when law reform projects are irrelevant to them.[31] There is indifference and disinterest in law reforms that do not directly improve the livelihood of the people.[32] The majority of Samoans still live a subsistence living, are not economically active in commercial farming or formal employment and most reside on their customary land. Therefore laws and law reform are the responsibilities of the state for the state's purposes.[33] It is difficult to persuade people of any responsibility on their part to participate in developing reforms.[34] There is no sense of ownership of parliamentary laws; people dislike, distrust and dismiss them as 'not theirs'.[35] Even

---

[25]Interview with VM Respondent 2 (Samoa, 9 March 2011).

[26]Interview with SOH Respondent 3 (Samoa, 4 April 2011).

[27]Interview with MOJ Respondent 5 (Samoa, 1 April 2011).

[28]Interview with MOJ Respondent 7 (Samoa, 4 April 2011).

[29]Interviews in Samoa with: GCE Respondent 1 (19 January 2011); GCE Respondent 2 (11 March 2011); GCE Respondent 3, (12 April 2011); GCE Respondent 4 (18 January 2011); GCE Respondent 5 (18 January 2011); GCE Respondent 6 (22 December 2010).

[30]Interviews in Samoa with: MOP Respondent 6 (24 December 2010); MOP Respondent 1 (22 December 2010); MOP Respondent 6 (24 December 2010); GEC Respondent 6 (22 December 2010).

[31]Email from SOH Respondent 8 to Lalotoa Mulitalo, 7 May 2012.

[32]Interview with LP Respondent 2 (Samoa, 21 February 2011).

[33]Interviews in Samoa with: GEC Respondent 2 (11 March 2011); GCE Respondent 1 (19 January 2011).

[34]Interview with LP Respondent 5 (Samoa, 14 March 2011).

[35]Interview with GCE Respondent 1 (Samoa, 19 January 2011).

where there is attendance at public consultation, disinterest is evident where 'people won't listen when the issues are discussed, people have no idea what is going on in a consultation, and they do not understand how those issues relate to them.'[36] There is lack of confidence in the state system and law reform. Some respondents who made some input in earlier consultations and do not receive feedback lose interest in law reform.[37] Others posited that law reform projects were predetermined exercises by the state[38] and that consultations are only carried out to influence the respondents into agreeing to state policies.[39]

4.1.5 Cultural Factors

Cultural dynamics is also an impediment to law reform in particular to law reform public consultations. Village protocols are necessary for any meetings or consultations to take place in the village, and the expenses required for village consultation may prove too costly for the state.

Some respondents point out that village protocols prevent or influence free and willing participation in law reform.[40] According to village hierarchy, the appropriate *matai* must be approached to seek the village's support and attendance at law reform consultation.[41] After the spokesperson is informed of the purposes of the consultations, the spokesperson extends the invitation to the village to attend a scheduled consultation session. The spokesperson acts as a middleman and a gatekeeper to the villagers. Non-compliance with these protocols may cause internal friction within the village or may create a rift between the villagers and the State, hindering effective law reform consultations.[42]

The lack of public attendance and participation in law reform consultations in some villages is due to customs that allow only a *matai* to speak as a representative of a village or families,[43] a cultural feature of the Samoan society as discussed in the opening chapter. The hierarchy in some villages require certain individuals holding certain chiefly titles to speak for and make decisions on the villagers' behalf.[44] Making an input to law reform consultations is similar to one making an opinion in

---

[36]Interviews in Samoa with: GCE Respondent 6 (22 December 2010); GCE Respondent 2 (11 March 2011).

[37]Interviews with LP Respondent 2 (Samoa, 21 February 2011).

[38]Interview with SOH Respondent 9 (Samoa, 21 March 2011).

[39]Interview with SOH Respondent 7 (Samoa, 22 March 2011).

[40]Interviews in Samoa with: SOH Respondent 9 (21 March 2011); SOH Respondent 4 (11 July 2011).

[41]Interview with GCE Respondent 1 (Samoa, 19 January 2011).

[42]Interview with GCE Respondent 1 (Samoa, 19 January 2011).

[43]Interview with SOH Respondent 9 (Samoa, 21 March 2011).

[44]Interview with VC2 Respondent 5 (Samoa, 15 March 2011).

4.1 The Ideological Principles Behind Law Making: Customary Laws and State Laws 55

public and being involved in decision making. In the village setting, this is the prerogative of *matais*.[45]

A further cultural hindrance is in the principles of respect for others as discussed in the preceding chapter, particularly the respect that is culturally required for elders. This usually takes place where the *matai* and the youth are present for consultation. In most occasions, the youth retreat in deference and out of respect to the elders, on the basis that the elders would adequately and effectively present their views on law reform issues.[46] However, elders are unable to participate at a lengthy consultation session due to unfamiliarity with the principles and values promoted by the state and due to their health and physical abilities, and would decline the opportunity to make representations and/or to ask questions. This can unfortunately result in an ineffective and unproductive but costly consultation.

4.1.6 Language Barriers

The interview data discloses a number of views on 'language' barriers as yet another impediment to law reform. Some observations are as follows. There are demands for the language of law reform consultations to be in Samoan and for cultural protocols to be respected.[47] The majority of lawyers and Ministry officials who carry out public consultations are not well informed or fully appreciative of the nuances of the Samoan language. Being fluent in and having a good command of the Samoan language can be problematic at times.[48] The use of the English language in law reform discourages public participation as people are unfamiliar with this language.[49]

4.1.7 Support from Secondary Data: Local Newspaper Research

Due to a lack of interest triggered by a lack of understanding of reforms, the costly village protocols, the cultural impediments and language barriers, little value is placed on law reform. To confirm this broad finding from a different dimension, a research was carried out on the Samoa Observer, the most circulated local newspaper. The objective of the data was to record the public opinions expressed through

---

[45] Interview with SOH Respondent 9 (Samoa, 21 March 2011).
[46] Interview with SOH Respondent 4 (Samoa, 11 July 2011).
[47] Interview with LP Respondent 3 (Samoa, 14 March 2011).
[48] Interview with LP Respondent 5 (Samoa, 14 March 2011).
[49] Interviews in Samoa with: LP Respondent 5 (14 March 2011); LP Respondent 3 (14 March 2011).

Table 4.1 Samoa observer newspaper findings

Public Opinion on Legal Reform
Road Transport Reform Act 2008 (Samoa) **RTR**
Land Titles Registration Act 2008 (Samoa) **LTR**
Casino and Gambling Control Act 2010 (Samoa) **CGC**

LTE: Letters to the editor	2008	2009	2010	Total
Total no. of LTEs on RTR, LTR, CGC	198	103	34	335
No. of writers with named residences	122	79	28	229
No. of writers without named residences	76	24	6	106
Overseas writers	64	51	12	127
Local writers	58	27	11	96
Employment and residence of local writers				
	2008	2009	2010	Total
Local writers	58	28	11	97
No. of LTEs with villages stated	47	12	6	65
Urban	45	10	6	61
Rural	2	2	0	4
No. of LTEs with professions stated	17	4	6	27
Nature of profession	Ex-politicians, business owners, university lecturers, lawyers, public servants	Business owners, taxi drivers	Business owners, lecturers, public servants	

letters to the editor (LTEs) and to identify the residences (where provided) of those that expressed those public opinions, on the most controversial executive and parliamentary reforms in the years spanning from 2008 to 2010. The villages and employment status (where indicated) of those that wrote LTEs from inside of Samoa were also noted for analysis. The findings of this research are recorded in Table 4.1 and discussed below.

As indicated in Table 4.1, in the three years chosen for this study, there was a significant difference in 2009 as compared to 2008 and 2010, in the numbers of those that expressed a public opinion on reforms from outside of Samoa and those that resided in Samoa. The first overall finding this book relies on is that in all years, there are more writers from overseas than in Samoa. In 2008, from 198 people that expressed a view, 64 wrote from outside of Samoa and 58 from within Samoa. In 2009, 51 wrote from outside of Samoa and 27 from within Samoa. In 2010, 12 wrote from overseas and 11 from inside Samoa. The second finding is the

4.1 The Ideological Principles Behind Law Making: Customary Laws and State Laws   57

residence of the local writers. Of the 65 writers that wrote from within Samoa and named their resident villages, an overwhelming 61 reside in the urban area and only 4 from the rural area. Thirdly, of the 27 that named their employment or professional background, all were employed in formal employment and engaged in different professions such as business owners, university lecturers, lawyers, public servants and former politicians.

A significant absence of local and rural village views on the most controversial reforms that were (from the public's view) envisaged to do more harm than good and causing public protests in Samoa[50] is a strong indication that there is little interest and a lack of value placed by the majority of the general public in Samoa on law reform. This confirms the interview findings and supports the broad challenges discussed above, that there is lack of value placed on law reform in Samoa.

Not all writers offered their residences and therefore are excluded in the count. However, the number of those that named their residence or location significantly outweighs those that did not. The numbers available for analysis were therefore sufficient to draw up an analysis and findings.

4.1.8 Challenges to Address

From the above discussion, the following are some of the social and cultural factors that present challenges for law reform in Samoa. A limited understanding of the state legal system indicates the public is unaware of individual rights and duties under that system. A lack of appreciation of State laws also creates uncertainty and suspicion that the State is imposing modern laws which would effectively reduce the importance of and consequently remove customary laws as the basis of the Samoan society.

Education is important in a legal pluralist society. The challenge is to develop a population educated in both the customary and the state systems. Formal education is required to further understand the state system, and embrace modern technology, economies and thinking that facilitate the inclusion of customary principles into formal laws. Emphasis is placed on formal education to facilitate the development of the state system and the meaning of parliamentary laws. However, this cannot be the only emphasis. Informal education on Samoan history, genealogies, customary rules and village protocols obtained from taking part in village activities are equally vital, to inform balanced laws that take account of the pluralist realities of the Samoan society.

The public lose interest in law reform projects that do not impact directly on daily life. There is a lack of regard for state laws where those laws have little

---

[50]The *Road Transport Reform Act 2008* (Samoa) and the *Casino and Gambling Control Act 2010* (Samoa) are referred to further in Chap. 5 on discussions relating to the NGOs influence on law reform in Samoa.

relevance to village life for example, subsistence farming. There is more interest and participation in village activities, developments and village projects on customary lands or the village fishing areas. The village sector cannot see how they can benefit from most State reforms. Village rules are more respected because they address the daily realities. Enforcement is ensured through village council processes which are speedier, more convenient and effective. Formal laws on the other hand, are usually removed from the village realities. Most villagers find it difficult to make an opinion on matters they are unfamiliar with.

The cultural challenge to law reform is how to obtain input from the youth, women, untitled men and children for law reform. The cultural principles such as respect for elders and the importance of traditional hierarchies significantly impact on the consultation inputs from the villages. These cultural aspects determine decision making in the Samoan society as seen above. Cultural influences that impact on public participation in law reform are not particular to Samoa. A separate research project in which interviews were carried out in Fiji showed a similar regard to the traditional hierarchical system.[51] The author noted that the village people were willing to let their chiefs speak on their behalf. Some may be interested in making an input but felt that people higher up in the traditional hierarchy contribute a more valuable input. Traditional systems still determine the decision makers and spokespersons in many Pacific Islands.

Where law reform consultations involve the English language at any stage, people are cautious and withdraw, or there is reluctance to attend a public consultation session. There is fear of being addressed in the English language, or that one would say something 'wrong' and therefore 'lose face' in public. This may have a negative impact on any good relationships amongst *matais* themselves or between *matais* and the law reform officers of the State, particularly if the officers are unable to present their purposes in a manner relevant to the customary setting the matais are more familiar with. To a large extent, the English language is viewed as the superior language and not being able to speak it is considered 'uneducated'. It is difficult to break through this attitude. These social and cultural factors create challenges in developing effective law reform in Samoa.

4.2 Demand for Customs and Respect for the Constitution

The third broad challenge is the overwhelming desire for custom to be incorporated into formal laws of Samoa. Under this broad challenge, there are two features of the complexities of undertaking the incorporation. There is an overwhelming desire for customary laws to be the basis of Samoa's legal system. Secondly, there is a demand to have state laws developed in the context of the Samoan customary environment. Despite these demands, the empirical data also suggests that there is a

---

[51]Le Roy (2012), p. 246.

4.2 Demand for Customs and Respect for the Constitution

gradual but growing respect to uphold the Constitution and the individual rights it protects. There is also uncertainty on which to uphold, the traditional values or individualism, and this is particularly relevant where there is an abuse of, or unreasonable exercise of traditional village authority powers.

4.2.1 Customary Laws as the Basis of the Legal System

It is argued that customary laws must form the basis of Samoa's legal system.[52] There are several reasons behind this argument, one being that customs entail identity and differentiate Samoans from all others.[53] It must therefore be the prevailing legal system over all other sources of law.

> The real power of the nation is in the *fa'a Samoa*, we had paramount Kings and chiefs from long ago. In the *faamatai* system we have accountability, transparency and good governance. Custom maintains social order where the police cannot. Customs and traditions are the major contributing factor to stability in Samoa, on people and its politics.[54]

Employing the customary legal system as the basis of the legal system puts the customary legal system in its rightful superior status, above other laws.[55] This made sense to many who argued that there is little impact of the state in the villages, where customary laws are more respected.[56] Village councils have been successful in regulating village activities and communal practices in Samoa for many years.

4.2.2 Laws in the Samoan Context

In addition to customs being the basis of Samoa's legal system, all parliamentary laws must be contextualised to fit the Samoan customary environment.[57] Customs must be recognised in formal laws and become part of formal law where feasible and beneficial.[58] Customs and usages must be adequately considered in laws as they

---

[52]Interviews in Samoa with: GCE Respondent 1 (19 January 2011); MOP Respondent 1 (22 December 2010); MOJ Respondent 5 (1 April 2011).

[53]Interview with MOP Respondent 1 (Samoa, 22 December 2010).

[54]Interview with MOJ Respondent 5 (Samoa, 1 April 2011).

[55]Interview with GCE Respondent 1 (Samoa, 19 January 2011).

[56]Interviews in Samoa with: MOP 1 (22 December 2010); MOP 2 (4 January 2011); MOP 5 (11 January 2011).

[57]Interviews in Samoa with: MOP Respondent 1 (22 December 2010); MOP Respondent 2 (4 January 2011); MOP Respondent 4 (7 January 2011); MOP Respondent 6 (24 December 2010).

[58]Interviews in Samoa with: MOP Respondent 3 (11 January 2011); MOP Respondent 5 (11 January 2011); VC2 Respondent 5 (15 March 2011); SOH Respondent 7 (22 March 2011).

can be contradictory to the Constitution or may not fit well in the western legal system.[59] One respondent's observations summarise most of the responses received:

> All laws must balance with customs. If the new laws are in conflict with the customs, we must review that law to protect customs. Our problem is we ignore customs in law making. Our only focus is to make laws and not give enough time to consider and apply what is important from customs. We cannot just discard customs merely because they may (seem to) conflict with the western laws. We only check if laws are compliant with the constitution; we must also check if new laws sit well with our customs.[60]

Other respondents expressed as follows. 'Laws must be developed in the Samoan context and drafted first in the Samoan language.'[61] 'Individual rights must be applied in the context of Samoa's communal setting.'[62] 'We must give our customs the recognition they deserve under the constitution and as per the intentions of our forefathers.'[63] 'When we apply the white man's perception on a society like Samoa, the village councils separate themselves from the government; this is not workable for law reform in Samoa.'[64]

4.2.3 Respect for the Constitution

In spite of the strong inspirations for customs to be at the apex of law making, there is slow but notable increasing respect for the Constitution and the protection of individual rights.[65] These are indicated in observations such as follows.

> Many people forget that the Constitution is a result of two Conventions in Samoa in the 1940s and the 1960s. Representatives from different villages were present at those conventions from which the Constitution was developed. Thus it is not an overseas Constitution, Samoa is responsible for it. It is very difficult to make people understand this.[66]

Interview respondents also acknowledged that customs are recognised within the scope of the Constitution.[67] Samoa is bound by its Constitution to protect the universally accepted fundamental rights.[68] Some point out that there is need to

---

[59]Interview with LP Respondent 1 (Samoa, 15 March 2011).
[60]Interview with GCE Respondent 1 (Samoa, 19 January 2011).
[61]Interview with MOP Respondent 1 (Samoa, 22 December 2011).
[62]Interview with GCE Respondent 2 (Samoa, 11 March 2011).
[63]Interview with MOP Respondent 2 (Samoa, 4 January 2011).
[64]Interview with GCE Respondent 3 (Samoa, 12 April 2011).
[65]Interviews in Samoa with: MOJ Respondent 3 (7 March 2011); GCE Respondent 1 (19 January 2011); MOP Respondent 2 (4 January 2011); MOJ Respondent 1 (28 March 2011); LP Respondent 1 (15 March 2011); LP Respondent 4 (2 March 2011).
[66]Interview with MOJ Respondent 2 (Samoa, 13 July 2011).
[67]Interview with MOJ Respondent 3 (Samoa, 7 March 2011).
[68]Interview with MOJ Respondent 5 (Samoa, 1 April 2011).

4.2 Demand for Customs and Respect for the Constitution   61

reform some old customary practices to fit the changing environment of Samoa.[69] Some village mayors responded that they appreciate the Constitution in that it upholds the individual rights accorded to the villagers, particularly where there is unreasonable exercise of village council powers.[70] These village mayors stated their villages were exploring the possibility of developing customary rules that are compliant with the Constitution.

4.2.4 Challenges to Address

There is demand that customary laws become the basis of the legal system, and secondly that state laws must be developed in the Samoan context. A review of experiences elsewhere shows that efforts to adopt customary laws as the primary laws of legal systems have been unsuccessful.[71] There is assertion that no modern state has achieved a legal system that relies predominantly on customary laws, as the existing customary structures cannot support the socio-economic features of modern society.[72] Like every other developing post-colonial society, Samoa lacks these modern features. However, Samoa strives to find ways to accommodate the modern socio-economic infrastructures into the existing customary structures. Making customary law the basis of Samoa's legal system may thus be fraught with difficulties, and pressure from a population that demands this is a challenge for institutions responsible for law reform. To take account of customs, the interview respondents require that parliamentary laws be contextualised in the Samoan context. In the absence of policies, government directives such as subjecting all reforms to a customs analysis and mechanisms to accommodate this, contextualising laws to the Samoan customs is a significant challenge for law reform.

Although there are strong sentiments to have customs as the primary laws and for Parliament to be charged with formulating laws in the context of customary laws, there is also a growing respect for individual rights and the rule of law entrenched in the Constitution. The diverse views from interview respondents indicate the presence of two mindsets in a plural society. On the one hand there is a desire to hold on to customs and traditions. The modern attitude however is to embrace the Constitution and move forward to how the two systems can be accommodated in Samoa. The conflicting views suggest approaches to reforms must be gradual and cautious and must involve the general population in order for those reforms to be relevant and effective. One of the ways suggested by the

---

[69]For example, interview with MOP Respondent 2 (Samoa, 4 January 2011).
[70]Interviews in Samoa with: VM Respondent 2 (9 March 2011); VM Respondent 5 (16 March 2011).
[71]For example Oba (2011), p. 69.
[72]Ntumy, above n 13, 13.

empirical data in which customs could become part of the formal laws in Samoa is through the process of codification. This is discussed next.

4.3 Should Customs be Codified in Samoa's Laws?

4.3.1 Opposition to Codification

4.3.1.1 Conflicting Values

As discussed in Chap. 2 (2.1.4.1) the codification of Samoan customary laws is largely opposed[73] for many reasons such as that Samoan customary laws conflict with the formal laws.[74] This opposition is evident from the observations that legislation cannot capture a full account of what is customary or fully describe customary powers.[75] The *Village Fono Act 1990* (Samoa) was referred to as an example of legislation that is unable to capture the complete village council powers as intended.[76] Rather than giving full effect to customary powers, the Act failed to fully reflect the real powers of the village council.

4.3.1.2 Flexibility

Some respondents expressed the same concerns as found in the writings on 'codification' discussed earlier in this book. Once customary law is legislated, it loses flexibility.[77] The flexible nature of customs is suitable to the village lifestyle and social rules in the Samoan villages. Customary laws are about boundaries and relationships, and people and things shift boundaries all the time.[78] Codification means customs are frozen in time and lose the suppleness conducive to communal living and the Samoan practices.[79] Codification will present problems for law enforcement in Samoa.[80] The flexibility of customs allows for the successful

---

[73] Interviews in Samoa with: MOJ Respondent 3 (7 March 2011); MOJ Respondent 4 (5 April 2011); MOJ Respondent 7 (4 April 2011); GCE Respondent 1 (19 January 2011); GCE Respondent 4 (18 January 2011).

[74] Interview with MOP Respondent 6 (Samoa, 24 December 2010).

[75] Interviews in Samoa with: GCE Respondent 4 (18 January 2011); MOJ Respondent 7 (4 April 2011).

[76] Interview with MOJ Respondent 7 (Samoa, 4 April 2011). The *Village Fono Act 1990* (Samoa) is discussed further in Chap. 5.

[77] Interviews in Samoa with: MOJ Respondent 4 (5 April 2011); MOJ Respondent 3 (7 March 2011); MOJ Respondent 7 (4 April 2011).

[78] Interview with SOH Respondent 1 (Samoa, 8 April 2011).

[79] Interview with MOJ Respondent 4 (Samoa, 5 April 2011).

[80] Interviews in Samoa with: GCE Respondent 1 (19 January 2011); GCE Respondent 4 (18 January 2011).

4.3 Should Customs be Codified in Samoa's Laws?   63

application of both the customary and state laws where convenient. According to a law enforcement official, no formal arrests have ever been made in Samoa.[81] The Samoan customary laws allow police officers to work with the villages towards a more peaceful approach to detaining suspects and curbing crime and maintaining social order.

4.3.1.3 Ascertainment and Uniformity

Codification is dangerous, as it is difficult to identify certainty in customs.[82] There are some 300 villages with their own set of customs,[83] and no two villages are likely to agree on customs.[84] As law reform is a state initiative, it is inappropriate for lawyers to define customary laws; this should be the prerogative of the villagers and villages.[85]

4.3.1.4 Serving the Interests of Non-Locals Only

The empirical data also suggests that if customs are codified they benefit only the foreigners and not the locals. It is argued that if an issue is addressed by customary law, there is no need to legislate it.[86] An example given is legislation on 'traditional knowledge'. Where traditional knowledge is codified, the duties, liabilities and offences will be imposed. The foreigners who seek to study traditional knowledge will be guided by the code. However, there will be some frustration for locals as written laws cannot fully capture the traditional practices in the same way people understand and practise traditional knowledge. Codification will therefore benefit non-Samoans more than the locals. The codification of certain traditional aspects of the *fa'a Samoa* should therefore be discouraged.

4.3.1.5 Absence of Customary Structures to Support Customs in Legislation

If Samoa codifies customs, it must be supported by customary infrastructures which are lacking throughout Samoa.[87] This view is in line with the law making principle

---

[81] Interview with MOJ Respondent 4 (Samoa, 5 April 2011).

[82] Interviews in Samoa with: MOJ Respondent 3 (7 March 2011); MOJ Respondent 7 (4 April 2011); MOJ Respondent 4 (5 April 2011).

[83] Interview with MOJ Respondent 7 (Samoa, 4 April 2011).

[84] Interview with MOJ Respondent 3 (Samoa, 7 March 2011).

[85] Interview with GCE Respondent 1 (Samoa, 19 January 2011).

[86] Interview with MOJ Respondent 1 (Samoa, 19 January 2011).

[87] Interview with SOH Respondent 1 (Samoa, 8 February 2011).

that laws must be supported by the relevant infrastructure to allow for successful implementation. A similar view was posed by Kirby in the question on whether to recognise Aboriginal tribal laws. Kirby commented that 'in the past those laws rested on religious beliefs and the unquestioned authority of the elders, and it may not be possible to resuscitate customary laws without a return to the old religion and the old power structures as they do not exist as they did before.'[88]

4.3.1.6 Difficulties for Legislative Drafters

Although Samoa has to some extent incorporated customary practices in legislation, 'local drafters find uncertainty in the cultural analysis and in how to translate and draft Samoan customs in the English language.'[89] This is aggravated by the fear of venturing into a new practice of drafting and uncertainty at the consequences. No Samoan terminology, literature and grammar is readily available to assist the drafters develop suitable legal terms.[90] On the one hand a local drafter would understand the context of the Samoan society[91] and this is a positive aspect. On the other, there is a lack of confidence in local drafters taking up this task as law graduates have a limited knowledge of customs.[92] Most of the legal and legislative drafting training received by Pacific legislative drafters is from Australia or New Zealand and a post graduate legislative drafting course offered by the University of the South Pacific.[93] However, none of this training addresses legislative drafting in plural societies. Legislative drafting in Samoa is currently guided by the Legislative Drafting Handbook 2014 Samoa,[94] a revised version of the original Handbook of 2008. The Handbook requires all drafters in Samoa and for Samoa to comply with certain principles and styles of drafting. However, there are no requirements for customary principles to be considered in legislative drafting and any guidance on how these may be achieved.

4.3.1.7 Secondary Data: Pacific Legislative Drafters Survey

Evidence of the difficulties for legislative drafters to draft laws that incorporate customs can be found in a survey on Pacific legislative drafters. There was general consensus amongst the 11 contributors to the survey that most if not all Pacific

---

[88]Kirby (1983), p. 125.
[89]Interview with LP Respondent 3 (Samoa, 4 March 2011).
[90]Interview with SOH Respondent 1 (Samoa, 8 February 2011).
[91]Interview with LP Respondent 1 (Samoa, 15 March 2011).
[92]Interview with VC2 Respondent 5 (Samoa, 15 March 2011).
[93]Professional Diploma in Legislative Drafting, Commonwealth Distance Learning Course offered through the University of the South Pacific, Suva Fiji.
[94]Office of the Attorney-General (Samoa) Handbook (2014).

4.3 Should Customs be Codified in Samoa's Laws?

legislative drafters face legal pluralism issues while drafting legislation for their respective Pacific islands. The following observations were offered. 'There is difficulty in harmonising customary principles within legislative provisions and give formal recognition within our legal system.'[95] The main challenge is 'the translation of traditional customs into western laws.'[96] In addition,

> there is always the issue that while drafting a law there is unconscious disregard of existing customs, and a lack of appreciation that a custom may adequately address the intended policies, and that this custom can be incorporated as part of the formal laws. For example, the village governance may at times be overlooked when trying to regulate certain social problems.[97]

The difficulties in drafting customs into formal laws are a challenge in the codification of customs. Overall, the Pacific drafters acknowledge that Pacific Island customs are still a very important aspect of life across the Pacific Islands. There are difficulties in accommodating customs into law but drafters must find strategies to address these through policy development by the state. Drafters must build capacity towards an appreciation and acceptance of traditional concepts, and be bold to advise incorporation into draft laws.[98]

The main challenges found in the interview data and supported by the literature that opposes codification of Samoan customary laws are as follows. The origins of a code and customs derive from two underlying philosophies. By virtue of their originating opposing principles, they are already in opposition to each other. In light of this, if codified, Samoan customs will lose flexibility. The police rely on customs and customary practices and where this approach is taken the village council is cooperative and assists the police in their investigations. For law enforcers, the two systems of laws must stay separated. It is difficult to ascertain and determine uniform customs of the 300 plus villages in Samoa. The *Village Fono Act* 1990 (Samoa), was identified as a written law that is unable to fully capture customs. Due to this inability to capture customs, written laws on 'traditional knowledge' for example cannot capture customs as the locals know them. Thus it will not be beneficial for locals but will only benefit those outside of Samoa who rely on the codified law. There is no customary structure to support legislated customs. Finally, there are complexities in drafting customs into law. It is difficult to decide on the provisions of a draft Bill in such a way that captures what customs are intended to address. The comparative data from the Pacific Islands legislative drafters' survey support the findings of the interview data in relation to those difficulties.

---

[95] Survey PL Drafter 3.
[96] Survey PL Drafter 8.
[97] Survey PL Drafter 11.
[98] Survey PL Drafter 8.

4.3.2 Benefits of Codification

4.3.2.1 Certainty and Constitutional Compliance

Codification allows certainty in laws, and this was expressed by the two respondents in favour of codification.[99] This certainty, it is believed will be of significant assistance to the Land and Titles Court of Samoa in its customary proceedings. This will also allow customs to be reviewed against the constitution for constitutional compliance. This may redress any harsh consequences of some customary legal applications where they are brought into compliance with the constitution in its written form. There are some customs which are unchristian and impinge on the morals of the Samoan people and should not be recognised.[100] The codification of customary laws will dispel doubts on the status of customary laws relative to the Constitution and other written laws.[101]

The main argument in support of codification is that it brings about certainty in customs that are formalised in laws and certainty in the relationship of customary laws and the written laws. The codification of customary laws may also redress any harsh consequences of some customary legal applications where they are brought into compliance with the constitution in its written form. However, from the empirical interviews, the challenges raised far outweigh the advantages of codification. Codification of customary laws is therefore not supported for Samoa.

4.4 Emerging Conceptual Challenges

4.4.1 Understanding the Dichotomy

In summary, there are 5 broad conceptual challenges which may be drawn from the above discussions. Firstly, there is reflective understanding that there are two different sources of laws in Samoa. This is important as in order to progressively respond to challenges, the conflicting ideologies must be appreciated as a predicament that can be addressed, before identifying possible responses and those best placed to drive those responses. Plural societies must be encouraged to appreciate that there are two or more legal systems which they can rely upon depending on their circumstances. The nature of legal pluralism is appreciating that not all legal answers are found in state laws[102] or in customary laws. The two legal systems are

---

[99] Interviews in Samoa with: GCE Respondent 6 (22 December 2010); MOJ Respondent 5 (1 April 2011).
[100] Interview with MOJ Respondent 5 (Samoa, 1 April 2011).
[101] Ibid.
[102] Griffiths (1986), p. 24:39.

relied upon at the convenience of the users; what works on the ground is the best legal response at a given time.

4.4.2 Need to Promote Understanding of State Laws

The empirical data suggests that as long as there is lack of understanding of state laws, little value is placed on state law reform. If the State is to engage the village communities in law reform it must make the effort to create public awareness of state laws as well as educate on its benefits. The state legal system dominates the process of law making and operates independently of the customary legal system. The village sector is unaware of state laws and the modern system of government. There is general understanding that the principles of individual rights promoted by the state legal system are in opposition to customary values and there are no significant efforts to provide awareness of what those opposing values stand for. Unless there is a system that offers that information, and creates public awareness on laws and the State legal system, the gap continues to widen between the two systems.

4.4.3 Customs to be Recognised in State Laws

As a majority population and a proud people, most Samoans wish for their customs to be given the highest regard, as Samoan customs signify identity, and differentiates Samoans from the rest of the world. There is overwhelming support for customs to be given legal recognition and to be given status similar to that of state laws. Although Samoa's Constitution gives some recognition to customs, it is very restricted, and the Constitution does not provide how that insignificant opportunity may be utilised. The constitutional limitations restrict judges from applying customary considerations in court decisions, and requires drafters to check draft laws compliance against the constitution and formal laws only and not against customary principles and values. This needs to change if state laws are to be more suitable and relevant to the Samoan population.

4.4.4 Emerging Acceptance of Modern Laws

Although there is overwhelming demand for customary laws to be the basis of Samoa's legal system, there is also a gradual acceptance of individual rights and the principles upheld by the Constitution. This trend must be seriously considered and taken advantage of where beneficial for Samoa. Changes driven through law reform must be gradual. Reforms driven only by the few who have capacity to develop laws without the support of the population will face difficulties in implementation.

4.4.5 Interdependency

Having adopted modern economic, social and political frameworks, as discussed above, a legal system based on customary laws is not an option for Samoa. However, the success and survival of the modern political, social and economic conditions still relies on customary laws and customary structures.[103] Parliament can make laws, but they are sometimes unenforceable without the support of the village councils.[104] In this regard, without the assistance of the village councils, state policies lack public support. This interdependence makes considerations of legal pluralism necessary in law making. In the current socio-economic environment, neither of the two systems can survive independent of the other. Collaborative strategies between the two legal systems are necessary to find ways both can benefit Samoa to potential. In the next chapter, discussions shift away from the social and cultural structures to the formal institutions of the State system, to draw out how the co-existence of two legal systems impact on law making by these institutions.

References

Griffiths J (1986) What is legal pluralism? J Leg Pluralism 24:39
Kirby M (1983) Reform the law. Oxford University Press, p 125
Le Roy KJ (2012) Participatory constitution making: lessons from Fiji and Solomon Islands. PhD Book, University of Melbourne, p 246
Ntumy M (1995) The dreams of a Melanesian jurisprudence: the purpose and limits of law reform. In: Aleck J, Jackson R (eds) Customs at the crossroads. UPNG Law Faculty, p 11
Oba AA (2011) The future of customary law in Africa. In: Fenrich J, Galizzi P, Higgins T (eds) The future of African customary law. Cambridge University Press, p 69
Office of the Attorney-General Samoa (2014) Legislative drafting handbook

Legislation

Casino and Gambling Control Act 2010 (Samoa)
Road Transport Reform Act 2008 (Samoa)
Village Fono Act 1990 (Samoa)

---

[103]Interview with MOP Respondent 2 (Samoa, 4 January 2011).
[104]Interview with MOJ Respondent 3 (Samoa, 7 March 2011).

Chapter 5
State Focused Law Reform: Constitutional Offices, Institutions and Agents

Contents

5.1	The Courts	70
	5.1.1 Jurisdiction on Customs	70
	5.1.2 Judicial Training	72
	5.1.3 Role of the Judiciary in Law Reform	73
	5.1.4 Expatriate Judges	74
	5.1.4.1 General Pacific Experiences	74
	5.1.4.2 Interpretive Function of the Court	74
	5.1.4.3 Village Agreement Unenforceable Under Contract Law	76
	5.1.4.4 Obiter Unsupported by Local Realities	77
	5.1.5 Overview: The Courts	78
5.2	The Parliament	78
	5.2.1 Lack of Systems in Place to Support Assembly of *Matai*	79
	5.2.1.1 Language in Parliamentary Proceedings	80
	5.2.1.2 Law Making Procedures: Assembly Process and Private Members Bills	80
	5.2.2 Unsuccessful Legal Transplants	82
	5.2.3 Acts of Parliament with Custom References 1962–2015 (Samoa)	84
	5.2.3.1 Acts 1962 (Independence) to 1989	85
	5.2.3.2 Acts from 1990 to 2000	90
	5.2.3.3 Acts After 2000	93
	5.2.3.4 Overview	96
	5.2.4 Analysis: Acts of Parliament and Acts with Customs References (2008–2016)	97
	5.2.5 Overview: The Parliament	99
5.3	The Executive	99
	5.3.1 Executive Law Making Process	99
	5.3.1.1 Cabinet Handbook	99
	5.3.1.2 Legislative Drafting Handbook	100
	5.3.2 Overview: The Executive	101
5.4	The Samoa Law Reform Commission (SLRC)	101
	5.4.1 Establishment and Personnel	102
	5.4.1.1 What Model of Law Reform Institution?	102
	5.4.1.2 The Initial Years	103
	5.4.1.3 Western Educated Personnel	103
	5.4.1.4 The SLRC Advisory Board	104
	5.4.2 Law Reform Process	105

© Springer International Publishing AG 2018
T.L. Mulitalo Ropinisone Silipa Seumanutafa, *Law Reform in Plural Societies*, The World of Small States 2, https://doi.org/10.1007/978-3-319-65524-6_5

                5.4.3   Public Consultation 107
                         5.4.3.1   Costly Cultural Protocols 107
                         5.4.3.2   Law Reform Consultation 108
                5.4.4   Overview: The SLRC 110
       5.5   Other Law Reform Agents 110
                5.5.1   Commissions of Inquiry (COI) 111
                         5.5.1.1   COIs for Customary Reforms 111
                         5.5.1.2   COI Investigations and Reforms to Date 112
                         5.5.1.3   COI Strengths 112
                         5.5.1.4   COI Challenges 113
                         5.5.1.5   Law Reform Driven by Both Matais (Customary) and Lawyers
                                   (Modern) 114
                5.5.2   The Samoa Law Society (SLS) 115
                         5.5.2.1   Law Reform Functions 115
                         5.5.2.2   Challenges 116
                5.5.3   Office of the Ombudsman 117
                         5.5.3.1   Law Reform Functions 117
                         5.5.3.2   Challenges 118
                5.5.4   Non-Government Organisations (NGOs) 119
                         5.5.4.1   Law Reform Influence 119
                         5.5.4.2   Challenges 120
       5.6   Emerging Conceptual Challenges 121
                5.6.1   Law Reform Framework Not Embedded in Customs 121
                         5.6.1.1   Laws Authorising Law Making 121
                         5.6.1.2   Procedures Guiding Law Making 121
                5.6.2   Limited Professional Training Opportunities 122
                5.6.3   Involving the Village Structures in the Law Reform Process 122
                5.6.4   Funding Constraints 122
       References 123

The existence of two legal systems in one society poses challenges to its justice and law making systems. This chapter explores these challenges as experienced within Parliament, the Executive, the Judiciary, the Samoa Law Reform Commission and other law reform agents existing in Samoa. The challenges of legal pluralism stem from the difficulties in giving both the customary legal system and the state legal system a balanced application in law making. In many occasions, customary law is marginalised in the process of law reform developed under the above mentioned institutions. The challenges posed in this chapter are informed by analysis of case law and local legislation and the empirical interviews. References will be made to the empirical interviews which support the challenges put forward in this chapter.

5.1   The Courts

5.1.1   Jurisdiction on Customs

The courts of Samoa have limited jurisdiction to apply Samoan customs and usages. Article 111 of the Constitution defines the 'law' applying to Samoa as follows.

'Law' being in force in Samoa; and includes this Constitution, any Act of Parliament and any proclamation, regulation, order, by-law or other act of authority made there under, the English common law and equity for the time being in so far as they are not excluded by any other law in force in Samoa, and any custom or usage which has acquired the force of law in Samoa or any part thereof under the provisions of any Act or under a judgment of a Court of competent jurisdiction.

The scope within which the courts may apply customs is where such custom or usage has been included as part of an Act of Parliament, or that such custom or usage has been ruled by a court of Samoa to form part of the law of Samoa. Details of the hierarchy and the constitution of courts can be found in other Pacific Islands research.[1] Relevant to this book is the statutory jurisdiction of courts to deal with customary matters. The Supreme Court has original, appellate and revisional jurisdiction[2] and the jurisdiction necessary to administer the laws of Samoa.[3] The District Court and its subsidiary division the *Faamasino Fesoasoani*, do not have jurisdiction on customary land matters.[4] The only court with exclusive jurisdiction on customary matters is the Land and Titles Court.[5] This court has its own Appeal Court,[6] and its decisions are not reviewable by any other court.[7] However, a Supreme Court decision in 1998[8] significantly reduced the powers impacted this, as will be further discussed below. The strict limitations posed by the Constitution on 'customs' being part of the 'law' in Samoa, was further enhanced by the courts. Customary laws are continually suppressed and struggle to form part of the 'law' of Samoa as apparent in the following discussions.

In the recent years, the courts have ruled in favour of individual rights over the long established customary powers of the village council to impose banishment. Three cases that demonstrate this have been discussed at length in other literature[9] and will not be explored further here. In *Sefo v Attorney-General*,[10] in applying the Constitutional freedom of religion provisions, the Court held that by virtue of Articles 11, 12 and 13 of the Constitution, the *Alii and Faipule* of the village of Saipipi have no jurisdiction or authority to prevent or restrict a particular religion or religious instruction within the village of Saipipi. In *Lafaialii v Attorney-General*,[11] in applying Article 111 of the Constitution protecting the freedom of religion, the court held that the banishment by the village council of the plaintiffs and their

---

[1] Corrin and Paterson (2011), pp. 338–343.
[2] *Constitution of the Independent State of Samoa* (Samoa) art 73.
[3] *Judicature Ordinance1961* (Samoa) s 31.
[4] *District Court Act 1969* (Samoa) s 26.
[5] *Land and Titles Court Act 1981* (Samoa) s 34.
[6] *Land and Titles Court Act 1981* (Samoa) Pt 9 - Appeals.
[7] *Land and Titles Court Act 1981* (Samoa) s 71.
[8] (Unreported, Supreme Court of Samoa, Young AJ, 4 November 1998).
[9] Care (2006), pp. 27–60; Corrin (2009), pp. 31–71; Forsyth (2004), 8(2).
[10] (Unreported, Supreme Court of Samoa, Wilson J, 12 July 2000).
[11] (Unreported, Supreme Court of Samoa, Sapolu CJ, 24 April 2003).

families on the basis they practised a different religion was a violation of the plaintiff's constitutional freedom. In *Mauga v Leituala*[12] the court held that within the meaning of Article 13 (1) (d) and (4) of the Constitution, the right of all citizens of Samoa to move freely throughout Samoa and reside in any part thereof is not limited by the powers of the village council under the *Village Fono Act 1990* (Samoa).

There have been earlier court judgments in which the courts decided in favour of customs[13] However, as indicated in the above cases, due to the shift over time, more emphasis is placed on individual rights. This exercise of those rights such as the freedom of religion has weakened the traditional powers of the *matai*.[14] The Chief Justice of Samoa considers that the Constitution is the paramount law of the land and the Courts must respect and uphold this.[15] The courts will consider and apply customs as long as they do not interfere with the constitutional rights and freedom entrenched in the Constitution.[16] The courts will continue to place emphasis on individual rights over communal rights, and customs will continue to be ignored in favour of individual rights.

5.1.2 Judicial Training

In addition to the limited scope given by the Constitution, there is a lack of judicial training and seminars available to create meaningful dialogue on how customary laws and the state laws may be reconciled or allowed to work alongside each other. The empirical data suggests that the lack of local judicial training is due to funding constraints.[17] There are suggestions that the concept of communalism as an individual right needs to be explored in the context of Samoa. It was observed that the intentions of the framers of the Constitution were clear in that the Constitution was to be read in the spirit of customs and usages; however, there are constraints in

---

[12](Unreported, Court of Appeal of Samoa, Cooke, P, Casey and Bisson JJA, March 2005).

[13]*Samoan Public Trustee v Collins* [1961] WSNZSC 1; *Olomalu v The Attorney-General* (1980–1993) WSLR 256; *Taamale v Attorney-General* (Unreported, Court of Appeal of Samoa, Cooke, P, Casey and Bisson JJA, 18 August 1995).

[14]Report on Matai Titles, Customary Land and the Land and Titles Court, December 1975 cited in *Taamale v Attorney-General* (Unreported, Court of Appeal of Samoa, Cooke, P, Casey and Bisson JJA, 18 August 1995).

[15]Sapolu (2011).

[16]The empirical data shows the respondents from the judiciary are in agreement on this.

[17]Interviews in Samoa with: MOJ Respondent 1 (28 March 2011); GCE Respondent 1 (19 January 2011).

interpreting individual rights in the context of Samoa.[18] Local and overseas training is lacking for judges to address how individual rights can be refined to fit the Samoan customary system.[19]

Western legal training usually dictates a strict application of state laws and the promotion of individual rights. It is left to the judiciary to grapple with the application of modern legal philosophies in a customary environment. Some members of the Judiciary interviewed indicated that these issues have not been addressed as there is lack of opportunities to address them.[20] As long as these issues are left unaddressed, it is easier to continue to interpret the current laws in light of western and modern philosophies, further marginalising customary laws.

5.1.3 Role of the Judiciary in Law Reform

A senior member of the Judiciary interviewed expressed that the local judiciary contributes to law reform substantially through submissions to the SLRC or the Office of the Attorney-General,[21] and secondly through suggesting reforms to relevant authorities in written decisions.[22] It is also appreciated that judges do make laws through judicial discretion[23] in Samoa.

By 2012, the judiciary of Samoa consisted of three judges of the Supreme Court and two judges of the District Court who were all local Samoans, a significant milestone achieved in Samoa at the celebration of its 50th anniversary. By 2016, with the exception of two Judges who were in Samoa to assist the Judiciary set up the Family Court and the Drugs and Alcohol Court, all Judges of the Judiciary were local judges. Samoa's Court of Appeal which sits twice a year consists of retired judges mainly from New Zealand and Australia. In Australia, as in Commonwealth countries, the appellate courts have an obligation to exercise judicial discretion, within the party's existing rights.[24] In time, the capacity of Samoa's local judiciary will increase in numbers and in seniority. This will provide further opportunity to advance the level of confidence in exercising judicial discretion on customary law arguments in the courts, assisted by the legal profession.

---

[18]Interview with MOJ Respondent 5 (Samoa, 1 April 2011).
[19]Interview with LP Respondent 2 (Samoa, 21 February 2011).
[20]Interviews in Samoa with: MOJ Respondent 5 (1 April 2011); MOJ Respondent 6 (4 April 2011).
[21]Interview with MOJ Respondent 2 (Samoa, 13 July 2011).
[22]Interviews in Samoa with: MOJ Respondent 3 (Samoa, 7 March 2011); MOJ Respondent 6 (4 April 2011).
[23]Interview with MOJ Respondent 1 (Samoa, 28 March 2011).
[24]State Government Insurance Commission v Trigwell (1979) 142 CLR 617.

5.1.4 Expatriate Judges

5.1.4.1 General Pacific Experiences

Expatriate judges have significantly contributed to the development of the legal systems of the Pacific Islands. However, engaging overseas judges is a mixed blessing. The judiciary may practice judicial independence without fear or favour. Conversely, expatriate judges are not necessarily well placed to adjudicate on matters involving customs.[25] In Vanuatu for example, expatriate judges have experienced tensions with the local systems resulting in the forceful resignation or even impeachment of the expatriate judges.[26] A court decision[27] in coup driven Fiji resulted in the revocation of all judicial appointments including those of expatriate judges; and expatriate judges faced many challenges after taking judicial appointments under the then illegal Fiji regime.[28]

For Samoa, expatriate judges in the appeal courts have exercised caution and respect for the local customs and a willingness to defer to and be guided by a local judge at the lower court.[29] Earlier case law shows how expatriate judges, following research and deliberations, upheld the importance of the Samoan traditional structures and practices.[30] However, there are occasions when expatriate judges bring their influences into play and thus are not well placed to adjudicate matters relating to customs. A comprehensive study of the effects of expatriate judges in Samoa is not provided here. Rather, a few examples are offered to demonstrate occasions in which expatriate judges' decisions run contrary to the spirit of customs, due mainly to unfamiliarity with the local customs and environment.

5.1.4.2 Interpretive Function of the Court

One of the significant legal developments in Samoa decided by an expatriate judge was the use of the interpretive functions of the court to define the powers of review of the Supreme Court over the Land and Titles Court of Samoa. As stated earlier, the LTC has exclusive jurisdiction over customary land and titles. In *Alaelua v*

---

[25]Hassall and Saunders (2013), p. 186.
[26]Ibid 186–187.
[27]Qarase v Bainimarama (Unreported, Fiji Court of Appeal, Powell, Lloyd, Douglas JJA, 9 April 2009).
[28]Corrin (2010), pp. 191–209.
[29]Toailoa v Sapolu (Unreported, Court of Appeal of Samoa, Ellis, Gallen, Salmon JJA, 26 April 2006).
[30]Samoan Public Trustee v Collins [1961] WSNZSC 1; Olomalu v The Attorney-General (1980–1993) WSLR 256; Taamale v Attorney-General (Unreported, Court of Appeal of Samoa, Cooke, P, Casey and Bisson JJA, 18 August 1995).

5.1 The Courts

Lands and Titles Court[31] where the jurisdiction of the LTC was first clarified, the court summed up the scope of the Land and Titles Court's jurisdiction as follows:

1. The LTC is a unique court, but not an inferior court.
2. It has exclusive jurisdiction over Samoan titles and customary land.
3. It has its own appeal procedure.
4. It governs a legal system different and separate from that of the Supreme Court.
5. The status of the LTC and its President is equal in some respects to that of the Supreme Court and its Chief Justice. The LTC is the supreme court of authority for Samoan custom.[32]

This decision clearly supports the perception that LTC is a unique court independent of the formal courts. The functions of the LTC relative to those of the formal courts in Samoa are made clear in the following statement by a former Prime Minister of Samoa.

> The respective roles and functions of the two Courts are different. One is for the maintenance of law and order, the other is for the protection of rights to customary lands and titles, the two basic and fundamental things which form the very core of our Samoan society. The decisions of the Criminal Courts will affect only those accused whereas the decisions of the Land and Titles Court have far reaching effect, for they are binding even on the unborn generations.[33]

Further, in the development of the LTC Act, the LTC was to be a superior court of record, stand independently and separate from the criminal and civil courts of Samoa, and its decisions be regarded as if it were a decision of the Supreme Court.[34]

In *Alomaina v LTC*[35] New Zealand's Justice Young, in interpreting the relevant provisions of the LTC Act, took a different view in holding that the LTC was an inferior court, and that the Supreme Court's inherent jurisdiction to review violations of individual rights includes jurisdiction to review the LTC's decisions alleged to breach those rights. Justice Wilson of Australia fully supported *Alomaina* in *Sefo v LTC*.[36] The next constitutional challenges against the LTC decisions *Lafaialii v The Attorney-General*[37] and *Mauga v Leituala*[38] relied on these precedents and it is settled law to date. The LTC's decisions are subject to judicial review like any western tribunal.

---

[31] [1980–1993] WSLR 507. This case was decided by then Acting Chief Justice Lussick who resided in Samoa.

[32] Alaelua v Lands and Titles Court [1980–1993] WSLR 519.

[33] Spring, (1970–72) 1.

[34] Vaai (1999), pp. 168, 170.

[35] Alomaina v Land and Titles Court (Unreported, Supreme Court of Samoa, Young AJ, 4 November 1998).

[36] (Unreported, Supreme Court of Samoa, Wilson J, 12 July 2000).

[37] (Unreported, Supreme Court of Samoa, Sapolu C J, 24 April 2003).

[38] (Unreported, Court of Appeal of Samoa, Cooke, P, Casey and Bisson JJA, 4 March 2005); see further *Asiata v Asiata* (Unreported, Supreme Court of Samoa, Nelson J, 2 February 2007).

The *Alomaina* decision is a positive legal precedent for Samoa as far as human rights compliance is concerned. On the other hand, customary powers and decisions are subject to judicial review where the Constitutional fundamental rights are alleged to have been breached. This marginalises the significance attached to customary laws and practices.

5.1.4.3 Village Agreement Unenforceable Under Contract Law

A second example of customs being diminished under the interpretive function of the court is *Pauli Elisara v The Attorney-General*.[39] One of the main issues was whether there was a binding agreement between the State and Salelologa village. The *tuua* (a prominent *matai*) of Salelologa, on behalf of the village accepted a monetary offer for compensation offered by the state. This offer was for the use of customary land at Salelologa for a new township. An agreement was signed to this effect. The Supreme Court judge (a Samoan) found that the *tuua* did have customary authority and held that there was a binding agreement between the village (represented by the *tuua*) and the State. On appeal, the Court of Appeal, made up of expatriate judges overturned this decision, holding that the agreement was unauthorised, in that it was questionable whether the whole village consented to be represented by the *tuua*.[40]

The expatriate judges were unfamiliar with the customary practices of parties to an agreement. The actions of the *tuua* and the villages did not correspond with the essential elements of a contract including offer, acceptance, and intention to be bound, consideration and having the requisite capacity to contract.[41] The court looked at the agreement objectively and held no agreement was entered into. A strict application of the law was adopted without regard to the social and cultural context of Samoa. This further diminishes the importance of customary practices and customary laws.

Perhaps the court could have referred the issue to the LTC which is better placed and has jurisdiction to determine matters of a customary nature.[42] In addition, the Court could have also been assisted more by counsel providing substantive research material to appreciate that the *tuua's* actions in this case amounted to a binding agreement in the Samoan traditional setting. As discussed in earlier chapters, a *matai* is the head of the family and only matais may be spokespersons or decision makers for a group of families, a village or villages.

---

[39](Unreported, Supreme Court of Samoa, Vaai J, 25 June 2004).

[40]Pauli Elisara v Attorney-General (Unreported, Court of Appeal of Samoa, Cooke, P, Casey and Bisson JJA, 17 December 2004).

[41]Morawetz (1925), pp. 87–90.

[42]Land and Titles Act 1981 (Samoa) s 34.

5.1.4.4 Obiter Unsupported by Local Realities

There are also occasions where expatriate judges, in their written decisions, make comments on the Samoan customary village powers which are erroneous. In *Mauga v Leituala*,[43] the court confirmed the decision of the local judge Justice Vaai that only the Land and Titles Court has jurisdiction to issue a banishment order as opposed to the village council. The Court of Appeal then expressed the view that,

> it was unthinkable that the legislature [in enacting the *Fono* Act] would have intended to endorse by silence as drastic a village power as banishment... We have no doubt that the omission of any corresponding power from the Village *Fono* Act was deliberate policy on the part of the Samoan legislators of 1990.

Although the quoted portion is obiter, it portrays the state of mind of the appellate judges and misleads those that rely on the judgment. There are two problems with this observation. Firstly, the traditional power of the village council to banish was indeed a policy that formed part of the Village Fono Bill 1990 (Samoa) when it was first introduced in Parliament in 1990.[44] This is discussed further below in Part C of this chapter. Second, banishment is a long standing traditional practice.[45] It is practised regardless of whether it is recognised and supported in written law, policy decisions or Committee recommendations.[46] As depicted in the 2012 case that introduces this book,[47] banishment is still practised and state law has yet to effectively prohibit this customary practice.1.4.5 New Developments in the Courts System of Samoa.

With assistance from the Judiciary of New Zealand, two new courts have started operation in Samoa. The first two are the Family Court and the Family Violence Court following the enactment of the Family Court Act 2014 (Samoa); the Family Court's first decision was available to the public on 15 August 2014. The third Court is the Alcohol and Drugs Court; its first decision was made available to the public on 9 Feb 2016. The Youth Court is established under the Young Offenders

---

[43](Unreported, Court of Appeal of Samoa, Cooke, P, Casey and Bisson JJA, March 2005).

[44]Samoa, Parliamentary Debates, Legislative Assembly, 1990a, 22–23 January.

[45]Report on Matai Titles, Customary Land and the Land and Titles Court, December 1975 cited in Taamale v Attorney-General (Unreported, Court of Appeal of Samoa, Cooke, P, Casey and Bisson JJA, 18 August 1995).

[46]Despite the 1975 Committee Report's recommendation that banishment orders should be the prerogative of the Land and Titles Court, this recommendation is unknown and to date has not discouraged the practice. The village councils continue to impose banishment orders. This is evident from some of the Supreme Court judgments where 'banishment' was taken into account (as required by the Village Fono Act 1990 (Samoa) s 8) in determining the appropriate sentences. See for example, Police v F (Unreported, Supreme Court of Samoa, Nelson J, 30 March 2009); Police v Lemusu (Unreported, Supreme Court of Samoa, Nelson J, 14 September 2009); Police v Luka (Unreported, Supreme Court of Samoa, Vaai J, 21 May 2008); Police v D (Unreported, Supreme Court of Samoa, Sapolu CJ, 7 November 2008); Police v Vaa (Unreported, Supreme Court of Samoa, Sapolu CJ, 24 January 2006).

[47]Leota Leuluaialii Ituau Ale et al v Alii & Faipule Solosolo (Unreported, Land and Titles Court of Samoa, LC.11469 P2, 17 February 2012).

Act 2007. These recent courts have been set up with the same objectives, to continue to upgrade the services of the justice system in Samoa.

5.1.5 Overview: The Courts

The challenges facing the Samoan courts are sourced by a Constitution that provides a restrictive scope for the recognition of customs by the courts. There is a lack of judicial training available to debate the application of state laws in a customary society. There is little local judicial capacity to develop a strong Samoan judicial base committed to adopting customs in the courts. Due to the lack of Samoan Judges with senior judicial capacity, Samoa continues to engage expatriate appellate judges who may be unfamiliar with the customary context of Samoa. These factors hamper efforts and opportunities for Samoa's courts to promote customs in a modern state legal system. It also presents obstacles for the courts to contribute to law reform that takes account of both the customary legal system and the state legal system. Some suggestions towards addressing these challenges are provided towards the end of this book. We now look at the challenges of having two legal systems for the Parliament of Samoa.

5.2 The Parliament

The Constitution and the electoral laws of Samoa provide the criteria for membership which emphasise the importance of customary values and duties. The electoral laws of other jurisdictions[48] show that several common candidacy criteria apply across common law jurisdictions. These include citizenship and age requirements, registration status, and the usual disqualification grounds ofw having been imprisoned for a period of time and being an undischarged bankrupt, to name a few. For Samoa, in addition to these common criteria, the electoral laws require electoral candidates to be *matais* and place emphasis on the candidate's *matai* connection to the village.[49] Samoa's electoral laws require that a *matai* candidate has not been banished from the village, has resided in the village and has served the

---

[48] Parliament of Queensland Act 2002 (Qld) s 64; Electoral Act 1993 (NZ) s 47; Representation of the People Act (Vanuatu) ch 146, s 24.

[49] Constitution of the Independent State of Samoa 1962 (Samoa) art 42; Electoral Act 1963 (Samoa) s 5. To be eligible for membership, one has to be a citizen of Samoa, hold a matai title, and be registered as an elector or voter. At any elections, a candidate must provide a declaration from a village mayor that the candidate has resided in Samoa for 3 years and satisfies village services requirements. The electoral laws are discussed further below under a review of the Electoral Act 1963 (Samoa) 1963.

5.2.1 Lack of Systems in Place to Support Assembly of Matai

A significant challenge for Parliament is the lack of systems in place to assist members elected on strict customary criteria to undertake duties of members of a modern Parliament. A Parliament appointed entirely on customary criteria to take up duties in a modern Parliament needs systems in place to assist them carry out their parliamentary duties effectively.

The empirical data shows that there are high expectations that a Parliament solely of traditional *matai* will allow Samoa to develop laws that support the traditional and customary systems.[51] This has not been achieved where the Parliament continues to promote individual values contrary to customary ideals. There is a strong desire for more laws to be customary oriented, for members to be more involved in customary related debates and to show more certainty and confidence in the laws passed.[52] Some interview respondents expressed their wish to be heard in Parliament through their members and for more input from the villages and constituencies to reach Parliament.[53] More interaction is sought between members and their constituencies, to explain laws for the benefits of the constituencies.[54] The data suggests there is some difficulty for the members to translate some laws of Parliament into the village environment, accounting for the lack of feedback to the villages and the substantial exercise of caution in contributing to parliamentary debates.[55]

Although unfamiliarity with modern Parliament procedures is a feature for any new Parliamentarian in any common law country, this study argues that Samoa's unique electoral laws set them apart from others. Members of Parliament practise village laws and law making in the village which is a way of life. The same members require some assistance in being informed of individual rights and the Constitution and how they impact on the parliamentary laws they make. There must be systems in place to offer relevant information, for example professional training

---

[50] Electoral Act 1963 (Samoa) s 5(3)(b). Other Pacific Islands have less strict requirements connecting the candidate to the constituency. Papua New Guinea requires a candidate to have been born in or had resided in the electoral continuously for not less than 2 years; see Constitution of Papua New Guinea (Papua New Guinea) s 103. Solomon Islands require that the candidate be an ordinary resident of the electoral constituency and for the three nominating persons to be persons whose domicile of origin is in that constituency.

[51] Interview with VC1 Focus Group (Samoa, 1 March 2011).

[52] Interview with VC1 Focus Group (MT) (Samoa, 1 March 2011).

[53] Interview with VC1 Focus Group (FK) (Samoa, 1 March 2011).

[54] Interview with VC2 Respondent 2 (Samoa, 10 March 2011).

[55] Interview with VC2 Respondent 5 (Samoa, 15 March 2011).

that informs and encourages members to develop parliamentary laws that are suitable and relevant to both Samoa's *faamatai* and the modern legal system. In the absence of seminars and workshops that provide some background training on policy and law making, members cannot fully participate in parliamentary debates. Secondly, Parliament will pass laws that uphold the Constitution and individual rights without putting much debate on where customary laws may fit in to Parliament laws. There are two modern parliamentarian procedural features which run in contrast with the customary criteria upon which a member is elected. These are the language requirements and the law making procedures.

5.2.1.1 Language in Parliamentary Proceedings

Whereas Samoan language proficiency is part of the customary criteria to qualify for Parliament, Parliament procedures require a good command of English. This is because the Bills are drafted in English, and although the debates and parliamentary proceedings are conducted in the Samoan language, the English text of a Bill is debated throughout its passage through Parliament. This is at introduction, the three Parliament readings, consideration in detail and in Select Committee consultation. In statutory interpretation, in the event of inconsistency, the Supreme Court is in favour of the text version in which a Bill is debated in Parliament as depicting the intentions of Parliament.[56] As long as Parliament debates on an English text of a Bill, the English text will prevail over the Samoan text in the event of an inconsistency, despite dialogue and debates being in the native Samoan language. In 2015, despite the author's submissions to the Parliament Committee to the contrary, the new Acts Interpretation Act 2015 (Samoa) now gives priority to the English text,[57] without opportunity for arguments to the contrary given the uncommon practice of deliberating over the English text of a draft Bill in the Samoan language. Unless a Bill was originally drafted in the Samoan language (which has never been attempted or encouraged), the English version of an Act takes precedent over the Samoan text.[58] A lack of understanding of the draft laws in the English language deters a member from making meaningful submissions as sought by the villages and constituencies. This is an obstacle to effective law reform.

5.2.1.2 Law Making Procedures: Assembly Process and Private Members Bills

The second parliamentary feature in conflict with customary characteristics is the law making procedure. Two aspects of the parliamentary law making procedures

---

[56]In re the Electoral Act Pita v Liuga (Unreported, Supreme Court of Samoa, Sapolu CJ, Vaai J, Nelson J, 19 July 2001).
[57]Acts Interpretation Act 2015 (Samoa) s 11(2).
[58]Ibid.

are discussed here, the standard procedures of assembly meetings and the use of Private Members Bills (PMBs).

Unlike Parliament law making, village procedures are unwritten but are well defined, understood and practised by all traditional chiefs. Rules and laws (*tulafono*) in the villages are not abstract principles, rules or regulations devoid of feeling or emotion.[59] Consultation, if not always a consensus through *soalaupule* (making decisions on a consultative basis), is the goal.[60] Voting is a foreign concept unheard of in the village.[61] Law making by the village councils is underpinned by communal philosophies, and closely linked to the behaviours of the people, and the characteristics of the environment and society. In contrast, the written, strict and formal Standing Orders of Parliament regulate Parliament's procedures. All questions in Parliament are decided by a majority vote of all members present,[62] for example in putting forward a motion for the introduction or the first reading of a Bill.[63] Law making in Parliament must be in line with the individual rights entrenched in the Constitution[64] as any law that is inconsistent with the Constitution is void.[65] Samoa's Parliamentarians experience varying degrees of conflict in deciding over state policies. This is not largely researched and written about, but indigenous leaders turned politicians are also conflicted over policy determinations which are contrary to customs.[66] Firstly, the member must identify policies that impact on customs, secondly decide how those policies fit into a customary environment and thirdly, modify relevant provisions of draft laws that may bring the policies in line with customs. Where a member is unable to make the transitional changes and accordingly comply with the requirements of the different capacities he holds, the member cannot, on behalf of the member's constituents, make effective contributions to law reform.

The lack of confidence in the procedures of a modern Parliament means the members are cautious in seeking all available avenues to bring customary and village concerns to Parliament. One such avenue is the Private Members Bills (PMB). No PMB has ever been introduced in the Samoan Parliament.[67] The Standing Orders of Parliament impose stringent and costly procedural rules[68] that

---

[59]For the six dimensions of law making by the village councils, see Suaalii-Sauni et al. (2009), p. 12.

[60]Vaai, above n 34, 42.

[61]Interview with VC1 Focus Group (MT) (Samoa, 1 March 2011).

[62]Standing Orders of Parliament 2016 (Samoa) O 93.

[63]Ibid, O 100(1), (2), (3).

[64]Constitution of the Independent State of Samoa 1962 (Samoa) pt II.

[65]Ibid art 2.

[66]All interview respondents are in favour of promoting customs in formal laws. This includes the respondents from Parliament. However, there is no record of members promoting customs in areas where the Constitution is relied upon. There appears to be a general understanding that the Constitution is the supreme law in Samoa.

[67]Interview with GCE Respondent 6 (Samoa, 22 December 2010).

[68]Standing Orders of Parliament 2016 (Samoa) O 46 and O 99.

can be overwhelming without any guarantee that a PMB will be acceptable for debate.[69] PMBs have not been fully pursued as an avenue to initiate input from the village sector. Ill-informed members cannot make full use of the opportunities available for village views to be heard in parliamentary law reform. This is a further challenge for law reform in a plural society that needs to be addressed.

As alluded to earlier, Samoa's Parliament is reserved for Samoa's *matais* only; it is therefore an assembly of traditional chiefs, a system consciously adopted for Samoan *matais* to take control of the country's affairs. While there is an increasing number of formally educated officials and business owners running for elections, Parliamentarians are largely appointed on the status of their *matai* titles and their commitment to village services. Samoa's electoral laws have given these customary characteristics legal recognition emphasising the importance of traditional leadership. A modern Parliament constituted of traditional *matai* has its implications as discussed above. *Matais* may be unfamiliar with the language of the draft Bills, the formal law making procedures of Parliament, and invoking avenues to promote the contributions from the village sector. In years to come there may be a gradual change in this scenario. However, as long as the *faamatai* is important to the Samoan population, relevant training is necessary to allow parliamentarians to embrace both the *faamatai* and the adopted western styled political setting. Suggested ways of responding to these Parliament issues are provided in the next chapter.[70]

The next section demonstrates further why there is need for professional seminars to increase capacity to make laws that are both relevant to the customary legal system and the modern legal system. Like other developing countries, Samoa adopts laws made by other Parliaments in the form of legal transplants. Unless members are in tune with modern parliamentary requirements, Parliament risks enacting unsuccessful legal transplants.

5.2.2 Unsuccessful Legal Transplants

Legal transplantation as a law reform theory is discussed in a previous chapter. This section gives an example of an unsuccessful legal transplant in Samoa using the measures of success posed by Nelken,[71] (The transplant has not fitted into the

---

[69]Interview with GCE Respondent 6 (Samoa, 22 December 2010).

[70]Following every general election, the Office of the Clerk of the Legislative Assembly runs a one-day workshop to familiarise members with the Constitution and Parliament procedures. On one occasion, the researcher was the presenter on behalf of the Attorney-General on the features of the Constitution. Similar seminars with specific focuses are beneficial as background information for new Parliamentarians, for example, an overview of the current laws; a summary of the development of laws since independence; or emerging trends of law making in Samoa and other Pacific Islands.

[71]Nelken (2001), p. 47.

Samoan environment) and Cotterrell[72] (The transplant has not fitted into the local culture).

The *Dogs Control and Registration Ordinance 1955* (Samoa) (the Ordinance) was enacted while Samoa was under the New Zealand administration. Following independence, the Ordinance was one of the many laws carried forward by the Constitution to become part of the laws of Samoa.[73] The Ordinance was repealed and replaced by the *Canine Control Act 2013* (Samoa) (the 2013 Act). Save for several additional administrative duties extended towards non-government authorities, the 2013 Act substantially continues the provisions of the Ordinance. The discussions below are on the limitations of the Ordinance before being replaced, and the limitations and strengths of the 2013 Act are discussed in the next chapter.

The Ordinance required all dogs to be registered with the Ministry of Police in Samoa, it was envisaged that there would be a dog pound and dogs would be sold or destroyed if unclaimed. By 2013, 58 years later, there is no committed dog pound for the purposes of the Ordinance,[74] there are no dogs registered with the Ministry of Police and Samoa has a serious dog problem.[75] There is an overpopulation of dogs both in the urban and rural areas causing social and health issues[76] and threatening tourism.[77] Research in 2012[78] showed that Samoa had one of the highest recorded levels of household dog ownership in developing countries (88%), with very low levels of vaccination (15%) and sterilisation (19%).

The Ordinance was impractical given the local realities of Samoa and was an unsuccessful legal transplant for the following reasons. First, the Ordinance assumed that the regulation and control of an introduced family friend or pet is possible through a law notwithstanding its social and cultural environment. As canines are an introduced breed and do not form part of the traditional structures such as the family setting or traditional pets, it is difficult to give them the same treatment as given elsewhere where they are part of the family.[79] Although there are

---

[72]Cotterrell (2001), p. 79. Also see Trubek and Galanter (1974), pp. 1062–1102 where legal transplant is said to have failed as it was too ethnocentric.

[73]*Constitution of the Independent State of Samoa* (Samoa) art 114.

[74]Editorial, *Samoa Observer* (Samoa) 11 April 2013.

[75]Various visitors to Samoa have raised concerns on the social media such as Salinas, 2010, http://www.samoadiaries.com/travel/samoa-howls/.

[76]Farnworth et al. (2012), pp. 477–486. Dog bites were at a frequency of 37 new bites per annum requiring hospitalisation per 10,000 head of population.

[77]Animal Protection Society (Samoa), 2009, 14 July, http://apssamoa.blogspot.com.au/2009/07/new-aps-website.html#comment-form. Some of the comments from concerned tourists on this website include those by Clair, posted 7 April 2012. 'I have just returned from Savaii, a lovely island, but a shocking place for cats and dogs. They are neglected, abused ... for a religious country, this is shocking. Never visit Samoa if you respect companion animals.'

[78]Farnworth et al., above n 77. This study found that of the 327 Samoans surveyed, only 16% had received education about dogs. The attitudes of the sample did not correspond to their behaviour. A majority (81%) believed that dogs must be vaccinated, however 72% of 81% had never visited a veterinarian.

[79]Boelman (2012), 29 December http://boelmaninsamoa.blogspot.com.au/p/dogs.html.

now modern (closed-up) dwellings, many Samoans prefer traditional open *fale*. The majority of Samoan land is customary land without fences or clear demarcation of boundaries; pets are therefore not restricted but are free to roam.

Second, in imposing registration fees and requiring dog collars and other duties of dog owners, the Ordinance assumed cash economy which is contrary to the local reality. The majority of Samoa is village based surviving on subsistence farming for everyday consumption. The costs of proper care for a dog are unaffordable for many families. The Ordinance also imposes responsibilities on the State that it cannot afford given other competing priorities. There are no other similar schemes for the registration of animals due to the lack of resources to fund such systems.[80]

The incompatibility of the transplant with the local environment is now causing social and health problems and discouraging tourists, causing more economic implications to Samoa. A transplant that fails to take root in the customary environment of Samoa is a challenge for law reform in Samoa.

Adopting an appropriate and successful legal transplant is a challenge for Parliament; however, it is equally difficult to develop laws locally to give effective legal recognition to customs. These challenges are explored next.

5.2.3 Acts of Parliament with Custom References 1962–2015 (Samoa)

By 31 December 2016, out of 285 Acts of Parliament, only some 53 can be said to have some regard to the Samoan context. However this number would be misleading as a total of 27 only make a mere mention of the local context and nothing further. A number of 26 makes more than a mere mention and are worth discussing here, in terms of their strengths and weaknesses, analysed from the provisions of the Acts. The 27 Acts with minor references will not be discussed as they do not promote the customary context of Samoa further as illustrated in the following examples.

1. Some of the 27 Acts counted in the 53 merely provides that customary land or a customary practice is exempted from those Acts; e.g. the Public Trust Act 1975, the Wills Act 1975 and the Slaughter and Meat Supply Act 2015.
2. Some make reference to 'purposes' or 'objectives' of the Act to be in line with customary practises and usages in the preliminary provisions, but do not say how these objectives are to be carried out in the substantive sections of the legislation. Some examples are the Samoa Law Reform Commission Act 2008, the Prisons and Corrections Act 2013, the Lawyers and Legal Practitioners Act 2014 and the Medical Council Act 2015.

---

[80]The closest to an animal registration system is the registration of cattle brands, see Animal Ordinance 1960 (Samoa) pt III.

3. In some of the 27 Acts, the only reference to custom is that an appointee must be knowledgeable of the Samoan custom, for example, this is one of the criteria for the position of the Ombudsman in the Ombudsman (Komesina o Sulufaiga) Act 2013. In complete opposition to this criterion, the Act does not require the Ombudsman to carry out the Ombudsman's functions with regard to the customs and traditions of Samoa.
4. Some make reference only to one customary related term e.g. 'traditional birth attendant' in the Ministry of Health Act 2006 and the Allied Health Professionals Act 2014. Samoa is grappling to find how to regulate these traditional based professions in Parliament law.

The purpose of this section is to highlight the strengths and limitations of those 26 Acts which give some recognition to custom. Of the 26, four are pre-independence laws and will not be discussed, as they were not enacted by a politically independent Samoa. These 4 are Cooperative Societies Ordinance 1952; Samoa Antiquities Ordinance 1954; Police Offences Ordinance 1961; and the Burials Ordinance 1961. This leaves 22 Acts which are discussed below, and Parliament's attempts to give statutory recognition to the customary context and practices. In the following discussions, a reference to an Act includes all the amendments made to that Act. Court decisions and empirical interview data are referred to, to support a proposition where relevant. The 22 Acts are divided into three categories and are discussed in the order of the years they were enacted.

5.2.3.1 Acts 1962 (Independence) to 1989

Samoan Status Act 1963 This Act makes provisions for the status of a Samoan person. It continues the provisions of the Samoa Status Ordinance 1934[81] prescribing the qualifications for holders of *matai* titles. It defines a 'Samoan' as a person who is a citizen of Samoa and has any Samoan blood[82] and restricts eligibility of a *matai* title to 'Samoans' only.[83] It allows Europeans who held validly conferred *matai* titles before 1963 to continue holding those titles after that year, as a complimentary honour only.[84]
The limitation in this Act is that while it declares that it (the Act) is in accordance with Samoan customs and usages[85] the criteria of eligibility for *matai* titles, where one is required to be a Samoa citizen, is not a Samoan custom. Under Samoan customs, *matai* eligibility is primarily determined in accordance with succession

---

[81]Samoan Status Act 1963 (Samoa) s 10.
[82]Ibid s 3.
[83]Ibid s 6.
[84]Ibid s 7.
[85]Ibid s 2.

principles, irrespective of citizenship.[86] In addition, 'citizenship' is not expressly a 'particular' required for the 'Register of Matais' in the Land and Titles Court.[87] Under the Act, Samoans who have opted to be citizens of other countries are ineligible to hold *matai* titles. Given that citizenship is not a customary criterion for *matai* eligibility, this statutory requirement contradicts Samoan customs and usages.

Electoral Act 1963 The Electoral Act has been referred to in earlier discussions under Sect. 5.2 (Parliament). This Act is an example of legislation which has had some success in accommodating both an adopted western style political framework alongside the established socio-political system of the *faamatai* which is central to Samoan culture. Throughout the years since enactment the Act has undergone several amendments to accommodate the two political systems. From independence in 1962, only *matais* could vote and stand as candidates for Parliament. This was unsuccessfully challenged as unconstitutional in 1982,[88] after the Court of Appeal held that on the basis that the Samoan cultural system was founded on the *faamatai*, *matai* suffrage was not discriminative of *non-matais*. In 1990, however, Samoa moved to embrace modern democracy further by amending the Act to replace *matai* suffrage with universal suffrage.[89] A second significant legislative amendment to accommodate both political systems came in 2005.[90] Gift giving, reciprocity and traditional presentations are central to the *fa'a Samoa*. The practice of gift giving at the election period was challengeable as a corrupt practice under the Act.[91] To continue to recognise traditional presentations and to also respect fair and democratic elections, the Act allowed a time frame for traditional presentations to be made without those presentations being caught under the offences provisions. Traditional presentations (*o'o ma momoli*) by a candidate or a person acting on behalf of the candidate cannot be challenged as a commission of bribery or treating if they are made any time in the period of three to six months prior to polling day.[92] This period was later amended by the Electoral Amendment Act 2015 (No.13) to within 12 months after the date of the declaration of the results of the poll'.

In 2009, the Act was further amended to allow the practice of *tautua fa'aauau* (traditional service or assistance) and exempting it from being challenged as bribery or treating if the *tautua fa'aauau* was carried out in the period before 90 days prior to elections.[93] In the same Amendment Act, several more criteria were added to

---

[86]Vaai, above n 34, 157.
[87]Land and Titles Act 1981 (Samoa) s22.
[88]Olomalu v The Attorney-General (1980–1993) WSLR 256.
[89]Electoral Amendment Act (No 20) 1990 (Samoa).
[90]Electoral Amendment (No. 2) Act 2005 (No. 14) (Samoa).
[91]Electoral Act 1963 (Samoa) ss 96–98.
[92]Electoral Amendment (No. 2) Act 2005 (No. 14) (Samoa) s 97A.
[93]Electoral Amendment Act 2009 (No. 21) (Samoa) s 97B.

5.2 The Parliament

candidacy requirements.[94] In addition to being a citizen, over 21 years and a holder of a *matai* title,[95] the potential candidate must provide a statutory declaration from the village mayor declaring that the candidate has lived in the village for not less than three years, is not banished from the village and has satisfied village service requirements of that village. Village service is defined as the *monotaga* or the compulsory services a candidate renders in respect of one or more of the candidate's villages located in the territorial constituency in which the candidate intends to stand.[96] What amounts to compulsory village services is determined by the customs of each village. Prior to 2009, in the forty-nine seat Parliament of Samoa, forty-seven were all required to be *matai* elected from the 'electors' roll'. Two seats were set aside for two members from the 'individual voters roll', a registration roll for part-Samoans. The 2009 Amendment Act required all forty-nine members of Parliament to be *matai* and removed further different treatment between Samoans and part-Samoans. This supported the practice in reality as most if not all members of Parliament from the individual voters roll already held *matai* titles, although they were not addressed under those *matai* titles in official sittings.

In 2015, certain provisions of the Electoral Act were revised through 5 Amendment Acts. This is a record number of amendments for any Act in one year. Samoa continues to grapple with a framework that suits the Samoan context. A significance of the 2015 amendments was renaming the 'individual voters 'roll (originally reserved for part Samoans) the 'urban constituencies' roll. This removed the different references and all voters were now recognized as Samoans. The urban constituencies are located on the traditional territorial constituencies of Faleata and Vaimauga. A voter residing in these areas now has the option of registering and voting (according to kinship) in any of the two 'territorial' constituencies Faleata or Vaimauga, or registering and vote according to residence in any the two 'urban' constituencies.

The most recent amendments to the Electoral Act positively advance customs in Parliament laws. The amendments show how Samoa has developed on both political systems through legislation, further extending legislative recognition to the *faamatai* in Samoa's electoral laws. These amendments are not free of court challenges[97]; however, the developments in this Act indicate the State has made some healthy and successful attempts to accommodate both political systems in Samoa.

---

[94] Ibid s 5.

[95] Electoral Act 1963 (Samoa) ss 5, 16. The Act only allows candidates to stand for a constituency to which his or her *matai* title has connections with.

[96] Ibid s 5(3A).

[97] See Tuitui v The Attorney-General (Unreported, Supreme Court of Samoa, Sapolu CJ, 25 February 2011) for the constitutional challenge against the 2009 amendments. See Ale v Electoral Commissioner (Unreported, Supreme Court of Samoa, Sapolu CJ, 23 February 2011) and Asalemo v Electoral Commissioner (Unreported, Supreme Court of Samoa, Sapolu CJ, 28 February 2011) for proceedings seeking clarification of the traditional powers of the village mayor.

Taking of Lands Act 1964 This Act provides for compensation for land taken for public purposes. As discussed above, this Act failed to give legal protection to a compensation agreement executed in the customary way, where the land in question was customary land. As alluded to above, the Supreme Court decision that there was a properly executed agreement was overturned by the Court of Appeal in 2004.[98] Following this decision, in 2005, the State amended the Act.[99] The relevant amendments state that in relation to customary land acquired under the Act, the Minister of Lands or any interested person may apply to the Land and Titles Court (LTC) to determine eligibility under customary law to enter into a legally binding agreement on behalf of the customary landowners claiming compensation.[100] Where there is any doubt as to who is eligible for compensation for customary land taken, this is to be determined by the LTC.[101] Any determination on compensation (by the Supreme Court and the LTC) that follows is binding on the courts of Samoa and on the relevant parties.[102]

The 2005 amendments favour customary practices in that they give specific recognition to the exclusive jurisdiction of the LTC to decide on matters relating to customary leadership and traditional hierarchies. In addition, the amendments provide an avenue through which a *matai* (determined by the LTC) can execute a legally binding agreement on compensation for customary land on behalf of a village or villages. Given that about 81% of land in Samoa is customary land, these considerations should have been filtered in at the time this Act was first developed. That they did not form part of the original policies behind this Act shows there was a serious disregard for Samoa's customary realities. Such limitations in Acts that purport to support and protect customs need to be addressed in developing future Acts of Parliament that regulate or have an impact on customary land and customary practices.

Alienation of Customary Land Act 1965 This Act regulates the process in which customary land is leased or licensed. One of the main objectives of the Act is for customary land to be exploited to benefit the customary landowners from the proceeds of the leases and licenses. Under this Act, some of the customary landowners were unable to claim from the government amounts allegedly owed by the lessee foreign company which had left Samoa years earlier.[103] The court held that the government is only a trustee under the Act and was not privy to the lease agreement between the plaintiff and the overseas company. The government was

---

[98] Elisara v Attorney-General (Unreported, Court of Appeal, Samoa, Cooke, Casey, Bisson, JJA, 17 December 2004).

[99] Taking of Land Amendment Act (No 19) 2005 (Samoa).

[100] Taking of Land Amendment Act 1964 (Samoa) s 57B(10).

[101] Ibid s 57B(9).

[102] Ibid s 57B(11).

[103] Tavita v Attorney-General (Unreported, Supreme Court of Samoa, 2002). Taken from the notes of the researcher, who was the counsel representing the Office of the Attorney-General in these proceedings.

therefore not liable for any alleged breaches by the overseas company. The landowners (and their lawyers) were misinformed or had misinterpreted the legislation intended to promote the interests of landowners. This resulted in court proceedings that were unsuccessful and incurred further costs to the customary landowners. Although this Act was intended to benefit customary landowners, in the absence of proper legal advice, it was misinterpreted and incurred further costs to the customary landowners.

Land Titles Investigation Act 1966 The Land Titles Investigation Commission is established under this Act to inquire into claims made into the ownership of State land and customary land.[104] The majority of land in Samoa is customary land and alienation of customary land is prohibited.[105] Vaai is critical of this Act, pointing out some examples where the Commission was able to hastily convert customary land into freehold land and avoiding the investigative process in the Act.[106] According to Vaai, without proper monitoring processes in this Act, the Commission is capable of investigating the status of customary land primarily for conversion into freehold land, to avoid the constitutional prohibition of alienation of customary land. Based on Vaai's assertions, this Act may be challenged as unconstitutional.

Land and Titles Act 1981 (LT Act) As discussed above under the topic of expatriate judges, despite the original intention for an independent customary court, the decisions of the Land and Titles Court (LTC) are now reviewable against individual rights. Although this is positive for individual rights and the state legal system, it marginalises customs as customs will continue to be restrictively applied in favour of individual rights. However, there have been recent amendments to the LT Act[107] which advance certain customary practices. The Act now requires all parties to exhaust customary dispute resolution mechanisms[108] such as the Samoan conciliation[109] and mediation before filing court proceedings with the LTC. The basic qualifications of a *matai* holder are now specified in this Act to be 25 years or above (subject to special circumstances), and the person must be prepared to serve his or her families, and village communities according to Samoan custom and usage.[110] These recent amendments support a long standing customary practice of traditional conciliation, and reinforce the duties of a *matai* to families and village communities.

---

[104]Land Titles Investigation Act 1966 (Samoa) s 10.

[105]Constitution of the Independent State of Samoa 1962 (Samoa) art 102.

[106]Vaai, above n 34, 158–159.

[107]Land and Titles Court Amendment Act 2012 No.14 (Samoa).

[108]Land and Titles Court Act 1981 (Samoa) s 34C.

[109]Section 2 of the LTC Act defines 'Samoan conciliation' as the process where the parties to a customary land or title dispute, identify the disputed issues, develop options and endeavour to reach an agreement according to Samoan custom and usages.

[110]Land and Titles Court Act 1981 (Samoa) s 20A.

5.2.3.2 Acts from 1990 to 2000

Village Fono Act 1990 This Act provides examples of the difficulties of legislating for customary powers and practices. This is the first Act in which the Parliament of Samoa discussed the implications of accommodating both the customary legal systems of Samoa and the introduced legal system. As its background and developments are relevant to this study, the Act is explored in some detail.

In 1990, the Parliament of Samoa sat to debate the Village Fono Bill 1990 (Samoa) (VF Bill). It is evident from the parliamentary debates[111] that the policy behind the VF Bill was to strengthen the village council by giving it legal recognition. As indicated earlier (under the discussions on expatriate judges) the traditional power of the village council to impose banishment as a traditional penalty was part of the original draft Bill when it was first introduced in Parliament.[112] A *Constitutional Amendment Bill 1990* (Samoa) was also prepared and introduced by the State at the same sitting, to relax the relevant constitutional freedoms[113] and allow for the traditional village council power of 'banishment' to be recognised and regulated in legislation.

Some arguments in the debates are noteworthy. Some members argued that as a traditional institution, the village council did not require legislation for recognition and validity.[114] It was also evident that the Bill was sparked by the Supreme Court decision in *Tuivaiti v Faimalaga*[115] the first court proceedings in Samoa where the powers of the village council of Falelatai[116] were challenged and set aside in favour of individual rights.

The bulk of parliamentary debate was devoted to deliberations on whether to embrace individual rights or support a long standing customary practice. All members that made presentations on the Bill agreed on the importance of the village council and that it must be protected and promoted in parliamentary laws.[117] However, members were clearly divided on whether to give statutory powers to a village council to banish an offender from the village. There were grave concerns that banishment violates the fundamental freedoms of expression and movement under the Constitution.[118] In addition, there were no mechanisms to control this power; it was open to the village council to abuse it without any

---

[111] Samoa, Parliamentary Debates, 1990a, 22–23 January; Samoa, Parliamentary Debates, Legislative Assembly, Report of the Select Committee Report on the Bill, 1990c, 2–4 July.

[112] Village Fono Bill 1990 (Samoa) cl 6(c); also see Samoa, Parliamentary Debates, 2–4 July 1990 (Aeau Peniamina) 189.

[113] Samoa, Parliamentary Debates, 22–23 January 1990b, 938 (Aeau Peniamina).

[114] Ibid 898.

[115] [1980–1993] WSLR 17.

[116] Samoa, Parliamentary Debates, 1990b, 22–23 January, 938, 921–922.

[117] Ibid 910. The report records powerful and patriotic speeches in favour of promoting and protecting the powers of the village council.

[118] Ibid 890, 899.

5.2 The Parliament

recourse for the villager.[119] The Samoa Law Society opposed the Bill on similar constitutional concerns.[120] Those in favour of banishment argued that if 'banishment' were removed from the Bill, it defeated the purpose of the Bill, which was to protect the powers of the village councils. The Member of Parliament representing the constituency and the first village council whose decision was held unconstitutional[121] supported the Bill. He stated that 'if the power of banishment is removed from the Bill, this Bill has no meaning. It is better to remove the whole Bill. Without the banishment provision we are only partially recognising the village councils.'[122]

The express reference to the power of banishment was removed from the Bill[123] and as this was not contrary to the final policy adopted by Parliament, the *Village Fono Act 1990* (Samoa) was passed. The *Constitutional Amendment Bill 1990* (Samoa) was also withdrawn.[124] In 2005, some 15 years following these Parliament debates on the Village Fono Bill 1990 (Samoa) and banishment, the Court of Appeal in *Mauga v Leituala*[125] (above) reaffirmed the proposition that the village council does not have powers to impose banishment, and that this is only within the jurisdiction of the LTC. Despite this decision, banishment is still imposed by the village councils as a social control mechanism in the villages to date. This clearly shows the conflicts between the written law and judge made law on the one hand, and the law practised on the ground on the other.

Following enactment, the *Village Fono Act* has not been without criticism. Some scholars point to the Act as being no more than a political appeasement of *matais* for the loss of automatic entitlement to parliamentary candidacy, at the introduction of universal suffrage in the same year 1990.[126] It has been blamed for actions by villagers that appear to directly challenge the authority of the formal law;[127] and it has been said that criminal jurisdiction violates the right to a fair trial and the right concerning criminal law in the Constitution.[128] Lacking public consultation, it causes difficulties in the administration of justice.[129]

The main limitation against legislating for this customary institution is that the Act does not portray the reality, depth, scope and meaning of the customary powers

---

[119] Ibid 899.

[120] Samoa, Parliamentary Debates, 1990, 2–4 July, 196. This was confirmed by the member of Parliament from Tuivaiti's constituency who was also a member of the Samoa Law Society. The member emphatically supported the inclusion of the power to banish in the Bill, in respect of the consensus reached by the village councils of his constituency.

[121] Tuivaiti v Faimalaga [1980–1993] WSLR 17.

[122] Samoa, Parliamentary Debates, 2–4 July 1990, 190–191 (Aeau Peniamina).

[123] Ibid 189.

[124] Ibid 199.

[125] (Unreported, Court of Appeal of Samoa, Cooke, P, Casey and Bisson JJA, March 2005).

[126] Macpherson (1997), p. 43.

[127] Vaai, above n 34,184.

[128] Powles (1997), p. 72.

[129] Powles (2005), pp. 404, 418.

and functions of the village councils as understood and appreciated by the people of Samoa. Although it is meant to protect the powers of the traditional leaders, it does not have influence over the realities in the villages, where the law of the land is the *matai* law.[130] This Act is limited where it does not realise its purposes and functions. An Act that was made to protect and strengthen the traditional village council has succeeded more in challenging and marginalising the traditional powers of that system. The Act continues to be Samoa's Act of Parliament through which the difficulties of accommodating customs in state laws are evaluated; it has again undergone recent assessment through a COI and the SLRC. The most recent developments and proposed amendments to this Act (Village Fono Bill 2016) including reaffirming the traditional power of banishment are discussed in the next chapter. It demonstrates Samoa's latest response to promoting customs in parliamentary laws.

Ministry of Women Affairs Act 1990 In 2009, the Act was amended to require that that there be a woman representative in each traditional village to promote the advancement of women in that village. This Act was enacted to establish a government Ministry to promote the interests of women through development and implementation of relevant programmes, projects and activities.

Internal Affairs Act 1995 The overall objective of this Act is to promote the wellbeing of villages and village authorities. It is commended for providing the framework for opportunities and collaborative partnerships between the state and the village sector, strengthening partnerships for village development.[131] This is facilitated through the appointment of *sui o le nuu* (village mayors) and *sui o le malo* (government representatives) by villages and the government respectively.[132] The appointees are responsible for creating and facilitating mutual cooperation between the state and the villages. The Ministry of Women, Social and Community Development is responsible under this Act for the promotion of the wellbeing of villages and village authorities.

The empirical data suggests that before village mayors were paid a state salary, they were more effective and respected in the villages. As this is a vital position for a workable relationship between the State and the villages, there is increasing demand for the village mayors to be more effective and committed to their duties under the Act[133]; to attend and actively contribute to seminars conducted by the State[134]; to be able to impartially relate state policies to the villages[135] and to promote policies that benefit the villages and not to land them personal or political

---

[130]Macpherson, above n 126, 47.
[131]Internal Affairs Act 1995 (Samoa) s 5.
[132]Email from an Officer of Internal Affairs (MWSCD) to Lalotoa Mulitalo, 19 November 2012. As of 2012, the Ministry recorded a number of 249 village mayors and 111 women representatives.
[133]Email from GCE Respondent 7 to Lalotoa Mulitalo, 19 April 2011.
[134]Interview with VC2 Respondent 4 (Samoa, 10 March 2011).
[135]Interview with SOH Respondent 9 (Samoa, 21 March 2011).

gain.[136] Further, guidelines setting out the responsibilities of the village mayors[137] are suggested for village mayor accountability.[138] Incorporating the traditional position of village mayor in legislation and giving it a state position has materially changed the traditional nuances and the cultural respect that were originally attached to it, or that which it demanded. This is one of the implications of attempts to merge two conflicting social and legal systems; there must be changes to the original status of the traditional position. However, this is a small cost to the positive developments resulting under this Act.

Fisheries Act 1998 In this Act, one of the functions of the Chief Executive Officer (CEO) of the Ministry of Agriculture and Fisheries is to consult with fishermen, industry and village representatives, concerning the conservation, management and any development measures for fisheries. In consultation with fishermen, the fisheries industry and village representatives, the CEO may prepare and promulgate by-laws not inconsistent with the Fisheries Act for the conservation and management of fisheries, including limitations to be imposed upon or the banning of the use of particular fishing methods.

5.2.3.3 Acts After 2000

Young Offenders Act 2007 Prior to 2007, a young offender (10–17 years) in Samoa was treated like any other adult offender. The Young Offenders Act changed this in 2007 by subjecting a young offender to a criminal justice system for young persons. A Youth Court is established in the District Court Division.[139] The court may determine that proceedings be conducted in a manner consistent with Samoan custom and tradition.[140] The pre-sentencing meetings are conducted in accordance with Samoan custom and tradition to consider penalties which are rehabilitative and community based.[141]

Community Justice Act 2008 Similarly, the Community Justice Act 2008 promotes a community based justice system by creating opportunities for Samoan customary structures and practices to be recognised and become part of the sentencing, rehabilitation and reintegration procedures. A Court may promote, encourage and facilitate a settlement, according to Samoan custom and tradition.[142] In

---

[136]Interview with SOH Respondent 6 (Samoa, 12 April 2011).

[137]Email from GCE Respondent 7 to Lalotoa Mulitalo, 19 April 2011.

[138]The development of clear guidelines on the duties of village mayors was supported following concerns raised in an electoral petition, see Lufilufi v Hunt (Unreported, Supreme Court of Samoa, Vaai, Nelson JJ, 26 April 2011).

[139]Young Offenders Act 2007 (Samoa) s 4.

[140]Ibid, s4(2).

[141]Ibid, Part 4.

[142]Community Justice Act 2008 (Samoa) s 6.

sentencing, the court may take into account any compensation made under Samoan custom and may postpone sentencing to allow for customary sentencing to take place.[143] A court may also impose a substituted or alternative penalty of community work under the supervision of village authorities, in place of imprisonment.[144] Under the Young Offenders Act and the Community Justice Act, the criminal justice system in Samoa has embraced customs and traditions in relation to a young offender and any offender at criminal sentencing.[145] Although customary issues are largely irrelevant at the criminal trial stage, the two Acts are nevertheless a constructive development for both the state legal system and the customary legal system. Each system has responsibilities in the administration of the criminal justice system, albeit at a lesser level for the customary system. The village councils and other traditional village organisations all have a role to play in these two Acts, there must therefore be sufficient public awareness of the Acts. Unfortunately, like most of the laws of Samoa, the two Acts are not well known. A 2011 Pacific region study on youth involvement in urban crime and violence undertaken in Apia urban area found that awareness of both Acts was lacking amongst the local participants during consultations.[146] This needs to be addressed for a successful implementation of the Acts.

Water Management Resources Act 2008 The Water Resources Management Act[147] requires that all water resources are to be managed and controlled by the government. The provisions of the Act cannot apply to deprive the customary landowners of any customary land and resources, to which they are entitled under the customs and usages of Samoa.[148] This Act advances the customs and usages of Samoa through the protection of customary landownership in legislation, a positive development in the recognition of customary laws, which are firmly connected to customary land.

Samoa Law Reform Commission Act 2008 This Act requires the Samoa Law Reform Commission to develop reforms that promote Samoan customs and usages and allow customary laws to work alongside state laws.[149] The challenges in achieving this are discussed towards the end of this chapter under Sect. 5.4.

Education Act 2009 This Act empowers a Village Council to set up a village school (primary to secondary level) upon approval of the requisite application by the Ministry of Education. The Act requires the Government and the Village Councils to work together in the administration and operations of the village

---

[143]Ibid, s 7.

[144]Ibid s 9.

[145]This is also available under the Village Fono Act 1990 (Samoa) s 8.

[146]Noble et al. (2011), pp. 119, 128.

[147]Water Resource Management Act 2008 (Samoa). This Act came into force in 2009.

[148]Ibid s 6(4).

[149]Law Reform Commission Act 2008 (Samoa) s 4.

schools. This calls for the working together of both the village and the state for a common purpose, for education.

Liquor Act 2011 One of the requirements to be fulfilled by an applicant for a licence under this Act whose premises to which the application relates is located in the village, is consent from the village council of that village The Board then makes a determination on an application for a wholesale, retail, food and beverages, bar licences. In this Act, a 'public place' includes a village *malae* (open village field reserved for village activities).

Tourism Development Act 2012 One of the principles in promoting tourism under this Act is that tourism development must be consistent with the existing traditions, customary practices and rights of the Samoan people. Regulations may be made under the Act to require the providers of in-bound tour services to respect local customs and traditional authority structures, and to engage Samoan citizens in the provision of services involving or impacting on such customs and traditions.

Customary Land Advisory Commission Act 2013 This Act sets up the Customary Land Advisory Commission to encourage, facilitate and promote greater economic use of Samoa's customary land, for the social, cultural, economic and commercial development of Samoa. The Commission has a number of functions under the Act. The Commission is to recommend to Cabinet suggested measures for the facilitation, encouragement and promotion of the economic use of customary land in Samoa. The Commission is also tasked with reviewing all laws affecting customary land in Samoa and make recommendations to Cabinet for changes to such laws to facilitate the economic use of customary land. This Act has been criticised by some members of the public as they believe it will lead to the alienation of customary land. However, the goal for government is that the Samoan people will make use of dormant land for the benefit of the customary landowners, within the confines of non-alienation of customary land stipulated in the Constitution.

Canine Control Act 2013 Under this Act, the Police Service which administers this Act may involve the village and local communities in developing and monitoring canine control measures, and prepare and promulgate by-laws for the proper management and control of canines in village and local areas. Having realised there is a dog problem in Samoa even with the Dog Registration and Control Ordinance 1955 in place, Parliament has now brought in the village communities to assist the police administer this 2013 replacement Act.

Samoan Language Commission Act 2014 This Act was enacted to ensure the Samoan language is and remains a vibrant language. It declares the Samoan language as an official language, and establishes a Samoan Language Commission with functions geared towards promoting the Samoan language. The objectives of this Act include to ensure respect for the Samoan language as an official language and to ensure that the Samoan language is accorded the status, right and privilege as to its use in all government institutions or State institutions, in particular with respect to its use in in parliamentary proceedings, in legislative and other instruments; and in communicating with or providing services to the public. This is a positive law in Samoa as language is a feature of customs. Unfortunately, to date this Commission has not been very active in achieving their functions and the objectives of the Act.

Fisheries Management Act 2016 Under this Act, the Chief Executive Officer of the Ministry responsible for fisheries may, by Order declare and mark an area as a village fisheries management area. Before declaring such area the Chief Executive Officer must consult the Village Fono of the area and of any neighbouring village taking into account of the size of the district; the population of the district; the ownership of customary land; any traditional fisheries practices; and any other factors that may be necessary to facilitate the process. A disadvantaged village community or a member of a disadvantaged community, has the right to participate on an equal basis in the management of a village fisheries management area, if they have any traditional links, affinity, familial or clan relationship to the area.

These provisions recognise the close family ties of the Samoan people. In this regard, it is a positive law as it allows families working together for the good of the community and the environment.

District Courts Act 2016 Under this Act, the jurisdiction of a Faamasino Fesoasoani is to hear and determine minor matters such as any action founded on contract or in tort if the debt, demand or damage, or the value of the chattels, claimed does not exceed the sum of $2000; and any action for the recovery of any expense, contribution or other demand which is recoverable by virtue of any law, if the amount claimed in the action does not exceed the sum of $2000. A positive feature of this Act is that it also provides that where a Fa'amasino Fesoasoani sits with a Judge to determine a matter, the Fa'amasino Fesoasoani's role is only to advise on any matter involving Samoan custom, or to advise as to penalty.

Although this Act was updated in 2016 from the repealed 1992 Act, it does not take account that the Judiciary of Samoa consists of Samoan judges only, and does not expressly require the District Court Judges to each take account of the Samoan customary context in their court decisions.

5.2.3.4 Overview

The 22 Acts discussed above provide useful observations on the challenges of incorporating and giving statutory recognition to customs and customary practices in legislation. Some limitations of the Acts, particularly the earlier Acts after independence include that they were solely enacted for the purposes of continuing a pre-independence office or framework into the post-independence period, with little or no regard to Samoan customs. Care must be given to general legislative provisions that declare an Act is enacted in accordance with customs and usage, efforts must be made to ensure the statutory provisions are customary compliant. This was the limitation in the Samoa Status Act. It is difficult to ascertain all customary practices that may be relevant and include them in legislation at the time the legislation is developed as is noted in the Taking of Lands Act. There are limitations in attempts to fully capture customs in legislation as observed in the *Village Fono Act 1990 (Samoa)*. There is generally a lack of awareness of state laws, such as the Young Offenders Act and the Community Justice Act, and this can result in the misinterpretation of laws as in the Alienation of Customary Land Act.

Perhaps the passing of the Village Fono Act 1990 opened a bolder stance, and the other four Acts passed in the span of 1990 to 2000 made reference and started to recognise that a workable partnership between the state and the village is viable and perhaps necessary for development. Those 4 Acts empowered the development by both the state and the village councils' subsidiary legislation to further support a collaborative effort of the two systems. There have been continuous amendments to the Electoral Act up to 2015 in attempts to accommodate the two political systems (state and village) as seen in the Electoral Act. The Acts enacted after 2000 provided further frameworks for effective partnerships between the state and the customary systems. As society evolves through changes, legislation that attempts to give effect to two or more legal systems are continuously subject to court challenges as seen in most of the Acts above and in particular the Electoral Act, the Land and Titles Act and the Village *Fono* Act.

The analysis of the 22 Acts provides a general indication of the extent to which the Samoan legislature recognises customary laws and traditions to 2016. Although there appears to be a recent increase in the number of Acts giving regard to customary practices, to date the recognition is generally limited, incomplete and uncoordinated. This is because the importance of recognition of customary laws alongside state laws has not been consciously and fully reviewed in Samoa. Due to the complexities of recognising customs in state laws, there must be a consistent approach to basic policy making. More focus needs to be given to enacting more Acts that consciously and genuinely promote customs and customary practices. The application of some of the above legislation provides a background against which further recognition must be considered, and thus are instructive for future law making. A worthy approach to law reform may be built on the lessons and experiences from the implementation of the above Acts.

5.2.4 Analysis: Acts of Parliament and Acts with Customs References (2008–2016)

A comparative exercise was carried out, in which the number of Acts of the Parliament of Samoa, was compared against the number of Acts which give some reference and recognition to the Samoan customary context in their practices and institutions. This is a span of 10 years, from 2007 to 2016. The results are set out in 'Table 5.1 - Acts of Parliament with Custom References in Percentage', and further demonstrated in 'Fig. 5.1; Acts of Parliament Table 2007–2016'.

Table 5.1 Acts of Parliament with custom references in percentage

Year	No of Acts of Parliament	No of Acts with Custom references	Percentage
2007	242	26	10.7
2008	258	31	12
2009	255	32	12.5
2010	262	34	12.9
2011	271	36	13.3
2012	270	38	14
2013	274	44	16
2014	278	47	16.9
2015	277	50	18
2016	285	53	18.6

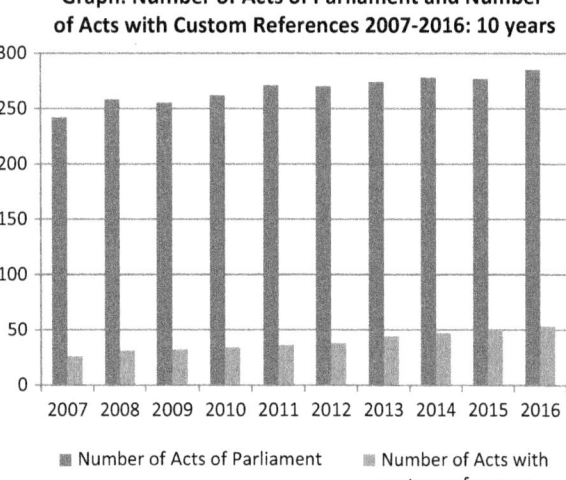

Fig. 5.1 Acts of Parliament 2007–2016

In the year 2007 Acts of Parliament totalled 242, of this total, only some 26 made references to Samoan customs and customary practices. This accounts for a mere 10.7% of all Acts of Parliament. In 2009, the Acts of Parliament totalled 255, some 32 made reference to customs; this is only 12.5%. In 2010, of the 262 Acts of Parliament, 32 made reference to custom, accounting for 12.9% of Samoa's laws. By 2016, there were 285 Acts of Parliament and only 18.6% made reference to the Samoan customary context and practices.

It is acknowledged that not all Acts of Parliament impact directly on custom, and in many a consideration of custom is not ideal or necessary. However, the gap between the total number of Acts of Parliament and those that make reference to the realities of the Samoan population shows too significant a difference to ignore. The 2011 census showed that the majority of the Samoan families are agriculturally active and rely heavily on subsistence farming for everyday consumption. Given

96% are indigenous Samoan citizens under the traditional governance of the village councils, these numbers beg the question - what percentage of the Samoan population have some appreciation of the close to 300 Acts passed by Parliament for their benefit? There is much work to do, to address the "legitimacy" of the Acts of the Parliament of Samoa enacted for the people of Samoa.

5.2.5 Overview: The Parliament

There is lack of professional training available to members of Parliament to develop capacity in modern law making. The law reform challenges for Parliament are as follows. Firstly, Parliament is an assembly of traditional leaders voted from the criteria of communal values to develop state laws that uphold individual rights principles. The foreign language of Bills and the modern procedures of a formal assembly impact on their performance and duties to their constituencies. This includes the lack of confidence to invoke avenues available such as the Private Members Bills (PMBs) to introduce and debate policies impacting on customary laws.

The legal transplant (Dogs Control and Registration Ordinance) earlier discussed had difficulties in finding root in Samoa. Some 53 Acts of Parliament to date give some recognition to customary structures and practices of Samoa. An analysis of those Acts provides valuable lessons in developing laws that genuinely and positively advance customs in legislation. These analyses must form part of the Samoan Parliament's professional training material as they offer real examples of the challenges of developing laws in Samoa. Some suggested responses to these challenges are offered in the next chapter. The next section discusses the law reform challenges for the Executive.

5.3 The Executive

A consideration of custom is not a conscious part of Cabinet's policy making. These results in laws that fail to recognise that some customary values and principles may be more relevant to the people of Samoan, than the modern values that form the laws developed and endorsed by Cabinet. Unless changes are made to this practice, state laws continue to undermine customs.

5.3.1 Executive Law Making Process

5.3.1.1 Cabinet Handbook

In 2011, for the first time in Samoa, the government procedures on law making were produced in bound consolidated documents. These recorded current and long standing government practices on law making. On 20 July 2011, through a Cabinet Directive,[150] the Samoan Cabinet approved two Handbooks, a 'Cabinet Handbook'[151] and the 'Ministerial Practice and Procedures Manual.'[152] The 2011 Cabinet Handbook provides general information to the public on how the Government works and serves as a working guide to the Public Service in improving its support services to Cabinet.[153] It also sets out the process and requirements to be met for proposed legislation (Bills and subsidiary legislation or regulations) to be in the form and substance for Cabinet consideration.[154] The Handbook requires a government Ministry seeking draft laws (Bill or regulations) to discuss their proposal with the Office of the Attorney-General. With the Attorney-General's support, the Ministry makes a submission to the Cabinet for approval for the drafting of relevant legislation. The submission must set out the policies to be pursued or implemented through this proposed legislative action. The Ministry must convince Cabinet why legislative action is most feasible to achieve policy objectives rather than other means. Where approval is given the relevant Minister and Ministry may proceed with drafting in consultation with the Attorney-General.

The government Ministries develop the policies for draft laws and Cabinet endorses government Bills to be presented for passage through Parliament, and subsidiary legislation for the signature of the Head of State. Generally, subsidiary legislation or regulations in Samoa are required by the authorising Act to be 'made' by the Head of State on the advice of Cabinet. In practice this is made by the Head of State upon his signature giving effect to the subsidiary legislation or regulation.[155]

A perusal and assessment of the Cabinet Handbooks underline that the process by which Bills and regulations are developed and endorsed by Cabinet does not require a conscious regard to customs and customary practices. Legal pluralism is not addressed at any level of policy development. State policies are thus not expressly required to be formulated with customary consideration. The effect of a policy on both the State and on customs are not consciously assessed and debated at any step of policy or law formulation. This limitation needs to be addressed.

5.3.1.2 Legislative Drafting Handbook

The first edition of the Legislative Drafting Handbook of Samoa was developed under the Office of the Attorney-General to guide all legislative drafting work in

---

[150]Government of Samoa, Cabinet Directive Faapitoa (Special) F K (11) 14, 20 July 2011.
[151]Ministry of the Prime Minister and Cabinet (Samoa), *Cabinet Handbook* (2011a).
[152]Ministry of the Prime Minister and Cabinet (Samoa), *Manual on Ministerial Practice and Procedures* (2011b).
[153]*Cabinet Handbook*, above n 151, 2.
[154]Ibid 33.
[155]Office of the Attorney-General (Samoa) (2008), p. 30.

Samoa. It was approved by the Attorney-General and came into effect on July 1 2008. All draft laws of Samoa must comply with the requirements and standards noted in this handbook. Part 1 of the handbook provides for the role of the Ministry in developing draft legislation. Part 2 sets out the general drafting requirements for all draft laws in Samoa.

A perusal of this handbook shows similar features to the Cabinet Handbook, there is no express requirement for customs to be consciously filtered into either policy development by the Ministries or the draft laws developed by drafters. In 2014 the Office of the Attorney General published a revised version (Legislative Drafting Handbook 2014), and a perusal of these revisions show there is no change to this stance. Similar to what was expressed above under the Cabinet Handbook, the absence of such directions means no obligation is placed on policy makers and drafters to include customary considerations in data and instructions that inform the policies and draft laws of the State.

5.3.2 Overview: The Executive

Both the Cabinet handbook and the Drafting handbook promote state based policies through the Ministries and state focused laws through the legislative drafters. If the State is serious about developing reforms relevant to the local customary environment, these handbooks must be modified to require State officers to filter in customary considerations at every stage of policy development and draft laws.

5.4 The Samoa Law Reform Commission (SLRC)

The SLRC experiences impediments to undertaking their functions of law reform in many forms. These setbacks are informed by an analysis of relevant legislation, empirical interviews, SLRC reports and other documentary research. The main challenges faced by the SLRC are experienced through the following: the SLRC establishment and personnel; overseas influence on structure and law reform process and through law reform public consultations. The challenges for the SLRC are discussed under those headings. All these impact on the overall challenge for the SLRC which is to develop law reform that supports the customs and usages of Samoa. In simple terms, the SLRC must find a way to effectively develop law reform in a plural society, upholding both the customary law and the state legal system. This is an onerous undertaking.

5.4.1 Establishment and Personnel

5.4.1.1 What Model of Law Reform Institution?

The first challenge faced by the SLRC is in its establishment. Samoa acknowledged that law reform is vital for development and looked at establishing a central institution to develop law reform relevant to the customary structures it wishes to protect. What form should it take?

The initial studies that identified the need for a law reform institution for Samoa date back to 1997 during discussions on an institutional strengthening project for the Ministry of Justice and Courts Administration of Samoa.[156] An Establishment Group consisting of government officials, representatives from the Samoa Law Society, the Chamber of Commerce and the SUNGO was set up in July 1999 to evaluate a Law Reform Commission.

In 2002, Parliament passed the *Samoa Law Reform Act 2002* (Samoa) establishing a Commission with law reform functions independent from the state. Section 1(2) provided that the Act was to commence on a date to be determined by the Minister of Justice and published in the *Savali*, a government newspaper. Such date was not determined and upon review in 2007, the Attorney-General determined that 'there were reportedly difficulties in securing a suitable and available person to be the Commissioner; there were challenges with resource allocation; and the structure and functions of the Law Reform Commission did not suit Samoa's current circumstances'.[157] Due to these restrictions, up to the time of the review in 2007, the Minister had yet to determine a commencement date.

Parliament passed the *Law Reform Commission Act 2008* (Samoa) to replace the unworkable 2002 Act. It reduced the independence of the Commission in that its law reform agenda is now to be in line with the government's agenda. It replaced a Commissioner with an Executive Director as the administrative head and provided for staff to be public servants. Part time commissioners, who may be chosen from judicial officers, may be engaged to undertake law reform projects. Rather than being a standalone office, it forms part of the Office of the Attorney-General. These changes were seen as more realistic given resource constraints and the lack of qualified personnel.

This was the initial establishment of the current SLRC. In 2011 the SLRC became independent of the Office of the Attorney-General, but its functions under the 2008 Act remain unchanged.[158] The functions of the SLRC are restricted to law reform, which involves a full review of particular subject matters stipulated in references from the Prime Minister, the Cabinet and the Attorney-General. The revision and consolidation of Samoa's statutes and subordinate legislation are under

---

[156]Leung Wai (2008), p. 5.
[157]Ibid 11.
[158]The new independent status of the Commission does not affect the functions of the SLRC under the Act which remains unchanged.

separate legislation.[159] The SLRC researches areas of law that are in need of reform, makes recommendations to the Attorney-General and Cabinet on new reforms, and liaises with both the government ministries and the public on areas requiring law reform. The SLRC has powers to conduct studies and public hearings and to engage suitably qualified persons to assist the SLRC with its work.

5.4.1.2 The Initial Years

Following its establishment, the SLRC experienced the challenges of being a newly set up institution that adopted best practices from overseas. It was faced with difficulties in developing effective reforms within its means. The first legislation resulting from an SLRC Project was passed by Parliament in 2013.[160] Within a very restrictive budget and limited expertise, the SLRC has been most active in developing Issues Papers, carrying out public consultations and developing draft legislation for passage through Parliament. It is envisaged that the increasing number of Bills resulting from SLRC projects will be enacted by Parliament in the latter half of 2013. The slow rate in which SLRC projects and recommendations have been realised is contributed by both new experiences and obstacles to a brand new setup trying to find root in Samoa.

5.4.1.3 Western Educated Personnel

The head and staff of the Commission are appointed under the public service laws.[161] The Commission of eight young western educated professional staff has faced several challenges in its initial years, in establishing itself in the customary environment.

Members of a Village Council interviewed were of the view that the village councils require time to be familiar with the SLRC and its purposes.[162] The hierarchy in the customary setting is disturbed when the young address the elders on important but somewhat foreign matters such as state law.[163] There is uncertainty on what the consultations entail when conducted by relatively young western educated lawyers. There are suggestions that those familiar with village protocols

---

[159]The Revision and Publications Act 2008 (Samoa) repealed the Reprint of Statutes Act 1972 (Samoa).

[160]Crimes Act 2013 No. 11 (Samoa).

[161]Law Reform Commission Act 2008 (Samoa) s 11.

[162]Interview in Samoa with VC1 Respondent (MT) and VC1 Respondent (FK) Focus Group, 1 March 2011).

[163]Interviews in Samoa with VC2 Respondent (15 March 2011) and LP Respondent 5 (14 March 2011).

and fluent in the Samoan language must take charge of public consultations[164] at least in these initial years of the SLRC, until the public is familiar with the work of the SLRC.

Western educated lawyers must keep a conscious check on the reforms they investigate and consult on, lest they put too much emphasis on western principles over communal values. Although there may be genuine attempts to import customs into law making, lawyers sometimes subconsciously move back to western ideals.[165] The empirical data suggests that those that conduct law reform public consultation must be able to speak the Samoan language and understand village protocols. Most Samoan lawyers are urban based and may be unfamiliar with oratorical language, village honorifics, genealogical salutations and the general cultural protocols. Such challenges require the SLRC to find strategic ways and methods of approaching public consultations in traditional communities.

5.4.1.4 The SLRC Advisory Board

An Advisory Board consisting of the heads of government ministries, civil society and community representatives assist the Commission in carrying out its functions.[166] One third of members are appointed on the basis of their community standing and having interest in law reform projects, and the rest are members by virtue of the government positions they hold.[167] The Act does not stipulate the functions of the Advisory Board. Apart from the government representatives who may have some experience in law reform from their official capacities as heads of departments, the rest of the Board are not required to have training in law reform, or knowledge of the legal system of Samoa in general. To date the Advisory Board has been instrumental in advising on the way public consultations are to be conducted; setting realistic timelines and advising on priority law reform projects.[168]

The empirical data suggest that the SLRC Advisory Board has found difficulties in setting out agendas and effectively carrying out their functions within the objectives of the Act.[169] In the absence of adequate funding, there is a lack of law reform training to enhance the capacity of the Board to assist the SLRC to develop a law reform process suitable for Samoa.

---

[164]Interviews in Samoa with VC1 Focus Group (1 March 2011); SOH Respondent 3 (4 April 2011); MOP Respondent 2 (4 January 2011); MOP Respondent 2 (4 January 2011).
[165]Interview in Samoa with LP Respondent 4 (2 March 2011); VC2 Respondent 5 (15 March 2011); GCE Respondent 1 (19 January 2011); LP Respondent 3 (4 March 2011).
[166]Law Reform Commission Act 2008 (Samoa) s 12.
[167]Law Reform Commission Act 2008 (Samoa) s 12(3).
[168]Interview with SOH Respondent 9 (Samoa, 21 March 2011).
[169]Ibid.

5.4.2 Law Reform Process

As the SLRC is a transplant and not a traditional Samoan institution, it needs assistance from outside of Samoa on its direction for development. Although the SLRC has received substantial assistance from overseas, it must develop a law reform process that is suitable for its own plural environment. This is a significant challenge for a newly setup institution to develop modern state laws.

In its initial years, the SLRC has had various overseas influences from partner commissions; the most notable are the Australian and Canadian law reform commissions.[170] There have been other influences including New Zealand, the UK, China, Japan, Thailand, and USA where the SLRC was represented at conferences or seminars related to law reform. Law reform training for the professional staff of the SLRC has been vital for professional development. Training was received from the ALRC on methodologies in conducting law reform inquiries and capacity building in legal policy and legislative review.[171] Since its establishment in 2008, the SLRC has participated at the Australasian Law Reform Commission Agency Conference (ALRAC).[172] The material from these conferences becomes an integral part of the professional and strategic development of the SLRC in the search for best practices for Samoa. Samoa's hosting of the biennial ALRAC in Samoa in 2014 is evidence of the importance of the ALRAC to the development of best practices of law reform in Samoa.

The *Law Reform Commission Act 2008* (Samoa) is modelled on the law reform legislation of the Australian states and Canadian provinces. Generally, law reform legislation including Samoa's and other Pacific Islands establish institutional law reform, provide for the functions of the Commission, its budget and staffing. Appendix C sets out the statutory functions of non-Pacific Island LRCs (Section 1) and Pacific Island LRCs (Section 2). The LRCs of the Pacific Islands are significantly influenced by the LRCs of their more advanced counterparts; this influence extends to the law reform processes adopted by the Pacific Islands.

A perusal of the law reform process of the Australian Law Reform Commission online shows six stages, the initial research and consultation; preparing the Issues Paper and inviting submissions on the Issues Paper; reviewing the submissions and carrying out further consultation; preparing the Discussion Paper and inviting submissions on it; reviewing the submissions and carrying out further consultation;

---

[170]Technical assistance and helpful insights on possible law reform approaches were received from the Australian Law Reform Commission; the Law Reform Commission of Western Australia; the New South Wales Law Reform Commission; the New Zealand Law Commission; the Maori Land Court; the Waitangi Tribunal; the Conference of the Federation of Law Reform Agencies of Canada; the British Columbia Law Institute; and the Alberta Law Reform Institute.

[171]Funded by Australia under the Pacific Legal Policy Twinning Programme with the Attorney-General's Department (AGD), Canberra, Australia.

[172]The SLRC presented an update of the work of the SLRC to the 2010 ALRAC held in Brisbane. In 2012, the SLRC was also represented to the ALRAC in Canberra.

and preparing the final report.[173] Each project depends on the inquiry, the scope of stakeholders and interest groups, the time period allocated, and the range of laws to review.[174] Samoa's law reform process set out in Appendix D adopts the same six steps[175] as those of the ALRC.

Caution however must be exercised in adopting overseas frameworks, in the same way vigilance must be applied in adopting law reform by legal transplantation. The overseas models have been developed in different socio-economic and more developed environments with much larger populations. Those models are more relevant to more modern social, political and economic systems. More importantly, the more advanced law reform frameworks promote the modern legal systems dominated by the state, and are unsuitable for societies with two equally dominant legal systems.

Pacific Islands must adopt law reform models that can assist them achieve their statutory functions relating to customs and usages. Whereas the law reform commissions of Canada, Australia (ALRC), Victoria, Queensland and New South Wales are not expressly required to promote customs and usages in law reform, this is a statutory requirement for Samoa's SLRC. The law reform commissions of Papua New Guinea,[176] Solomon Islands[177] and Vanuatu[178] are also tasked to reconcile customs with formal laws through law reform. New Zealand's legislation contains a similar obligation; it requires the Law Commission to 'take account of Maori and multicultural New Zealand society'.[179] Given these significant distinctions, Samoa and other Pacific Islands must develop a law reform process that not only adopts overseas best practices but must also take account of customary laws.

The SLRC is a relatively new experience for Samoa. It is too early to tell whether the investment of overseas governments and law reform institutions into Samoa will yield effective laws and whether legal change through the SLRC will bring about significant changes for Samoa. Other studies point to an assumption that law reform promotes development; however, in truth law reform has little effect on some societies.[180]

Overseas assistance is well received and appreciated, in particular as it gives useful guidance at the initial setup of institutional law reform for Samoa. However,

---

[173] Australian Law Reform Commission, Law Reform Process http://www.alrc.gov.au/law-reform-process.

[174] Kirby identifies 10 law reform techniques some of which are unique to the Australian Law Reform Commission, and which have contributed to the success of the ALRC as an institution, see Kirby (2003). Although these techniques are outside of the context of Samoa in terms of scale and application, they provide possible models for future adoption by the SLRC.

[175] Samoa Law Reform Commission, Law Reform Process http://www.samoalawreform.gov.ws.

[176] Constitutional and Law Reform Commission Act 2004 (Papua New Guinea) s 12.

[177] Law Reform Commission Act 1994 (Solomon Islands) s 5.

[178] Law Commission Act (Vanuatu) cap 115 s 7.

[179] Law Commission Act 1985 (New Zealand) s 5.

[180] Trubeck and Galanter discuss this uncertainty in the relationship between scholarship and action in third world countries in Trubek and Galanter (1974), pp. 1062, 1083.

a significant challenge for the SLRC is to adopt a law reform approach that is fitting to the local circumstances of Samoa and its customary systems. It must apply best practices that take account of pluralism in the Samoan context. This is no doubt an ongoing challenge for the SLRC.

5.4.3 Public Consultation

As noted in the first edition of the Legislative Drafting Handbook Samoa 2008,[181] consultation is the cornerstone to effective law reform. This section discusses the lack of resources and costly protocols as obstacles to effective law reform consultation, and the empirical data on the adequacy of the law reform consultation. The insights that inform the empirical data on consultations are not restricted to or are directed at the consultations of the SLRC which was first established in 2008. The empirical data made reference to consultation (of the lack thereof) in general, by both the SLRC and other state Ministries. In these discussions, reference is made to the SLRC's consultation practices as consultation is a core function of the Commission.

5.4.3.1 Costly Cultural Protocols

Law reform operations are costly and this significantly impacts on general law reform work by state authorities, including the SLRC.[182] The SLRC follows the government's agenda, as the budget of the SLRC is government funded,[183] and subject to the normal scrutinies of a public financed office. The lack of funding is a challenge to effective and adequate consultation.[184] Public consultations are costly and the burden of cultural protocols adds to financial constraints. However, cultural protocols are a necessary part of consultations.[185] The attendance of various respondents at consultations must be reciprocated by the visitors (SLRC), usually with monetary donations to the village, in the same way the author had to reciprocate the kindness and food offered at the interviews carried out for this study.[186] As one interview respondent puts it, 'by giving, we are actually reinforcing customary practices of giving otherwise we cannot advance with law reform consultations.'[187]

---

[181] Office of the Attorney-General (Samoa), 2008, 15.
[182] Interview with LP Respondent 5 (Samoa, 14 March 2011).
[183] Interview with GEC Respondent 3 (Samoa, 12 April 2011).
[184] Email from GEC Respondent 7 to Lalotoa Mulitalo, 19 April 2011; Interviews in Samoa with LP Respondent 5 (14 March 2011); LP Respondent 1 (15 March 2011).
[185] Interview with LP Respondent 4, (Samoa, 2 March 2011).
[186] See discussions on reciprocity, Chap. 3 on methodology.
[187] Interview with LP Respondent 5 (Samoa, 14 March 2011).

There are some suggestions that costs should not prevent adequate consultation, and that consultation is less costly than the consequences of a population ignorant of the law.[188] On this basis, the government should be more concerned about the outcomes of the consultation rather than budget constraints.[189] Customary protocols are a necessary part of law reform consultation. Unfortunately for law reformers, on many occasions, tending to customary protocols does not guarantee constructive participation in consultations.

5.4.3.2 Law Reform Consultation

As stated at the beginning of the discussions on the SLRC, since establishment, the SLRC has been active in carrying out public consultations. The empirical data found a mixture of views on the adequacy of law reform consultation.

The majority of the village interview respondents observed that law reform consultation is hardly heard of in Samoa, it is uncommon and therefore inadequate.[190] Several concerns were raised on the lack of law reform consultation in the villages. It is observed that there is lack of public notice,[191] insufficient circulation of information and material on law reform,[192] and no opportunity given to read and understand law reform material before the actual consultations.[193] Some say that the government carries out consultations as a formality to be complied with, without genuine attempt to involve the public in law reform.[194] People are only aware of reforms when they had already become law.[195] Where some input was made to consultations, there has been no feedback on whether inputs were considered, used or made any difference to law reform proposals.[196] This invokes mistrust against the state. Consultation does not reach the majority of areas of Samoa.[197] Some village respondents were unsure if the consultations they attended were law reform consultation, village mayor seminars, or other government ministry consultation for example the Ministry of Health on public health issues.[198] The public is

---

[188] Interview with SOH Respondent 5 (Samoa, 20 July 2011).

[189] Interview with MOP Respondent 3 (Samoa, 11 January 2011).

[190] Interviews in Samoa with VC1 Focus Group (1 March 2011); VC2 Respondents 1-5 (15 March 2011; 10 March 2011; 7 March 2011; 10 March 2011; 15 March 2011 respectively); and with VC2 Respondent 2 (10 March 2011).

[191] Interview with SOH Respondent 6 (Samoa, 12 April 2011).

[192] Interview with SOH Respondent 5 (Samoa, 20 July 2011).

[193] Interview with SOH Respondent 7 (Samoa, 22 March 2011).

[194] Interview with GCE Respondent 1 (Samoa, 19 January 2011).

[195] Interview with VC1 Focus Group (Samoa, 1 March 2011).

[196] Interview with SOH Respondent 9 (Samoa, 21 March 2011).

[197] Interview with GCE Respondent 5 (Samoa, 18 January 2011).

[198] Interviews in Samoa with GWR Respondent 1 (21 March 2011); GWR 2 (21 March 2011); SOH Respondent 7 (22 March 2011).

5.4 The Samoa Law Reform Commission (SLRC)

unfamiliar with the state system and the sources of authority behind public consultation programmes.[199]

The inadequacy of law reform public consultation was also echoed by several members of the government sector.[200] One government member stated that 'consultations are inadequate to bring out the voices of the village sector; we are not getting that voice in law making. We are not listening at consultations, and when we don't, our laws are more influenced from overseas.'[201] There was however common appreciation that consultation is a costly exercise and that Samoa lacks the resources for big scale consultations.[202] Some respondents observed that consultations would have reached outer areas if the requisite resources were available.[203]

The empirical data also recorded opposing views. There is data that suggests 'there is no need to consult with too many communities, a few selected villages is sufficient for the purposes of consultation.'[204] 'The government Ministries cannot afford consultation costs and all consultation expenses are borne by the state which is already stretched of resources.'[205] Some of the government respondents question the accessibility to and clarity of, public invitations.[206] Others suggest that there was public awareness[207] but attendance before government officials or a Parliamentary Committee was overwhelming and intimidating for a villager.[208] There is a lack of interest in making a contribution to draft laws,[209] as the reforms under discussion may have no bearing on the realities in the villages.[210] Public consultations are not being fully utilised by the public.[211]

There are conflicting views on the adequacy of law reform consultation. While the village sector overwhelmingly believes there is inadequate consultation and sought more accessible and effective law reform consultations, lawyers and state

---

[199] Interviews in Samoa with VC2 Respondent 3 (7 March 2011); VC2 Respondent 2 (10 March 2011); VM Respondent 3 (8 March 2011). GWR Respondent 2 (21 March 2011); VC2 Respondent 5 (15 March 2011).

[200] Interviews in Samoa with MOP Respondent 5 (11 January 2011); MOP Respondent 2 (4 January 2011); MOP 3 (11 January 2011), GEC Respondent 1 (11 January 2011); GEC Respondent 2 (11 March 2011); GEC Respondent 6 (22 December 2010); GEC Respondent 5 (18 January 2011); Email from GEC Respondent 7 to Lalotoa Mulitalo, 15 April 2011.

[201] Interview with MOP Respondent 2 (Samoa, 4 January 2011).

[202] Interview with LP Respondent 4 (Samoa, 2 March 2011).

[203] Interview with LP Respondent 5 (Samoa, 14 March 2011).

[204] Interview with GEC Respondent 2 (Samoa, 11 March 2011).

[205] Interview with LP Respondent 1 (Samoa, 15 March 2011).

[206] Interviews in Samoa with LP Parliament 5 (14 March 2011) and LP Respondent 3 (4 March 2011).

[207] Email from SOH Respondent 8 to Lalotoa Mulitalo, 7 May 2012.

[208] Interview with VC2 Respondent 2 (Samoa, 10 March 2011).

[209] Interviews in Samoa with GCE Respondent 6 (22 December 2010) and VC2 Respondent 4 (10 March 2011).

[210] Interview with SOH Respondent 9 (Samoa, 21 March 2011).

[211] Interview with MOP Respondent 2 (Samoa, 4 January 2011).

officials consider there is adequate consultation given the limited resources available to the state. The state officials also point out that the public are given opportunities to be heard but these consultations are not fully utilised. The conflicting views suggest there are some consultations but they do not reach the majority of the villages in Samoa due to the lack of resources. The village sector may also argue there is a lack of consultation yet what this translates to is that they do not understand law reform and are cautious and reluctant to take part in it. This requires the state through the SLRC to develop strategies to involve the villages in organising and coordinating consultations. The data further suggests there is a need for better communication and more coordinated efforts between the villages and the State. The gap between the state and the villages must be bridged. There is a general consensus that the lack of funding hampers effective consultation. If public interest on law reform is to be improved, the state must give some priority to funding consultation in the villages.

5.4.4 Overview: The SLRC

The SLRC has yet to find its roots in Samoa. With its establishment, the future for customary laws is bright. However, the SLRC has an onerous task of developing reforms that uphold the customs and usages of Samoa. The SLRC must have a clear focus of its objectives and a realistic plan of how this may be achieved.

It will take time for the public to appreciate the work of the SLRC. The SLRC needs to raise its profile through public awareness programmes. The State must be strategic in establishing good relationships with a society entrenched in the *faamatai* and hierarchal village norms. Customary protocols can be costly but they are necessary for village support. A good command of the Samoan language including the oratorical, genealogical addresses and village protocols is beneficial for constructive dialogue. The villages must see some relevance in reforms and they must be involved in the law reform process. As a relatively new office, the SLRC requires substantial funding and resources for office material, professional training and modern technology support. Significant funding constraints result in difficulties in carrying out adequate public consultation on law reform. The next chapter provides some suggestions to address the challenges of legal pluralism for the SLRC discussed in this chapter. The next discussions explore the law reform work of ad hoc commissions and other law reform agents.

5.5 Other Law Reform Agents

The literature on the development of law reform machineries discussed earlier in Chap. 2 informs that the use of ad hoc commissions and law reform agents to undertake law reform in the absence of, or while awaiting the full operation of an

5.5 Other Law Reform Agents

institutional law reform is a common practice in the history of law reform institutions. Before the establishment and during the initial years of the SLRC, Samoa relied heavily on Commissions of Inquiry (COI) to investigate and recommend on law reform inquiries. Other statutory offices such as the Samoa Law Society (SLS)[212] and the Office of the Ombudsman[213] have law reform investigative powers under empowering legislation. Non-government organisations (NGOs) by the very nature of their focus significantly impact on how laws are shaped. This section discusses the law reform functions of these agents, their strengths and limitations in developing law reform in the plural environment of Samoa.

5.5.1 Commissions of Inquiry (COI)

Given the success of COIs in developing reforms in Samoa, an overall challenge for the state is to be able to continue COIs within its limited resources. Before examining the impediments on COIs as law reform agents, a brief background to the work and strengths of the COIs is provided. The advantages of a law reform agent constituted of *matais* and legal officers conclude the discussions in this section.

5.5.1.1 COIs for Customary Reforms

In the period 2001–2010, the State had set up six COIs for law reform, all having a common feature. The areas of potential reform they were to investigate were matters closely linked to Samoan traditional systems. These include the electoral system and *matai* candidacy,[214] the relationship between the village councils and the formal courts,[215] laws that impact on *matai* titles,[216] and possible reforms on the 'freedom of religion' in Samoa's customary context.[217]

Opeskin posited that whether law reform recommendations result in law reform is not a measure of success. However, legislation resulting from law reform projects is a helpful performance measure for governments. It indicates possibilities and scope for policy development.[218] In applying this to COIs in Samoa, it is useful for the government to understand the effectiveness of COIs, and whether such

---

[212] Law Practitioners Act 1967 (Samoa).

[213] Ombudsman (Komesina o Sulufaiga) Act 2013 (Samoa).

[214] Samoa, Commission of Inquiry into the Electoral Act, Final Reports (2001), (2006), (2011).

[215] Samoa, Commission of Inquiry on Matters Relating to the Divergence between the Decision Making Authority of the Alii and Faipule and the Formal Courts, Final Report (2007).

[216] Samoa, Commission of Inquiry into Matai Titles, Final Report (2010).

[217] Samoa, Commission of Inquiry into the Freedom of Religion, Final Report (2010).

[218] Opeskin (2005), p. 204.

commissions effectively meet their objectives of investigating into reforms to law in Samoa's plural environment.

5.5.1.2 COI Investigations and Reforms to Date

Commission of Inquiry on Matters Relating to the Divergence The results are recorded in Appendix B and overall show a high level of success in terms of the number of recommendations for legislative change and those actioned. The majority of the recommendations for legislative amendments have been actioned to date. For the COI into the Electoral Act (2001),[219] there were 22 recommendations made, 17 proposed changes to the law and 13 changes were made.[220] For the COI into the Electoral Act (2006)[221] out of 25 total recommendations, 20 sought legislative changes. A total of 16 out of the 20 recommendations led to changes to the electoral laws.[222]

For the COI into Matters relating to the Divergence Between the Decision Making Authority of the Alii and Faipule and the Formal Courts (2007),[223] 15 overall recommendations were made, 12 requested legislative changes and four were actioned.[224] The COI into the Freedom of Religion (2010)[225] recommended two legislative changes out of six overall recommendations, both recommendations for legislative change are proposed amendments in the Village Fono Bill 2016 currently before the Parliament of Samoa.[226] For the COI into Matai (Chiefly) Titles 2010,[227] one legislative amendment was made and this has resulted in the 2012 amendments to the criteria of a *matai* under the Land and Titles Amendment Act (No 14) 2012 (Samoa).[228]

5.5.1.3 COI Strengths

There are several reasons for the success of COI's in Samoa. They are appointed by Cabinet and therefore have the political support to sustain their temporary life.

---

[219] Samoa, Commission of Inquiry into the Electoral Act, Final Report (2001).

[220] See the Electoral Amendment Act (No.3) 2005 (Samoa).

[221] Samoa, Commission of Inquiry into the Electoral Act, Final Report (2006).

[222] Electoral Amendment Act (No 3) 2005 (Samoa); Electoral Amendment Act (No 21) 2009 (Samoa); Election Candidate Regulations S.R. 2006/6 (Samoa).

[223] Samoa Commission of Inquiry (2007), above n 215.

[224] Land and Titles Amendment Act (No 14) 2012 (Samoa); Internal Affairs Amendment Act (No 3) 2010 (Samoa).

[225] Samoa Commission of Inquiry (2010), above n 219.

[226] Samoa Law Reform Commission, Village Fono Act 1990, Final Report 09/12 (June 2012).

[227] Samoa Commission of Inquiry (2010), above n 216.

[228] Land and Titles Amendment Act (No 14) 2012 (Samoa) s 6.

5.5 Other Law Reform Agents

Customary related matters are urgent matters and are given top priority. Secondly, compared with the SLRC which is staffed with young lawyers with little customary knowledge and experience, their membership is diverse consisting of *matai* and village elders, church and government leaders as well as members of the private sector. As suggested by the empirical interviews, in relation to COI's created after the establishment of the SLRC in 2008, COIs are preferred over the SLRC on reforms relating to customs as the COIs are constituted of *matai* and Samoan elders.[229] A COI setup has more rapport with the public due to the relevance of its composition and status to both the village and state sectors. Their procedures are more relaxed with the use of *Talanoa* styled conversation giving a more relaxed atmosphere. Traditional hierarchy is not an obstacle as *matai* members of the public are deemed to be making law reform submissions to other *matai*. Overall, the number of legislative amendments made relative to their recommendations indicate that COIs have been very effective in developing law reform in Samoa.

5.5.1.4 COI Challenges

The first challenge for the State in relying on COIs to develop law reform is that the State cannot fund a COI for every customary related challenge that arises in Samoa, they are expensive establishments. A second challenge is the ad hoc nature of COIs. Membership changes with each new COI and members lose official capacity at the end of each final report. The empowering Act which is relatively unknown to the public requires that a COI is answerable to Cabinet only.[230] COI members are therefore not answerable to the public for the recommendations they make. In contrast, the SLRC is a permanent office subject to public opinion. Temporary establishments do not have established methods of consultation, procedure and representation similar to that of a permanent body. The standard law reform procedures of the SLRC are more transparent by comparison, in that they are advertised on the SLRC's website.

There is also the danger of a possible duplication of work between the SLRC and the COIs as evident in the developments on the *Village Fono Act 1990* (Samoa). The COI (Freedom of Religion) carried out the first set of consultations under its TOR and formulated recommendations.[231] Cabinet referred those recommendations to the SLRC which in turn made legal recommendations on reforms. After those recommendations were approved by Cabinet, the SLRC carried out further public consultations on the same project.[232] This duplicates costs, technical work and time which are not available in a resource constrained economy.

---

[229]Interview with SOH Respondent 3 (Samoa, 4 April 2011).

[230]Commissions of Inquiry Act 1964 (Samoa) s 4.

[231]Samoa Commission of Inquiry (2010), above n 217.

[232]Samoa Law Reform Commission Final Report (2012), above n 226, 4.

However, in overview, a satisfactory review of the *Village Fono Act 1990* (Samoa) was only achieved when two processes were completed; that of consultations by the COI (obtaining customary perspectives) and further review by the SLRC (for legal implications). This combination prompts confidence that the Act regulating the most important traditional institution of Samoa, the village councils, does reflect the views of the people of Samoa. The collaborative work of the COI and the SLRC leads to a proposition that a law reform agent constituting both the *matai* and lawyers working in partnership is more likely to produce law reform results that gain public confidence. The merging of both customary and legal expertise in one specialised authority is found in a recently enacted legislation in Samoa, discussed next.

5.5.1.5 Law Reform Driven by Both Matais (Customary) and Lawyers (Modern)

In the first half of 2013, the Parliament of Samoa enacted legislation[233] to establish a Customary Land Advisory Commission (CLAC) to address the complexities of customary land issues. Amongst other duties, it receives references made to it by Cabinet, conducts public consultations on areas of law (affecting customary land) considered to be in need of reform and reports its recommendations for reform to Cabinet.[234] The main function of the CLAC is to facilitate greater economic use of customary land to enhance cultural and economic development in Samoa.[235] The three Commissioners must be *matais* and possess a significant understanding of Samoan culture. To comply with their function of reviewing all laws affecting customary land, the Commission will require legal staff and this is to be provided by the Public Service Commission of Samoa. This is a new setup in Samoa, where law reform of a specific nature is assigned under statute to a permanent body. Time will tell of the effectiveness of this setup. The establishment of another statutory Commission (CLAC) in Samoa to develop law reform on a specific area may appear to undermine the existence of Samoa's independent law reform institution, the SLRC. However, it is evidence of Samoa's continuous search for an appropriate model of law reform agent that can develop effective law reform that protects and promotes Samoa's customary land and traditional structures.

COIs have been an effective means of investigating and instigating reforms in Samoa. However, they are costly, they have a time and budget limit and they are ad hoc in nature. Their procedures are flexible and uncertain due to the absence of a proper consultation process. The members of a Commission are appointed for the term of the reform investigation and are only accountable to the State. Despite the

---

[233]Customary Land Advisory Commission Act 2013 No 9 (Samoa).
[234]Ibid s 6.
[235]Customary Land Advisory Commission Act 2013 No 9 (Samoa). Expressed in the long title of the Act.

establishment of an institutional law reform, the importance of customary land to Samoa led to the establishment of the CLAC. It is the first statutory body with law reform functions with a specific focus. The inclusion of both *matai* and legal officers in one law reform authority may be the model law reform agent for Samoa. Its success will provide useful considerations for a law reform institution setup and law reform process suitable for Samoa.

5.5.2 The Samoa Law Society (SLS)

In 2016, 159 lawyers were registered as practitioners in Samoa, 81 were in-house lawyers, 9 were employed by organisations and regional offices and 69 made up the private practice.[236] This is a significant increase from the recorded 103 financial members in 2011, of which 52 were in-house counsels and[237] forty lawyers were in the private practice. The increase in private lawyer numbers means more service available to the public from the ratio of about 1 to about 4000 people for a population of 187,820[238] in 2011. Currently, SLS Council members, who are private practitioners or fulltime government employees, service the SLS's administrative and operational functions on a voluntary unsalaried basis.

5.5.2.1 Law Reform Functions

The *Law Practitioners Act 1976* (Samoa) (the 1976 Act) regulates the practice of law in Samoa. The functions of the Law Society relevant to this book are to 'consider and suggest amendments of the law'.[239] This function is currently best implemented through making submissions on draft laws to the relevant Ministry, to the SLRC and to the relevant Parliamentary Select Committees. The 1976 Act however makes no requirement for the SLS to promote customs or customary laws. Although the SLS is empowered to make suggestions on the laws, they are not required to take account of customs.

The recent Lawyers and Legal Practice Act 2014 continues the functions of 'considering and suggesting amendments to the law'. A new function for the SLS has been incorporated. It states as follows:

> to promote and encourage the maintenance of the rule of law, and the development of the laws of Samoa and the practice of the law in Samoa, in order to promote Samoan custom and traditions and enhance the social, economic and commercial development of Samoa.[240]

---

[236] Executive Council, Samoa Law Society (2016).

[237] South Pacific Lawyers Association, 2001, http://www.southpacificlawyers.org.

[238] Samoa Bureau of Statistics, Population and Housing Census, 2011, 60.

[239] Law Practitioners Act 1976 (Samoa) s 13(f).

[240] Lawyers and Legal Practice Act 2014 (Samoa) s 5.

This is a positive development which is likely to enhance the customary law focus of the SLS.

5.5.2.2 Challenges

The SLS is not legally required to take account of customs in suggesting reforms to the law. There are no known requirements obligating the SLS members to contribute to law reform. The SLS members however have made submissions on draft laws to the state Ministries and the SLRC. Apart from these consistent practices, for reasons below, the SLS has not been able to consistently 'consider and suggest amendments to the law'.

In terms of formal training, Samoa's legal profession are mostly western trained. Individual rights are promoted by western training. Except for biennial seminars where presentations are made on specific legal topics, little emphasis is placed on legal education and training that address the conflicts brought about by legal pluralism on the work of the legal profession. The lack of resources to fund the society's operations adds to the challenges of creating a vibrant and relevant legal profession. Except for an insignificant annual per diem set aside for the Secretary of the Executive Council, all work carried out by the Executive Council and all Society Committees, for example the Continuing Legal Education Committee responsible for coordinating conferences is on a voluntary and unremunerated basis. On 19 April 2013, the first permanent office for the SLS was opened at the Court Complex in Apia. It consists of a conference room and a room for a computer and printing facilities.[241] This is an important milestone for the SLS intended to facilitate more local dialogue through seminars.[242] Finally, keeping a legal practice afloat is expensive in Samoa and forces law reform and customary considerations into the background of priorities.[243]

At the regional level, a review of the objectives of the South Pacific Lawyers' Association (SPLA)[244] of which Samoa is a member shows that the conflicts between customary laws and state laws are absent as core issues of regional concerns.[245] No conscious regard is given to the complexities of legal pluralism in the Pacific law societies. These societies may be more encouraged to consciously

---

[241]Ta'ateo (2013), 22 April.

[242]Identified as a primary goal of the Samoa Law Society as reported in the South Pacific Lawyers Association, Needs Evaluation Survey above, n 238.

[243]Interview with LP Respondent 1 (Samoa, 15 March 2011).

[244]Formerly South Pacific Bars' Secretariat (SPBS), SPLA was established in 2007 to assist developing law societies and bar associations in the South Pacific and to promote the interests of the legal profession in the South Pacific. One of the objectives of the Constitution of SPLA is 'to be a united body to represent SPLA in all matters involving reform and uniformity of laws, and legal practice in the region'.

[245]South Pacific Lawyers Association, Constitution of the South Pacific Lawyers' Association, 2011, 11 July http://www.southpacificlawyers.org.

promote customary laws alongside state laws if this is supported at the regional level.

A commitment to developing reforms generally, including reforms that impact on customs, is hampered in the work of the SLS in three ways. There is a lack of legal prerequisites and policies that obligate the SLS to actively take part in law reform. Secondly there is lack of training, conferences and seminars to facilitate an active and constructive dialogue on customs and laws. Further, it is difficult to create interest in law reform without the relevant funding and resources within the means of the SLS. The new permanent SLS office will hopefully be a positive start towards seminars and conferences. In addition to the local obstacles, the complexities of legal pluralism are not a priority in the agenda and focus of the association of Pacific law societies. There is no regional support towards an individual country's efforts to facilitate legal pluralism in Pacific societies.

5.5.3 Office of the Ombudsman

Unlike some Pacific Islands,[246] Samoa's Ombudsman is a constitutional officer,[247] appointed to investigate complaints against administrative authorities, independently of state intervention.[248] The current Ombudsman is a law graduate with substantial work experience in government and international relations offices. Samoa's Ombudsman office has affiliations with the Commonwealth Ombudsman of Australia through which assistance is received from the government of Australia.[249]

5.5.3.1 Law Reform Functions

Initiating law reform is not a central function of the Samoan Ombudsman under its empowering Act. The Ombudsman's office is explored in this book as there are statutory powers that can be effectively invoked to support considerations of customs in reforms. In 2013, Parliament repealed and replaced the *Komesina o Sulufaiga (Ombudsman) Act 1988* (Samoa) with the *Ombudsman (Komesina o Sulufaiga) Act 2013* (Samoa). Under the 1988 Act, at the conclusion of investigations, the Ombudsman is authorised to initiate law reform on any law upon which

---

[246]Ombudsman Act 1998 (Vanuatu); and a constitutional officer in Solomon Islands, Constitution of Solomon Islands 1978 (Solomon Islands) arts 96, 97.

[247]Constitution of Samoa 1962 (Samoa), art 82A.

[248]Ombudsman (Komesina o Sulufaiga) Samoa, What we do? http://www.ombudsman.gov.ws.

[249]Commonwealth Ombudsman, Samoa - Commonwealth Ombudsman Annual Report 2008–2009, (9 December 2009) http://www.ombudsman.gov.au.

his or her decision, recommendation, act, or omission was based.[250] These provisions were continued under the 2013 Act.[251] The Ombudsman must refer an opinion for law reform to the appropriate Ministry or organisation together with reasons for the opinion.[252] The 2013 Act gave additional duties to the Ombudsman to recommend reforms. The Ombudsman may recommend legal reforms to prevent or redress human rights violations.[253]

5.5.3.2 Challenges

The Ombudsman has not invoked his law reform functions (under the 1988 Act) to date[254] including in its most recent investigations in 2007.[255] This is substantially due to a lack of funding and the limited capacity of a small office.[256] Further, until recent, the office was not assisted by legal expertise in developing procedures through which the Ombudsman's law reform functions may be realised. Until recent (2015), apart from the Ombudsman who is a qualified lawyer, the staff of the Ombudsman's office had no formal legal training.

There is no known Ombudsman report (Samoa) that discusses a situation when the Ombudsman investigated an administrative decision that impacted on customary laws or customary practices. It may well be that no such situation has occurred, or that there exists a mistaken belief that customary arguments are irrelevant. Where customs are still strongly practised in Samoa, the Ombudsman must take account of customary issues where relevant in his investigations, inquiries and recommendations. Given the Ombudsman's new functions to recommend legal reforms to uphold human rights,[257] the Ombudsman must explore, investigate and uphold human rights in the context of a customary society. Each case will be decided on its merits; however, this is another avenue through which reforms

---

[250]Komesina o Sulufaiga (Ombudsman) Act 1988 (Samoa) s 19(3)(e).

[251]Ombudsman (Komesina o Sulufaiga) Act 2013 (Samoa) s 28(2)(e).

[252]Between the years 2010 and 2011, the Ombudsman role was reviewed and new functions were developed, see Pacific Ombudsman Alliance, Pacific Ombudsman Alliance - Network News, 2012: 27. http://www.pacificombudsman.org. The original policies to these changes relate to setting up of an office of a Human Rights Commissioner in Samoa. Due to resource constraints, the functions of a human rights commissioner became part of the functions of the Ombudsman. The substantial additions to the role of the Ombudsman led to a complete overhaul of the Act resulting in the Ombudsman (Komesina o Sulufaiga) Act 2013 (Samoa).

[253]Ombudsman (Komesina o Sulufaiga) Act 2013 (Samoa) s 40(1)(a)(i).

[254]Discussions with a representative of the Office of the Ombudsman: Komesina o Sulufaiga (Samoa, 6 April 2010).

[255]Samoa, Ombudsman: Komesina o Sulufaiga Final Report on Sexual Harassment, Samoa Tourism Authority (2007); Samoa, Ombudsman: Komesina o Sulufaiga, Final Report on Review of Fraud Investigations, Ministry of Health (2007).

[256]Discussions with the Office of the Ombudsman, above, n 254.

[257]Ombudsman (Komesina o Sulufaiga) Act 2013 (Samoa) s 33(a).

must be recommended with pluralism in mind. With the recent addition in 2015 and 2016 of qualified lawyers with some work experience into the office of the Ombudsman, legal assistance to invoke law reform functions of the Ombudsman is another avenue, through which customs and laws can both be promoted through law reform.

5.5.4 Non-Government Organisations (NGOs)

The administering organisation for all non-government organisations in Samoa is the Samoa Umbrella Non-Government Organisation (SUNGO) which was founded in 1997 to provide input into government policy from the non-government organisations.[258] The Constitution of SUNGO refers to civil societies and NGOs interchangeably as NGOs. In these discussions, a reference to NGOs is also a reference to civil societies. By 2011, the SUNGOs membership had reached 139. The significant role of SUNGO that is relevant to this study is that it promotes the interests of the customary and grass roots level of Samoa. The activities of the NGOs extend to the rural areas of Samoa where the government services seldom reach. Through its strategic plan, SUNGO targets development projects in the village communities. Its goals include fostering effective communications and services amongst civil societies; providing quality services to local communities; empowering effective organisations and coordinating effective research and data collection to better inform civil society initiatives.[259] SUNGO is therefore an important ally in promoting customs through law reform. A study on the work of civil societies in Samoa reported the success of development projects assisted by the civil societies in the local communities, a feature fully acknowledged by overseas donors.[260]

5.5.4.1 Law Reform Influence

Some of SUNGO's significant influences in law reform are apparent through its activist role in opposing reforms that members believe are unfavourable for Samoa. When the Casino Bill 2008 (Samoa) was first developed, SUNGO took opposition

---

[258]Samoa Umbrella For Non-Governmental Organisations Incorporated, Constitution of Samoa Umbrella For Non-Governmental Organisations, Incorporated, 2007, 26 October, http://www.sungo.ws.
[259]Samoa Umbrella For Non-Governmental Organisations Incorporated, Strategic Plan 2011–2016 http://www.sungo.ws.
[260]Lidimani, 2000, https://www.usp.ac.fj/index.php?id=13206.

to it, encouraged and facilitated a collection of written submissions.[261] SUNGO strongly advocated the view that a casino would not only increase crime but it would break up the most important traditional institution in Samoa, the family.[262] In 2009, SUNGO was again instrumental in assembling supporters for a public march under the banner 'People Against Switching Sides', opposing the Road Transport Reform Bill 2009. This law changed the side of the road for vehicles to be driven on. SUNGO filed court proceedings against the State, seeking a declaration from the Supreme Court that this Bill was unconstitutional.[263] Although they were unsuccessful, they gained respect from the private and public sectors alike. In 2010, SUNGO publicly opposed the membership of a Commission of Inquiry on the basis that it was discriminatory towards females and minority churches.[264] At the regional level, SUNGOs membership with the Pacific Islands Association of Non-Governmental Organisations (PIANGO)[265] strengthens its activist projects as a state watchdog.

5.5.4.2 Challenges

There are three main challenges SUNGO faces in relation to law reform in Samoa. First is a lack of a basic understanding of laws and the legal system of Samoa. Second there is limited funding to take policy arguments to a higher authority or legal challenges to the courts. Third SUNGO does not have a legal officer to offer advice on law reform initiatives before it challenges the State on the objectives of the reforms. At times, SUNGO acts out of good faith but a misinterpretation of a proposed law reform may prove costly to SUNGO and supporters. Despite these challenges, SUNGO remains a useful ally for the promotion of customary laws. The NGOs experience challenges similar to other law reform agents. In the absence of any legal assistance to bring the reforms that are contrary to customary principles to the attention of SUNGO and to seek financial support to contest them, NGOs are unable to effectively assist with law reform developments.

---

[261] The main objectives of the Casino Gambling and Control Act 2010 (Samoa) are to raise proceeds to fund sporting teams and activities in local, regional and international competitions. See Samoa, Parliamentary Debates, 2010, 12 October. 703.
[262] Radio NZ International 2010, 8 April http://www.solomonstarnews.com.
[263] Jackson v Attorney-General (Unreported, Supreme Court of Samoa, Nelson J, 28 August 2009).
[264] Radio NZ International, 2010, 24 March, http://www.solomonstarnews.com.
[265] Pacific Islands Association of Non-Government Organisations, Constitution (2007 http://www.piango.org/. PIANGO was formally established in 1991 to assist the national non-government organisations in the Pacific Islands to work collaboratively and become more influential as a collective voice. PIANGO's primary role is to be a catalyst for collective action, to facilitate and support coalitions and alliances on issues of common concern, and to strengthen the influence and impact of NGO efforts in the region.

5.6 Emerging Conceptual Challenges

Four broad conceptual challenges may be drawn from the discussions above. These are discussed below and conclude this chapter. The next chapter endeavours to provide possible responses to the challenges of legal pluralism, under these conceptual challenges.

5.6.1 Law Reform Framework Not Embedded in Customs

5.6.1.1 Laws Authorising Law Making

Samoa's laws that authorise law making were made in the absence of a consideration of Samoa's customary environment. Although the preamble of Samoa's Constitution declares that the Constitution is adopted based on the customs and usages of Samoa, in relation to law making, this declaration is unsupported by constitutional provisions. The Constitution does not expressly obligate law makers to develop laws in Samoa's customary context. Rather, it gives little scope for the application of customs under Article 111 discussed above. The court decisions (above) illustrate that the rule of law in the Constitution must be respected above all legal rules including customary laws. The existing laws of Samoa which are required to be developed within the ambit of the Constitution pay scant regard to customs.

Where legislation requires that customs and usages are to be promoted in legislation, for example the Samoa Law Reform Commission Act, those laws lack guidance as to how this may be achieved. In addition, where legislation empowers a body to develop reforms such as the Samoa Law Society and the Ombudsman, the authorising laws do not require those law reform agents to have regard to customs in fulfilling their law reform functions.

5.6.1.2 Procedures Guiding Law Making

Until recently, there has been a lack of guidelines setting out procedures for law making. Where such guides are available (Cabinet and Drafting handbooks discussed above), they do not expressly require policy makers and law drafters to have regard to customs in their line of work. The law reform officers, who are mostly western trained thus tend to apply western concepts without due regard to customs. Without specific requirements to take account of customs, it is convenient for officers to apply western concepts to their western styled offices in the urban area. This marginalises customs further.

5.6.2 Limited Professional Training Opportunities

There are no systems in place to accommodate a conscious regard to customs in law making. These systems include professional training for the judiciary, Parliament, the executive, the government ministries, and the legal profession, that facilitate an appreciation of the customary legal system in law making. There is a lack of opportunity for judicial training especially in areas of conflict between the two legal systems. As has been seen above, the *matai* assembly of chiefs in Parliament does not have ready access to professional training on the law making functions of a modern Parliament with emphasis on the customary context of Samoa. The western educated legal profession is also in dire need of interactive opportunities, open dialogue and legal debates on accommodating customary laws in a modern legal system. The lack of professional legal training limits a more balanced consideration of both the customary values and individual rights philosophies in law reform.

5.6.3 Involving the Village Structures in the Law Reform Process

There are various views on the adequacy of consultation. Each sector views adequacy from their position. The lack of resources makes consultations uncoordinated and inadequate. Notwithstanding the lack of resources, to increase village participation in law reform, to obtain public support and to give laws the legitimacy they require, the State must involve the village structures in the law reform process, in particular in coordinating public consultations.

5.6.4 Funding Constraints

Funding and resource constraints hamper efforts for law reform across all sectors. Funding is required for professional training to cover material for training and professional trainers. Funding is also required for doctrinal and socio-legal research for the SLRC as well as the provision of internet facilities. The lack of funding means there are few resources to work from, and this further attracts a lack of commitment to promote customary laws in law reform.

The above conceptual challenges suggest Samoa operates an unbalanced law reform framework in that western based values are given more emphasis in law making over customary considerations. This is perpetuated by the laws and law making procedures that guide the conduct of law making. In addition, there is limited professional training to facilitate dialogue on identifying the factors hindering the development of effective laws and possible ways to address those challenges. The State also fails to include the village sector in the law reform process accounting for the lack of interest for law reform. Attempts to develop strategies to promote customs in state laws are hampered by the lack of resources. The next chapter suggests some responses to the challenges raised in both Chap. 4 and in this chapter.

References

Care JC (2006) A green stick or a fresh stick?: locating customary penalties in the post-colonial era. Oxford Univ Commonw Law J 6(1):27–60
Corrin J (2009) From horizontal and vertical to lateral: extending the effect of human rights in post-colonial legal systems of the South Pacific. Int Compa Law Q 58(1):31–71
Corrin J (2010) Judge or be judged: accepting judicial appointment in an unlawful regime. Int J Leg Prof 16(2&3):191–209
Corrin J, Paterson D (2011) Introduction to South Pacific law, 3rd edn. Palgrave Macmillan, pp 338–343
Cotterrell R (2001) Is there a logic for legal transplants? In: Nelken D, Feest J (eds) Adapting legal cultures. Hart, Oxford, p 79
Executive Council (2016) Lawyers issued with practicing certificates. Samoa Law Society, Apia, Samoa
Farnworth MJ et al (2012) Incidence of dog bites and public attitudes towards dog care and management in Samoa. Anim Welfare 21:477–486
Forsyth M (2004) Banishment and Freedom of Movement in Samoa: Leituala v Mauga, Kilifi et al. J South Pac Law 8(2)
Government of Samoa, Cabinet Directive Faapitoa (Special) F K (11) 14, 20 July 2011
Hassall G, Saunders C (2013) Asia-Pacific constitutional systems. Cambridge University Press, p 186
Kirby M (2003) The ALRC: a winning formula. Remarks at the rededication of the Michael Kirby Library of the ALRC Sydney, 17 February
Leung Wai MC (2008) Samoan's experience with the establishment of a law reform commission. Paper presented to the Australasian Law Reform Agencies Conference, Vanuatu 10–12 September
Macpherson C (1997) The persistent of chiefly authority in Western Samoa. In: White GM, Lindstrom L (eds), Chiefs today – traditional Pacific leadership and the postcolonial state. Stanford California, p 43
Ministry of the Prime Minister and Cabinet (Samoa), Cabinet Handbook (2011a)
Ministry of the Prime Minister and Cabinet (Samoa), Manual on Ministerial Practice and Procedures (2011b)
Morawetz V (1925) The elements of a contract. Am Bar Assoc J 11:87–90
Nelken D (2001) Towards a sociology of legal adaptation. In: Nelken D, Feest J (eds) Adapting legal cultures. Hart, Oxford, p 47
Noble C, Pereira N, Saune N (2011) Urban youth in the pacific: increasing resilience and reducing risk for involvement in crime and violence. UNDP Pacific Centre, Pacific Islands Forum Secretariat, pp 119, 128
Office of the Attorney-General Samoa (2008) Legislative Drafting Handbook
Opeskin B (2005) Measuring success. In: Opeskin B, Weisbrot D (eds), The promise of law reform. Federation Press, p 204
Powles G (1997) Common law at bay? J Pac Stud 21:72
Powles G (2005) Law reform in the Pacific Island states. In: Opeskin B, Weisbrot D. The promise of law reform. Federation, vol 404, p 418
Samoa, Parliamentary Debates, 2–4 July 1990, 190–191 (Aeau Peniamina)

Report on Matai Titles, Customary Land and the Land and Titles Court, December 1975. In *Taamale v Attorney-General* (Unreported, Court of Appeal of Samoa, Cooke, P, Casey and Bisson JJA, 18 August 1995)
Samoa Bureau of Statistics, Population and Housing Census (2011) 60
Samoa, Commission of Inquiry into the Electoral Act, Final Reports (2001), (2006), (2011)
Samoa, Commission of Inquiry on Matters Relating to the Divergence between the Decision Making Authority of the Alii and Faipule and the Formal Courts, Final Report (2007)
Samoa, Commission of Inquiry into Matai Titles, Final Report (2010)
Samoa, Commission of Inquiry into the Freedom of Religion, Final Report (2010)
Samoa, Commission of Inquiry into the Electoral Act, Final Report (2001)
Samoa, Commission of Inquiry into the Electoral Act, Final Report (2006)
Samoa Observer Editorial (2013) Welcome to Samoa, where fat people pay more and dog meat is a treat. 11 April
Samoa, Ombudsman: Komesina o Sulufaiga Final Report on Sexual Harassment, Samoa Tourism Authority (2007)
Samoa, Ombudsman: Komesina o Sulufaiga, Final Report on Review of Fraud Investigations, Ministry of Health (2007)
Samoa Parliamentary Debates (1990a) Legislative Assembly, 22–23 January
Samoa Parliamentary Debates (1990b) Legislative Assembly, 22–23, 938
Samoa Parliamentary Debates (1990c) Legislative Assembly, Report of the Select Committee Report on the Bill 2–4 July
Samoa Parliamentary Debates (1990d) 2–4 July, 190–191
Samoa Parliamentary Debates (2010) 12 October, 703
Sapolu T (2011) Freedom of religion. Paper presented to the Judicial Training, Samoa, 25 October
Suaalii-Sauni et al (eds) (2009) Su'esu'e manogi: In search of fragrance, Tui Atua Tupua Tamasese Ta'isi and the Samoan indigenous reference. National University of Samoa, p 12
Ta'ateo J (2013) Samoa Law Society opens first office. Samoa Observer (Samoa) 22 April 2013
Trubek DM, Galanter M (1974) Law and society, scholars in self-estrangement: some reflections on the crisis in law and development studies in the United States. Wisconsin Law Rev 1062, 1083
Vaai S (1999) Samoa faamatai and the rule of law. National University of Samoa, pp 168, 170

Legislation

Acts Interpretation Act 2015 (Samoa)
Animal Ordinance 1960 (Samoa)
Casino Gambling and Control Act 2010 (Samoa)
Constitution of Papua New Guinea (Papua New Guinea)
Commissions of Inquiry Act 1964 (Samoa)
Community Justice Act 2008 (Samoa)
Constitution of Samoa 1962 (Samoa)
Constitution of Solomon Islands 1978 (Solomon Islands)
Constitutional and Law Reform Commission Act 2004 (Papua New Guinea)
Crimes Act 2013 No. 11 (Samoa)
Customary Land Advisory Commission Act 2013 No 9 (Samoa)
District Court Act 1969 (Samoa)
Electoral Act 1993 (NZ)
Electoral Act 1963 (Samoa)
Electoral Amendment Act (No 20) 1990 (Samoa)
Electoral Amendment Act (No 3) 2005 (Samoa)

Electoral Amendment Act (No 14) 2005 (Samoa)
Electoral Amendment Act (No 21) 2009 (Samoa)
Election Candidate Regulations S.R. 2006/6 (Samoa)
Internal Affairs Act 1995 (Samoa)
Internal Affairs Amendment Act (No 3) 2010 (Samoa)
Judicature Ordinance 1961 (Samoa)
Komesina o Sulufaiga (Ombudsman) Act 1988 (Samoa)
Land and Titles Amendment Act (No 14) 2012 (Samoa)
Land and Titles Court Act 1981 (Samoa)
Land Titles Investigation Act 1966 (Samoa)
Law Commission Act (Vanuatu) Cap 115
Law Commission Act 1985 (New Zealand)
Law Practitioners Act 1976 (Samoa)
Law Reform Commission Act 1994 (Solomon Islands)
Law Reform Commission Act 2008 (Samoa)
Lawyers and Legal Practice Act 2014 (Samoa)
Ombudsman Act 1998 (Vanuatu)
Ombudsman (Komesina o Sulufaiga) Act 2013 (Samoa)
Parliament of Queensland Act 2002 (Qld)
Representation of the People Act (Vanuatu)
Reprint of Statutes Act 1972 (Samoa)
Revision and Publications Act 2008 (Samoa)
Samoan Status Act 1963 (Samoa)
Standing Orders of Parliament 2016 (Samoa)
Taking of Land Amendment Act (No 19) 2005 (Samoa)
Taking of Land Amendment Act 1964 (Samoa)
Village Fono Bill 1990 (Samoa)
Water Resource Management Act 2008 (Samoa)
Young Offenders Act 2007 (Samoa)

Case Law

Alaelua v Lands and Titles Court [1980-1993] WSLR 519
Ale v Electoral Commissioner (Unreported, Supreme Court of Samoa, Sapolu CJ, 23 February 2011)
Alomaina v Land and Titles Court (Unreported, Supreme Court of Samoa, Young AJ, 4 November 1998)
Asalemo v Electoral Commissioner (Unreported, Supreme Court of Samoa, Sapolu CJ, 28 February 2011)
Asiata v Asiata (Unreported, Supreme Court of Samoa, Nelson J, 2 February 2007)
In re the Electoral Act Pita v Liuga (Unreported, Supreme Court of Samoa, Sapolu CJ, Vaai J, Nelson J, 19 July 2001)
Jackson v Attorney-General (Unreported, Supreme Court of Samoa, Nelson J, 28 August 2009)
Lafaialii v The Attorney-General (Unreported, Supreme Court of Samoa, Sapolu CJ, 24 April 2003)
Leota Leuluaialii Ituau Ale et al v Alii & Faipule Solosolo (Unreported, Land and Titles Court of Samoa, LC.11469 P2, 17 February 2012)
Lufilufi v Hunt (Unreported, Supreme Court of Samoa, Vaai, Nelson JJ, 26 April 2011).
Mauga v Leituala (Unreported, Court of Appeal of Samoa, Cooke, P, Casey and Bisson JJA, March 2005)

Olomalu v The Attorney-General (1980-1993) WSLR
Pauli Elisara v Attorney-General (Unreported, Court of Appeal of Samoa, Cooke, P, Casey and Bisson JJA, 17 December 2004)
Pauli Elisara v Attorney General (Unreported, Supreme Court of Samoa, Vaai J, 25 June 2004)
Police v D (Unreported, Supreme Court of Samoa, Sapolu CJ, 7 November 2008)
Police v F (Unreported, Supreme Court of Samoa, Nelson J, 30 March 2009)
Police v Lemusu (Unreported, Supreme Court of Samoa, Nelson J, 14 September 2009)
Police v Luka (Unreported, Supreme Court of Samoa, Vaai J, 21 May 2008)
Police v Vaa (Unreported, Supreme Court of Samoa, Sapolu CJ, 24 January 2006)
Qarase v Bainimarama (Unreported, Fiji Court of Appeal, Powell, Lloyd, Douglas JJA, 9 April 2009)
Samoan Public Trustee v Collins [1961] WSNZSC 1
Sefo v Attorney-General (Unreported, Supreme Court of Samoa, Wilson J, 12 July 2000)
State Government Insurance Commission v Trigwell (1979) 142 CLR 617
Taamale v Attorney-General (Unreported, Court of Appeal of Samoa, Cooke, P, Casey and Bisson JJA, 18 August 1995)
Tavita v Attorney-General (Unreported, Supreme Court of Samoa, 2002)
Toailoa v Sapolu (Unreported, Court of Appeal of Samoa, Ellis, Gallen, Salmon JJA, 26 April 2006)
Tuitui v The Attorney-General (Unreported, Supreme Court of Samoa, Sapolu CJ, 25 February 2011)
Tuivaiti v Faimalaga [1980-1993] WSLR 17

Online Databases

Animal Protection Society (Samoa) (2009) Working together to help the animals of Samoa, 14 July 2009 http://apssamoa.blogspot.com.au/2009/07/new-aps-website.html#comment-form
Australian Law Reform Commission, Law Reform Process http://www.alrc.gov.au/law-reform-process
Boelman B (2012) Dogs. In Boelman B. The continuing adventures of Boelman B in Samoa. 29 December http://boelmaninsamoa.blogspot.com.au/p/dogs.html
Commonwealth Ombudsman, Samoa - Commonwealth Ombudsman Annual Report 2008-2009, (9 December 2009) http://www.ombudsman.gov.au
Lidimani D, Law and the role of non-state actor: A Review of the Legislative Framework Governing Civil Society Organisations in Samoa, University of the South Pacific https://www.usp.ac.fj/index.php?id=13206
Ombudsman (Komesina o Sulufaiga) Samoa (2009) What we do? http://www.ombudsman.gov.ws
Pacific Islands Association of Non-Government Organisations, Constitution (2007) http://www.piango.org/
Pacific Ombudsman Alliance (2012) Pacific Ombudsman alliance - Network News, Issue 27 (April 2012) http://www.pacificombudsman.org
Radio NZ International, 'Samoa NGO criticises govt's commission of inquiry choice' Solomon Star (online) 24 March 2010a. http://www.solomonstarnews.com
Radio NZ International 'Samoa NGOs oppose casino plans' *Solomon Star* (online) 8 April 2010b. http://www.solomonstarnews.com
Salinas EM (2010) Samoa howls. In Salinas EM Samoa diaries. 17 September http://www.samoadiaries.com/travel/samoa-howls/
Samoa Law Reform Commission, Law Reform Process http://www.samoalawreform.gov.ws

References

Samoa Umbrella For Non-Governmental Organisations Incorporated, Constitution of Samoa Umbrella For Non-Governmental Organisations, Incorporated (26 October 2007) http://www.sungo.ws

Samoa Umbrella For Non-Governmental Organisations Incorporated, Strategic Plan 2011-2016 http://www.sungo.ws

South Pacific Lawyers Association (2011) Needs Evaluation Survey for South Pacific Lawyer Associations 18 October http://www.southpacificlawyers.org

Spring BC (1970-1972) The Land and Titles Court of Western Samoa. Melanesian Law J 1 http://www.vanuatu.usp.ac.fj/sol_adobe_documents/usp%20only/Pacific%20law/Spring.htm

Chapter 6
Towards Responsive Law Reform

Contents

6.1	Public Awareness of State Laws	130
	6.1.1 Develop Community Awareness	130
	6.1.2 Facilitate Public Access to Acts and Court Decisions	131
6.2	Professional Training: Judiciary, Parliament, Legal Profession	133
	6.2.1 The Judiciary	133
	6.2.1.1 Judicial Training	133
	6.2.1.2 Judicial Guidance Clause	134
	6.2.1.3 Code of Judicial Conduct	135
	6.2.1.4 Court Benchbooks	136
	6.2.1.5 New Developments in the Courts of Samoa	137
	6.2.2 Parliament	137
	6.2.2.1 Professional Training	137
	6.2.2.2 Customary Duties to Village Communities	139
	6.2.2.3 Private Members Bill (PMB)	140
	6.2.2.4 Recent Developments for Parliament	141
	6.2.3 Legal Profession	142
	6.2.3.1 Professional Training on the Rule of Law and Samoan Customs	142
	6.2.3.2 Training on Samoan Language and Cultural Protocols	142
	6.2.3.3 Engaging in Academic Conferences and Quality Research	144
6.3	State Responsibilities in Law Reform	145
	6.3.1 Constitutional and Legislative Review, Drafting Handbooks	145
	6.3.1.1 Reference Guide to Customary Practices	147
	6.3.1.2 Village Fono Act (1990) Review	148
	6.3.1.3 Cabinet and Drafting Handbooks	149
	6.3.2 Promote Formal Education	149
	6.3.3 National Plans	151
	6.3.3.1 Samoa's National Plan 2012–2016	151
	6.3.3.2 Law and Justice Sector Plan	152
6.4	Village Responsibilities in Law Reform	152
	6.4.1 Change of Village Mayor Criteria	153
	6.4.2 Develop Constitutionally Compliant Village Rules	154
6.5	Managing Funding Constraints	155
	6.5.1 Involving Customary Structures in Law Reform Consultation	155
	6.5.2 Prioritising and Justifying Costs for Customary Reforms	156
6.6	Local Jurisprudence: Customary Law as the Basis of Common Law	157

© Springer International Publishing AG 2018
T.L. Mulitalo Ropinisone Silipa Seumanutafa, *Law Reform in Plural Societies*,
The World of Small States 2, https://doi.org/10.1007/978-3-319-65524-6_6

6.7   Legislative Drafters and Draft Laws 159
    6.7.1   Pacific Specific Drafting and Law Reform Training 159
    6.7.2   Drafting in the Samoan Language, Legislative References, Context 160
    6.7.3   Review of Draft Laws for Customary Compliance 162
6.8   Summary of Responses to Legal Pluralism 164
References 165

How can the challenges identified in the last two chapters be effectively addressed? A starting point is to acknowledge that the State must create collaborative and meaningful partnerships between the customary legal system and the state legal system to allow for a suitable law reform framework for Samoa. The responses to the issues raised can be formulated under the following broad headings:

1. creating public awareness programmes;
2. facilitating professional training and law making guidelines;
3. identifying key state responsibilities;
4. village sector accountability;
5. managing funding constraints;
6. developing a local jurisprudence; and
7. adopting legislative drafting techniques relevant to drafting laws in a plural society.

These responses are also informed by empirical interviews, relevant literature, current and recent State projects and national plans to analyse the viability of the suggested responses.

6.1   Public Awareness of State Laws

6.1.1   Develop Community Awareness

The first approach proposed to address the conflicts between individualism and communalism philosophies is to create public awareness of state laws. This includes awareness programmes on—what is law? What are individual rights?

Community programmes and public awareness campaigns developed on a holistic approach are necessary, to inform of the differences between statute laws, customary laws and how they interrelate or conflict.[1] They must include information on individual rights and the state legal system. Village participation in law reform will increase if the villagers understand what is meant by 'law' that is

---

[1] Interviews in Samoa with: VC2 Respondent 5 (15 March 2011); SOH Respondent 1 (8 April 2011).

advocated through law reform[2] and what 'law' entails in relation to the village sector. Information on human rights and state laws must be made more accessible.[3] Village mayors, in collaboration with the state ministries responsible for village welfare, must work together with the State to coordinate information seminars in the villages to explain current laws as well as proposed new laws.[4]

The empirical data is divided on how many legal systems exist in Samoa, whether there is one or two. However, there is a notable willingness to be informed of state laws, and to be given the opportunity to understand state laws better. If this leads to positive developments, there was enthusiasm in support of what works best. This enthusiasm must be fully utilised to an advantage.

A sustainable and realistic approach is to raise awareness in the village sector through the village councils, community and church leaders. Community workshops on formal laws and individual rights, and advertising the services available in the state legal system must be the first focus of these workshops.[5] A review of experiences elsewhere reveals that these were the focuses successfully applied for the community education programmes in other jurisdictions, for example Liberia. Although the Liberian programmes were at a higher scale with the use of a formal Justice and Peace Commission on a much bigger population, these are helpful considerations for similar community programmes for smaller populations like Samoa. The Ministry of Women, Social and Community Development Samoa which is responsible for village welfare is best placed for public awareness programmes, with the assistance of state or private lawyers. Similar workshops may be coordinated through non-government organisations.

The public awareness programmes must however be approached with clear objectives. The villages must not be expected to immediately accept individual rights concepts or principles of state laws. Community workshop programmes must therefore be conducted for public awareness and be made readily available at the request of a village or a district.

6.1.2 Facilitate Public Access to Acts and Court Decisions

A second proposal is for the State to facilitate more access to laws than is currently available. Access to laws is a basic principle of the rule of law to aid access to justice. However, there is restricted access to the laws of Samoa. The population is unaware of their individual rights under the Constitution and there is little commitment to make laws accessible in a language that is understood. The current rate of

---

[2]Interviews in Samoa with: GWR Respondent 1 (21 March 2011); GWR Respondent 2 (21 March 2011).
[3]Interview with SOH Respondent 7 (Samoa, 22 March 2011).
[4]Interview with SOH Respondent 6 (Samoa, 12 April 2011).
[5]Mgbako and Baehr (2011), p. 186.

accessibility is insufficient, and this contributes significantly to the gulf between customary laws and state laws.

The insights received from the empirical data illustrate that most believe state laws are the domain of the state only and apply to the urban areas only. It is costly to access laws[6] and only a few who possess modern technology such as computers and internet[7] have access to laws. The decisions of the courts are only in the English language. This restricts further access to laws in a language that can be understood. While there is current effort to convert Land and Title Court (LTC) decisions (which are in the Samoan language) into electronic copies, there is no indication that the decisions of the formal courts (District Court, Supreme Court, Court of Appeal) will in the short term be made accessible in the Samoan language.

To create an awareness of laws through court decisions, the decisions of the formal courts must be available in the Samoan language. Given the lack of resources and competing priorities, such an initiative is not likely to be forthcoming in the near future. In the interim, in relation to court decisions that impact on customs, such as a judicial review of a LTC decision, court decisions may be made available in summaries in the Samoan language. This one page summary may be entitled 'Summary of the Decision in the Samoan Language' or '*Aotelega o le Faaiuga i le Gagana Samoa*'. It may contain only the decision and reasons for the decisions and the laws that were relied upon. It must be clarified in the document that it is not a complete official LTC legal decision, but a supplement of the full court decision produced for the information of the traditional chiefs and petitioners who were parties to the LTC decision.[8] These Samoan language decisions or summaries may be made available to the public, particularly to the village councils.

Proposal

The state must develop and fund public awareness programmes through community education on state laws in the villages, in collaboration with village councils. The State must remove or lower the costs of state laws and make court decisions accessible to the public in a language they understand. Educating the public is the first step towards addressing the conflicts between customary laws and state laws.

---

[6]Email from Officer of the Office of the Clerk of the Legislative Assembly, Samoa to Lalotoa Mulitalo, *Costs of Acts and Regulations* (2 April 2013). Copies of Acts and Regulations may be obtained from the Legislative Assembly in the Samoan or English language at the cost of 40 *sene* (cents) (AUD$0.20) per page excluding GST. Copies of the Constitution, the Standing Orders and List of Acts of Parliament each cost ST$65 (approximately AUD$32).

[7]The Acts and some regulations may be accessed at the Parliament of Samoa's official website, http://www.parliament.gov.ws/. They are also accessible at the Samoa Legal Information Institute (SamLII), official website www.samlii.org. The costs are unaffordable to the general public where most are involved in subsistence farming and lack access to internet facilities (see Chap. 1).

[8]Some of the words of the Samoan language may be perceived differently by different readers. It must be clarified at the outset it is not a legal document and it cannot be relied upon in any court proceedings.

6.2 Professional Training: Judiciary, Parliament, Legal Profession

The second approach to responding to legal pluralism challenges is to make professional training available to all sectors that carry out law reform. These include the constitutional offices (the courts, the Parliament and the executive), the SLRC and the legal profession. The discussions below also explore the production of relevant handbooks and guidelines to further promote custom in these constitutional offices and the legal profession.

6.2.1 The Judiciary

6.2.1.1 Judicial Training

The judiciary must undertake continuous judicial training to find the best legal responses in judicial proceedings that impact on customary laws. This will build judicial commitment and confidence towards the application of customary laws within the scope of the Constitution.

This proposal is supported by the empirical data. Judicial training is encouraged for the judiciary to actively engage in discourse[9] on responses to legal pluralism.[10] In consideration of the supremacy of the Constitution, the courts will continue to respect the rule of law to the detriment of customary laws.[11] Judicial dialogue is encouraged to ascertain when and in what scenarios customs can be applied in the formal courts,[12] if at all. There are Supreme Court decisions that in reality cannot be enforced by the police under the formal law without the support of the village communities.[13] Such issues remain active and in need of constructive judicial dialogue, research and development.[14] Other suggested training includes best

---

[9]Interview with MOJ Respondent 5 (Samoa, 1 April 2011).

[10]Interview with GEC Respondent 6 (Samoa, 22 December 2010).

[11]Interview with MOJ Respondent 1 (Samoa, 28 March 2011).

[12]Ibid.

[13]Interview with MOJ Respondent 3 (Samoa, 7 March 2013). This is where for example a village council decision of 'banishment' is declared unconstitutional and therefore void. The court and the state cannot return the plaintiff to the village; he or she returns only if called and accepted back by the village. Similarly, there is little benefit where the village council are found guilty of burning and damaging property. Even if damages are awarded in favour of a banished plaintiff, in most cases the village councils cannot meet the damages awarded. No research has been undertaken on village councils that cannot make the payments, but the next recourse for the plaintiff is to seek for contempt of court in the district court. The members of the village council would most likely serve imprisonment terms for non-payment. Overall, the banished villager and the village council do not benefit from pursuing resolutions in the formal courts. The formal court system cannot offer a satisfying resolution to an aggrieved party in these circumstances.

[14]Interview with SOH Respondent 1 (Samoa, 8 April 2011).

practices in alternative dispute resolution[15] which is now a pre-condition in both the formal courts and in the Land and Titles Court.[16] ADR has been practised informally in Samoa for a long time and is a traditional form of dispute resolution. The courts are encouraged to adopt ADR for a more effective LTC justice system.[17] The LTC judges who are not required under the LT Act 1981 (Samoa) to have a legal background, require training on the Constitution and the state legal system as they are obligated to uphold the constitutional rights in their LTC decisions.[18]

The areas in need of judicial professional training are identified as follows. Given the existence of conflicting values of individualism and communalism, the judiciary plays a significant role in identifying legal responses to these pluralist complexities. The Samoan judiciary require ongoing dialogue to develop local frameworks to respond to these issues. The re-introduction of the alternative dispute resolution is intended to reduce the backlog in the formal courts.

Judicial training is achievable as it is in line with the intentions and long term plans of the judiciary. A judicial training of all judges of the formal courts and the LTC in October 2011 focused on the role of each court in Samoa's judicial system.[19] The conflicting functions of the two systems (individualism based and communalism based) were also the subject of dialogue. Although there are international and regional judicial conferences attended by the judicial members, due to restricted funding, local judicial trainings are few and far between. More judicial training is possible when funding is secured. Judicial training is perhaps the first step towards building confidence and commitment in the judiciary to find ways in which customs may be applied in both the formal and the Land and Titles Court proceedings. This also builds the professional capacity of local judges towards taking up senior positions in appeal courts, removing the need to engage expatriate judges.

6.2.1.2 Judicial Guidance Clause

As discussed earlier, the jurisdictions of the various courts of Samoa are defined by the Constitution and relevant legislation.[20] The application of custom is rather limited which further marginalises the recognition of customs in the courts. Article 111 however should be used to its potential. It recognises customs as law where it is

---

[15]Interview with MOJ Respondent 1 (Samoa, 28 March 2011).
[16]Land and Titles Amendment Act (No 14) (Samoa) s 8.
[17]Interview with MOJ Respondent 4 (Samoa, 5 April 2011).
[18]Interviews in Samoa with: MOJ Respondent 5 (1 April 2011); MOJ Respondent 3 (7 March 2011).
[19]Interview with MOJ Respondent 1 (Samoa, 28 March 2011).
[20]*Constitution of the Independent State of Samoa 1962* (Samoa) pt VI; *Judicature Ordinance 1961* (Samoa); *District Court Act 1969* (Samoa); *Land and Title Court Act 1981* (Samoa).

given the force of law by a court judgment. The courts must be empowered to facilitate this within the scope of the Constitution being the supreme law of Samoa.

Within the Pacific region, the *Underlying Law Act 2000* (Papua New Guinea), the *Customs Recognition Acts 1963* (Papua New Guinea) and the *Customs Recognition Act 2000* (Solomon Islands) provide helpful statutory provisions on how the courts may take account of custom. However, given the common view that these pieces of legislation have largely struggled to fulfil their obligations,[21] and given also that the same restrictions exist in Samoa's Constitution,[22] adopting legislation similar to those of Papua New Guinea and Solomon Islands (mentioned above) will not be helpful for Samoa.

It is proposed here that the Constitution is amended to insert a 'judicial guidance clause', to require the courts to give regard to customs and usages of Samoa in the determination of court decisions. This gives the courts constitutional authority to consider the application of customs at the commencement of proceedings and not at sentencing only,[23] and it will still be within the scope of the Constitution.

This provision is available in other Pacific jurisdictions. Section 11, Clause XI of the Constitution of the Federated States of Micronesia (FSM) provides that 'Court decisions shall be consistent with this Constitution, Micronesian customs and traditions, and the social and geographical configuration of Micronesia'. Other states of the FSM incorporated similar constitutional provisions into the national Constitution.[24] This clause has played a role in bridging the gap between the customary laws of Micronesia and the introduced laws[25] allowing parties to present customary evidence to prove their claim.[26]

6.2.1.3 Code of Judicial Conduct

It is also proposed that the proposed Code of Judicial Conduct for Samoa (discussed further below) should contain a provision that expressly requires a commitment to consciously pursue the application of customs as part of the judicial procedures of the Samoan judiciary, where appropriate.

---

[21] Care and Haller (2004), 8(2); Corrin and Paterson (2011), p. 9; Zorn and Care (2002), pp. 61–91; Weisbrot (1988), 10(1).

[22] Customary laws can be applied if they are not contrary to the Constitution. *Constitution of the Independent State of Samoa 1962* (Samoa) art 11; *Underlying Act 2000* (Papua New Guinea) s 4(2); *Customs Recognition Act 2000* (Solomon Islands) s 6.

[23] See the discussions on the *Young Offenders Act 2007* (Samoa) and the *Community Justice Act 2008* (Samoa) in Chap. 5; also see *Village Fono Act 1990* (Samoa) s 8.

[24] For example, the Judicial Policy Clause in *Pohnpei Constitution* (Pohnpei, Federated State of Micronesia) art 10 s11.

[25] Sharma (2006), 10:1. More discussions on FSM's Judicial Guidance Clause can be found in Zorn (1990), p. 470; Tamanaha (1989–1990), p. 72.

[26] *Alfons v FSM* 5 FSM Intrm.402 (App. 1992).

This is possible according to the Final Report which preceded the development of 3 Codes of Judicial Conduct in the Pacific under the Pacific Judicial Development Programme.[27] In 2012, the Pacific Judicial Development Programme developed 3 codes of judicial conduct for Niue, Tuvalu and Kiribati which were endorsed by the Chief Justices of those Pacific Islands.[28] Samoa was to follow suit with the 'Samoa Judicial Conduct Guidelines' catered for the Samoan judiciary and context. For customs to be part of the ethical guidelines for the judiciary, references to customs must be expressly made in the Codes that guide the work of the judiciary. It is encouraging that customary considerations were part of the preliminary workshops from which the first 3 Pacific codes were built upon.[29] For example, Kiribati's Code of Judicial Conduct combines the Bangalore Principles of Judicial Conduct[30] and a reference to Kiribati customs.[31]

6.2.1.4 Court Benchbooks

It is further suggested that the court benchbooks of Samoa must include references to customs where appropriate. Samoa's Land and Titles Benchbook[32] requires that the LTC upholds individual rights and freedoms in its court proceedings, further promoting the supremacy of state laws over customary laws. While both the LTC Benchbook 2003 and the District Court Benchbook 2009[33] are useful guides to the rules of evidence and procedure, they make no reference to the social context of Samoa upon which these rules are imposed and enforced. A benchbook setting out a brief outline of the socio-cultural basis of Samoa is helpful to put these guides into context. The 'Equal Treatment Benchbook' of the Supreme Court of Queensland provides a helpful example of a benchbook with context. It contains references to the indigenous population, their traditional languages,[34] the cultural barriers to effective communication,[35] and a judge's role in criminal trials involving indigenous witnesses and/or accused.[36] Rather than a benchbook for judges only, this benchbook informs both the judges and the litigants. It is framed in such a way that judges can manage matters that come before them in a manner that is fair to all litigants and other parties to a court proceeding.[37]

---

[27]Pacific Judicial Development Programme, 2001.
[28]Pacific Judicial Development Programme, 2012.
[29]Pillans (2011).
[30]United Nations Rule of Law, 2002.
[31]Pacific Judicial Development Programme, 2011, cl 4.2.
[32]Pacific Judicial Development Programme, 2003, 34.
[33]Pacific Judicial Development Programme, 2009.
[34]Supreme Court of Queensland, 2005, 105.
[35]Ibid 113.
[36]Ibid 124.
[37]Ibid 13.

6.2.1.5 New Developments in the Courts of Samoa

Chapter 5 noted that Samoa has four courts recently added to the judicial system. The proposals for proper training and professional judicial guidelines that promote the recognition of customs in the work of the judiciary must apply and be made available for the judges of the new courts. This way, the new Family Court, the Family Violence Court, the Alcohol and Drugs Court, and the Youth Court would assist the superior courts to provide a more relevant justice system for Samoa.

Proposals
To reiterate, judicial training is required in four areas. The first is to develop judicial discourse on areas where the decisions of the formal courts cannot be enforced in the customary village setting. The second is to identify when customs can be recognised in the formal court proceedings. Judicial expertise on the application of alternative dispute resolutions must be encouraged over adjudication. Finally, the judges of the LTC are to be adequately informed of the Constitution and the principles of individual rights. A judicial empowerment (Judicial Guidance Clause) is essential to sanction and encourage legal debates on the application of customs in the formal courts of Samoa. Expatriate judges will also be governed by the same provisions, as courts at all levels will be required to take account of customs. This facilitates a local jurisprudence based on Samoan customary laws. It is also proposed that the Code of Judicial Conduct of Samoa contain a conscious regard for customs as part of the ethical principles of the Samoan judiciary. Given that customs are a way of life in Samoa, the benchbooks of the Samoan courts should include information such as that contained in the Supreme Court of Queensland benchbook,[38] to give a social and cultural context to the rules of evidence and procedures by which the judiciary and litigants are guided. These benchbooks must be both in the Samoan and English language.

6.2.2 Parliament

To address challenges posed by legal pluralism for law reform developed by Parliament, professional training is required for Parliamentarians. In addition, a handbook on duties of members is proposed to encourage compliance with parliamentary and customary duties to the constituencies and villages.

6.2.2.1 Professional Training

Parliamentarians require professional guidance to assist them in their functions of law makers in a modern Parliament. Although there are members of Parliament

---

[38]Ibid pts 8 and 9.

who have work experience with the state system and are therefore aware of the functions of a modern Parliament, not all members have benefitted from the same opportunities. The Members of Parliament are elected while serving the villages from inside the villages. These proposals are supported by the empirical data, where it is proposed that members must undergo parliamentary procedure training, and awareness training on the existing state laws, the Constitution and the state legal system of Samoa.[39]

Due largely to the electoral candidacy criteria that only traditional chiefs may become a candidate, members of Samoa's Parliament require more than a procedural training. There must be seminars on what the modern parliamentary system entails, including an understanding of the Constitution, parliamentary procedures[40] and familiarisation with all laws[41] that govern the work of members. Some members are unable to voice their constituencies' input due to uncertainty, caution and cultural respect towards other members. Parliamentary seminars must target member familiarisation with the formal law making processes of Parliament. Members must be encouraged to understand and question the policies of the state through proposed laws and be given the infrastructure and means to carry out their own research to debate the policies in new laws.

Professional training may also involve the use of current examples of laws that are enacted but not implemented, and looking at why they were not implemented. An example is the Dogs Ordinance discussed in the previous chapter (under Parliament). It is helpful for Parliament to review enacted or repealed laws and question their suitability in Samoa's environment, and avoid enacting similar unsuccessful transplants. As presented in Chap. 5, Parliament reviewed and amended the unworkable *Dogs Registration and Control Ordinance 1955* (Samoa) in 2013. The relevant more workable amendments are as follows.

There are three features of the 2013 Act which render it to be more relevant to Samoa's environment. First is the inclusion of the village councils into the administration of the Act. The police services and the villages may develop bylaws[42] for the proper management and control of canines in the village.[43] Second, other

---

[39]Interviews in Samoa with: MOP Respondent 2 (4 January 2011); MOP Respondent 4 (7 January 2011); MOP Respondent 5 (11 January 2011).

[40]Standing Orders of the Parliament of Samoa 2006.

[41]*Legislative Assembly Powers and Privileges Ordinance 1960* (Samoa), *Parliamentary Pension Scheme Act 1998* (Samoa), *Parliamentary Under-Secretaries Act 1988* (Samoa).

[42]*Canine Control Act 2013 No 6* (Samoa) s 26.

[43]Samoa's local town Apia is located in the village Apia which also has its own village council. All areas of Samoa are distinguished by villages governed by village councils. Efforts towards reducing the number of dogs and preventing further health and social problems can therefore be effectively implemented with the support of the village councils. Without a commencement day for the registration of canines' provisions of the new Act, this is Samoa's only hope towards curtailing canine problems.

agencies and non-government organisations[44] are empowered to assist in the administration of the Act. Third, there is less express government commitment.[45]

These features show that the State has devolved administrative functions outside of the state, acknowledging it cannot take responsibility alone. Village councils are relied upon where state laws cannot work. Canvassing the assistance of the village empowers its structure and acknowledges that pluralism may work. It is too early to tell whether the new Act will now achieve its objectives. However as at the time of writing the relevant Minister has yet to determine a commencement date for the registration of canines under the Act,[46] any immediate relief to the dog problems in Samoa is placed on the village councils.

The review of the weaknesses or strengths of past laws and lessons learnt provide more realistic assistance than overseas training for members of Parliament, undertaken in the absence of Samoa's customary realities. The review of the limitations and strengths of the 12 Acts of Parliament that purport to recognise customs in the previous is instructive for future parliamentary reforms suitable to Samoa's environment.

6.2.2.2 Customary Duties to Village Communities

It was a consensual view from the empirical data that Parliamentarians must be required to actively engage the villages and constituencies and seek views to inform submissions in Parliament.[47] As members are appointed due to having satisfied village services,[48] the village councils argue that these duties to the families, village and constituencies should not cease when a person becomes a Member of Parliament. A member is entitled to a Parliament seat by virtue of the member being a *matai* from a village of the constituencies.

In a small jurisdiction like Samoa, where communal living is the current norm, this proposal is beneficial to the communities and relevant to the legitimacy of parliamentary laws. Requiring the Members of Parliament to take draft laws or

---

[44]The Animal Protection Society of Samoa and the Australian Royal Society for the Protection of Cruelty to Animals (RSPCA) have carried out numerous clinics for de-sexing dogs in the town and in the rural areas. See for example an article in Samoa Observer Staff, '1 million less dogs in Samoa' 2012a.

[45]Whereas the 1955 Ordinance indicated the state may be responsible for a dog pound, the 2013 Act empowers the Police Service to approve places as pounds. The 1955 Ordinance required the Ministry of Police to keep supplies of collars for registration purposes; the 2013 Act does not have this same requirement, but rather, allows the Commissioner to approve registration marks including collars. Specific duties are replaced with general powers to carry out a duty.

[46]*Canine Control Act 2013 No 6* (Samoa), section 6 says that Part III of the Act (Registration of Canines) 'commences at such time and for such places within Samoa as the Minister determines by notice'.

[47]Interviews in Samoa with: VC1 Focus Group (1 March 2011); VC2 Respondent 2 (10 March 2011); VC2 Respondent 5 (15 March 2011); VC2 Respondent 1 (15 March 2011).

[48]*Electoral Act 1963* (Samoa) s 5(3).

enacted laws to their constituencies for information and input would not only allow for better and diverse participation to inform Samoa's laws, but it again takes advantage of the assistance rendered by the local chiefly system. The village communities will likely be more open in discussions with their own traditional *matai* (Member of Parliament) than making an input in public consultation. The absence of a conventional guideline setting out the responsibilities of Parliamentarians to their constituencies in Samoa means Parliamentarians may discard this moral[49] and cultural obligation without repercussions. The absence of parliamentary assistance to constituencies is counter-productive to the judges advising the public the only way to amend a law is through their Members of Parliament.[50]

A possible model is 'A Guide for Members of Parliament' of New Zealand containing provisions on how individual members contribute to parliamentary functions.[51] The members participate in determining laws by bringing in ideas for laws to the House, participating in debate, considering Bills in select committees and consulting constituents and interested parties outside Parliament. Similar provisions can be incorporated in the 'Samoa Parliamentary Practice and Procedure Manual' first launched in 2013. There must be an express function for members to make periodical visits to the village, to take draft laws that may directly affect customs and to seek views on those draft laws. Although these duties may be unenforceable in law, they signify a Samoan Parliament that acknowledges it has duties under both the customary legal system and the modern legal system. Parliamentary members must observe and fulfil their moral and cultural duties and advocate for customs in legislation.

6.2.2.3 Private Members Bill (PMB)

From the empirical data, there is argument that the PMB is an available avenue through which customary laws can be introduced and discussed in Parliament.[52] The PMBs must be utilised to enable wider public and village aspirations to be considered, debated and become part of parliamentary laws.[53]

As stated in Chap. 5, PMBs have not been put to the test in Samoa. A review of the Standing Orders of Parliament governing PMBs[54] shows similar procedural and structural constraints as those of other common law jurisdictions.[55] In addition, if the Bill is rejected by the Assembly, which the UK experience shows is the reality for almost all PMBs, the cost of preparation and printing of a PMB is borne by the

---

[49]Email from SOH Respondent 8 to Lalotoa Mulitalo (Monday 7 May 2012).
[50]Interview with MOJ Respondent 1 (Samoa, 28 March 2011).
[51]Office of the Clerk of the House of Representatives (New Zealand), 2001, 15, 16.
[52]Interview with GEC Respondent 6 (Samoa, 22 December 2010).
[53]Interview with MOP Respondent 5 (Samoa, 11 January 2011).
[54]*Standing Orders of Parliament 2006* (Samoa) O 115.
[55]For example, the Parliament of UK as discussed in Marsh and Marsh (2002) 8(1).

mover of the Bill. A study was carried out on the UK Parliament on the hypothesis that an electoral connection exists between MPs and the PMBs in the UK.[56] It involved testing whether the district vote margins prompt members to propose PMBs. The evidence suggests there is a component of an 'electoral connection' that shapes behaviour of MPs in the UK Parliament as well as other legislatures.[57]

Samoa's situation is different from many other countries in that the electoral laws and membership criteria guarantee a connection between the members and their constituencies. A member has familial, customary and genealogical connections to the villages and constituencies. Customary matters are of significance to generally all Samoans including its parliamentarians. Thus, a customary rule may be promoted through a PMB; it may appeal to the 'Samoan *matai*' aspirations of parliamentarians and gain support not only amongst parliamentarians but also from the country. PMBs can be taken advantage of this way in Samoa, but first the Standing Orders on PMBs must be relaxed and the relevant assistance made accessible to members.

The Office of the Clerk of the Legislative Assembly must provide the facilities, legal advice and legislative drafting services to assist the members utilise the opportunities to develop PMBs. A manual for drafting non-government legislation similar to that of New South Wales can be developed to facilitate the use of PMBs. This manual sets out the drafting arrangements and guidelines for PMBs.[58] Professional training must include comparable information such as the use of PMBs in other jurisdictions.[59]

6.2.2.4 Recent Developments for Parliament

The Parliament of Samoa recently received some professional training through the Samoa Parliamentary Support Project funded by AusAID and coordinated by the UNDP with the assistance of the Pacific Parliamentary Partnership (PPP). In November 2012 the first 'Samoa Parliamentary Practice and Procedure Manual' was handed over to the Speaker of the House developed under the support of the PPP.[60] This Manual was updated in 2016 and offered to the newly elected members of the XVIth Parliament of Samoa after the general elections in March 2016. The recent professional training is a positive development for the Parliament of Samoa. However, the professional training must acknowledge the pluralist nature of Samoa. Developing guidelines on applicable considerations when debating

---

[56]Bowler (2010), pp. 476–494.

[57]Ibid 491.

[58]New South Wales Office of Parliamentary Counsel, 2011.

[59]Davies (2005), pp. 32–39. Davies for example states that for a PMB to be successful, in addition to many other restrictions, it must not introduce complex and technical measures and it must support government agenda.

[60]Samoa Observer Staff, Samoa Observer, (Samoa) 30 November 2012b.

customary policies in Parliament is one way of acknowledging pluralism in laws. Professional training on law making must instruct on features of laws applicable to Samoa and the requisite processes must be in place to facilitate the achievement of those features.

Proposals

Relevant professional training for Parliamentarians on law making must include training on developing laws in a customary environment. Handbooks providing guidelines on a member's duties as a law maker in Parliament (in a plural society) and duties to the villages are recommended. Relevant services must be made available to members to facilitate the use of private members Bills.

6.2.3 Legal Profession

6.2.3.1 Professional Training on the Rule of Law and Samoan Customs

A legal profession operating in a plural environment requires professional training that explores responses to the conflicts between the two systems if customary laws are to be seriously regarded as law. As discussed in the previous chapter, there are no avenues through which such dialogue is promoted in the Samoa Law Society (SLS). Before 2014, the SLS was not expressly required to promote customs in any way. However, this limitation is now addressed under the society's new Lawyers and Legal Practice Act 2014 (Samoa). The Act requires the SLS to promote and encourage the maintenance of the rule of law, to promote Samoan custom and traditions and enhance the social, economic and commercial development of Samoa.[61] Although this is a general function, the SLS must utilise this general power to advantage to benefit the majority of the population governed under customary rule.

6.2.3.2 Training on Samoan Language and Cultural Protocols

The legal profession and in particular those conducting law reform consultations from the SLRC legal staff will find Samoan language and cultural protocols training useful. A strong command of the language and protocols allow for a more fluent and effective dialogue in law reform consultations.

This proposal is supported by the empirical data. In Samoa, the best way to make people understand a new message is through the Samoan language, communicating in relevant 'speak', in nuances and meaning.[62] Where the message is misunderstood or not understood at all due to the use of a different language, one loses the attention

---

[61] *Lawyers and Legal Practice Act 2014* (Samoa) s 5.
[62] Interview with SOH Respondent 1 (Samoa, 8 April 2011).

of the audience.[63] The use of Samoan proverbs and seeking to conduct *Talanoa* sessions in groups is another effective means of conducting consultations. The staff of the SLRC must also be knowledgeable of general village cultural protocols[64] and have a basic comprehension of general genealogical addresses of Samoa.[65]

Language and cultural training is imperative for effective law reform in Samoa especially if one does not occasionally participate in traditional village activities. Lawyers must have some knowledge of general genealogical links. Texts on genealogies, traditional addresses and Samoan proverbial expressions are available in Samoa and overseas where there is a Samoan population. Some examples of proverbial texts are 'Palefuiono'[66] and 'Alaga'upu Fa'a Samoa: Samoan Proverbial Expressions'.[67] Examples of texts on identity and genealogies include 'O le Tusi o Faalupega' (Booklet of Genealogies),[68] O le 'Faasinomaga' (Identity)[69] and 'Fa'afaigofieina o Fa'alupega o Samoa,'[70] a text on Samoan genealogies. There are also publications funded by the State on the oral traditions and legends of Samoa, in both the Samoan and the English language.[71] These texts provide invaluable information on Samoan history, genealogical links to ancestral gods and to each other, salutations, cultural addresses and proverbial Samoan sayings. These materials do not form part of western education. Local lawyers must make time to be familiar with these and similar material to be able to connect to the village communities. The most effective teachers however, are the *matais* themselves, assisting individuals through the trials and errors of participation in cultural activities. Consistently attending village meetings and activities and constantly making errors and corrected during such customary activities is tough, but the best way to learn. Indeed, this was how the most influential of all orators and leaders were schooled.

SLRC training initiatives such as the Samoan oratory (*Lauga Samoa*) teaching under the guidance of a prominent Samoan *matai* and writer[72] is encouraged. This training involved the conduct of the traditional welcoming ceremony, oratorical speech and other core values of the Samoan culture. It offered crucial knowledge to facilitate the cultural aspects of public consultations.[73] Training in the Samoan language, Samoan salutations and village protocols is highly relevant to effective law reform.

---

[63] Efi (2008), p. 12.
[64] Interview with LP Respondent 5 (Samoa, 14 March 2011).
[65] Interview with GCE Respondent 1 (Samoa, 19 January 2011).
[66] Atonio (1992).
[67] Schultz (2008).
[68] Tuvale et al. (1981).
[69] Le Tagaloa (1997).
[70] Tavae (2005), Le Tagaloa (1997).
[71] Ministry of Education, Sports and Culture (Samoa) (1997), Vols 1–7.
[72] Also author of Samoan oratory texts including Amosa (1999) and 2002.
[73] Samoa Law Reform Commission http://www.samoalawreform.gov.ws.

6.2.3.3 Engaging in Academic Conferences and Quality Research

The empirical data also highlighted the need for the legal profession and the law makers to engage in academic conferences. A prominent Samoan academic has encouraged discourse on cultural ideologies and philosophies in the Samoan context.[74] The Measina Samoa Conference which targets the core values of the Samoan customs is now a biennial event at the National University of Samoa. This conference addresses key cultural topics such as identifying the core values of the *fa'a Samoa*, the changes that influence these values and which cultural principles are to be preserved, for example in legislation. Such themes lead research and presentations into Samoa's history, traditions and culture recorded by song, poetry, chants, dance and lyrics. One must understand the basis and foundations of Samoan culture before proposing changes intended to recognise Samoan customs and culture.[75] Research partnerships can be developed between the SLRC and the local university (the National University of Samoa) to create active dialogue on various research areas, particularly on socio-legal research. The existing literature on Samoa in areas of anthropology, archaeology and history are useful sources that may inform reforms inquiries. The SLRC must be equipped with a proper library and electronic database systems for legal research. If funding is prioritised for these purposes, these may be realistically achieved.

Quality research also extends to attaining empirical evidence as strongly advocated by Kirby.[76] According to Kirby, empirical data is a foundation for a thorough understanding of how the law operates in practice. It is not sufficient to study legal problems through judicial opinions. It is essential to get out into the field and to discover how the law actually operates and affects ordinary people. In the context of Samoa, a visit to the villages to observe how reforms may likely impact the local environment and provide persuasive policies for effective laws. The strong links that the SLRC may forge with others in the local community, in both the private and the public sector will enable it to benefit from the pooled knowledge and skills available from a multidisciplinary approach.[77] Importantly, the reports and recommendations of the SLRC are better informed where the area for reform has been researched and reports and published research are available from the academics.

Proposals
Samoan cultural and language training must become part of the SLRC and the SLS professional seminars and training. Undertaking a language and customary protocol training can also be a prerequisite for admission and for renewal of practising certificates. This can be considered in a future review of Samoa's law practitioners' legislation. Professional training and funding is necessary for the legal profession to

---

[74]Interview with SOH Respondent 3 (Samoa, 4 April 2011).
[75]Interview with SOH Respondent 1 (Samoa, 8 April 2011).
[76]Kirby (2003).
[77]Commonwealth Secretariat, 17–20 Oct 2005.

effectively contribute in shaping a justice system that is fitting for Samoa. This justice system is where the customary legal system and the state legal system are given equal importance. The legal profession and the SLRC staff must also undertake Samoan language and cultural protocols training to assist the profession to conduct law reform consultations that respect cultural protocols. Finally, the SLRC staff must carry out research and present findings at conferences to obtain feedback from academics, engage in legal database training, and carry out empirical research to inform law reform projects. The next suggested responses explore improvements and changes that can be driven by the state.

6.3 State Responsibilities in Law Reform

6.3.1 Constitutional and Legislative Review, Drafting Handbooks

The empirical data suggests that one of the ways in which customs may be promoted on the same level as state laws is to revise the Constitution to for example, insert in it a reaffirmation, that customary laws is part of the formal laws of Samoa, and to provide direct guidelines for its progressive application.

It was observed that the Constitution must be reviewed[78] to clarify the scope and status of customs in the formal laws of Samoa.[79] The rule of law prevails; but due recognition must be given to customs being the major contributing factor to political and social stability.[80] Individual rights undermine customary authorities; they must be reviewed and refined in the context of Samoan customs.[81] Parliament must give the same certainty to the application of customary laws as afforded to individual rights, and provide guidelines for the application of customary laws.

The proposition to reaffirm the status of customs and define individual rights in the context of the customary system in the Constitution is fraught with difficulties. The flexible nature of customs is a challenge to the ascertainment of customary rules against which individual rights may be assessed. Unless all villages of Samoa agree to an identifiable, specific and certain list of customary rules, an assessment of individual rights in the context of customary rules is complex. Each of the 330 villages of Samoa has its own set of customary rules. It is therefore difficult to ascertain uniform customary rules against which individual rights can be refined, for a set of individual rights said to be developed in the context of Samoan customs.

The proposal is not impossible however. It requires a systematic and gradual approach to the revision of the supreme law of the country, and should not be

---

[78]Interview with LP Respondent 2 (Samoa, 21 February 2011).
[79]Interview with MOJ Respondent 5 (Samoa, 1 April 2011).
[80]Interview with MOP Respondent 2 (Samoa, 4 January 2011).
[81]Interview with SOH Respondent 4 (Samoa, 11 July 2011).

rushed. It is similar to the initiatives such as in post-colonial African societies seeking an elevation of customary laws in state laws.[82] The literature on the ascertainment of customary laws for the purposes of codification and restatement[83] provides valuable guidance for Samoa. Namibia's self-stating of customary law project has been rated as successful to date. According to Manfred O Hinz, self-statement of customary laws in this sense 'does not render the non-ascertained parts of customary law obsolete, the non-ascertained part continues to exist, and the ascertained part may even be revisited by the underlying customary laws in existence before the ascertainment'.[84] The purpose of the self-stated project was for the traditional communities of Nigeria to identify the customary laws they were to be governed by.[85] Although the African states are larger in population size and total land-area, and feature numerous traditional communities with unique vernacular languages, the past and present experiences of African communities on ascertaining customary laws provide helpful experiences which Samoa and other Pacific Islands can draw from.

There appears to be no published systematic research or projects on restatement of the ascertainment of customary laws of many Pacific Islands. The ascertainment of customary rules is largely left to specific bodies such as tribunals and courts. For example, the Constitution of Vanuatu requires the Vanuatu Parliament to establish village and island courts with jurisdiction over island matters[86] and to 'provide for the manner of the ascertainment of relevant rules of custom.'[87] It is uncertain whether there is attempt to ascertain customary rules and there seems to be no published study on this. However, indirectly, under specific legislation, the Parliament of Vanuatu has referred the ascertainment of customary land rules to be developed from the proceedings of the Customary Land Tribunal.[88] The relevant rules of customs to a particular land area are ascertained by the tribunal and parties in the course of the proceedings and disputes are resolved under those rules.[89]

Given the lack of restatement experiences in the Pacific region and the failures of restatement projects experienced by other countries informed by the literature, a gradual rather than an urgent Constitutional review to restate customary laws for the purposes of reaffirming their status in the Constitution of Samoa is more viable at this stage. A more realistic project is to identify and record the most common customary rules and practices[90] of Samoa in the form of a manual to guide the

---

[82]Ochich (2011), p. 153, 126.
[83]Salman (2006).
[84]Hinz (2011), pp. 153, 155.
[85]Ibid 167–168.
[86]*Constitution of the Republic of Vanuatu 1980* (Vanuatu) s 52.
[87]Ibid s 51.
[88]*Customary Land Tribunal Act* (Vanuatu) ch 271, s 28(1).
[89]Email from Parliamentary Counsel of Vanuatu to Lalotoa Mulitalo, 1 July 2013.
[90]See discussions in Twining (1963), p. 221.

6.3.1.1 Reference Guide to Customary Practices

As highlighted in Chap. 2, there are a number of problems with the ascertainment and restatement of customary laws. Those experiences however are from large scale restatement projects.[91] In contrast, Samoa is a Pacific island society with less than 200,000 people and two official languages. The main source of Samoan customary laws, the *faamatai* (chiefly system) is respected (though in varying degrees) by all Samoans. Samoa may learn from lessons of other jurisdictions and adopt best practices suitable for Samoa. The main objective is to have a record of customary practices currently practised in Samoa for the use of the judiciary and the Parliament, the legal profession (SLRC staff and the legislative drafters). It must not be given legislative effect and must be subject to periodical review to allow for the evolution of customs. This project can be entitled the 'Reference Guide to Customary Practices'. Where this guide is combined with legal textbooks, it may achieve some certainty, objectivity and flexibility in the application of customary laws[92] in Samoa.

Arguably, the absence of such a guideline makes it easier and convenient to ignore customs; the fact that customs exist and are widely practised is not disputed, however they cannot be referred to in a physical form. The Report on Matai Titles, Customary Land and the Land and Titles Court, October 1974 to November 1975 which the courts in a number of cases relied upon[93] is an example of a document which has guided the work of the Samoan judiciary. The significant relevance of this report to those decisions may form part of the preliminary considerations on the need for and feasibility of this proposed project.

Proposal

An immediate review of the Constitution to specify the status of customs is not viable at this stage without further research. Successful and unsuccessful studies elsewhere provide useful backgrounds on the feasibility of this study for Samoa. A Reference Guide to Customary Practice would be more realistic at this stage where the customary laws of Samoa are collected, collated and recorded for the purposes of guiding the judiciary, the Parliament and the executive. These guidelines may be reviewed periodically to ensure that customary laws are not frozen in time and are updated from time to time. The experiences and further reviews may start the

---

[91] Ibid. For example the Restatement of African laws covered 16 countries in Africa, consisting of several hundreds of different bodies of customary law.

[92] Epiphany (1991), p. 289.

[93] *Taamale v Attorney-General* (Unreported, Court of Appeal of Samoa, Cooke, P, Casey and Bisson JJA, 18 August 1995); *Mauga v Leituala* (Unreported, Court of Appeal of Samoa, Cooke, P, Casey and Bisson JJA, 4 March 2005).

process of confirming the customs and practices towards a meaningful and comprehensive Constitutional review.

6.3.1.2 Village Fono Act (1990) Review

The *Village Fono Act 1990* (Samoa) (VF Act) must be reviewed to affirm the powers of the village council. The empirical data supports a review of the VF Act for two purposes. These are to empower the village councils to make bylaws to regulate village governance[94] and to reaffirm the powers of the village council.[95] The gist of the empirical data argument is that this Act is the only Act of Parliament law that recognises the customary powers of the village councils. Effort must be made to, as much as possible, portray the true depth, scope and meaning of the customary powers and functions of the village councils.

The requirement for the state to consult with the village councils in developing village bylaws for specific purposes is already expressed in several Acts of Parliament.[96] It appears this is the new trend in law making, where village councils are drawn in to assist administer legislation.[97] In relation to reaffirming the powers of the village councils, this section provides the most recent developments to the VF Act which includes proposed legislative provisions on the powers of the village council.

The VF Act has undergone extensive reviews.[98] Relevant to this book are the attempts at making customs and state law work in the framework of the VF Act. Two recommendations highlighted in the said review are significant as they relate to a verification of the powers of the village council as proposed in this section. The first recommendation[99] is for the State (MWSCD) to draw up a draft set of standard village rules and bylaws on punishments and penalties for village misconduct with the assistance of the Registrar of Lands and Title Court for review by the Attorney-General for constitutional compliance. The village *Fono* may choose to accept or reject or modify the standard village rules. Where they are accepted, they can be registered before the Registrar of the Land and Titles Court. Alternatively, each village council can draw up its own set of village rules and bylaws in line with the Constitution. Registration does not automatically give the full effect of law to these rules and bylaws. Only those which comply with the Constitution and all other laws will have the full effect of law.

---

[94] Also see similar powers in the *Fisheries Act 1988* (Samoa) s 3.

[95] Interviews in Samoa with: LP Respondent 4 (2 March 2011); GEC Respondent 6 (22 December 2010).

[96] *Fisheries Act 1988* (Samoa), *Internal Affairs Act 1995* (Samoa).

[97] More recent examples include the *Canine Control Act 2013* (Samoa) s 26 discussed above; the *Water Resources Management Act 2008* (Samoa) s 33; *Waste Management Act 2010* (Samoa) s 40.

[98] Samoa Law Reform Commission, *Village Fono Act 1990*, Report No. 09/12 (2012).

[99] Ibid 25.

6.3 State Responsibilities in Law Reform

The second recommendation[100] is that the traditional power of 'banishment' continues to be the prerogative of the village councils, but there should be general guidelines to guide village councils on steps to be taken before making their decision to banish. Such guidelines should take into account natural fairness and justice; justified banishment relative to social order; and the right to appeal a village council decision. At the time of writing, a Village Fono Bill 2016 containing the above recommendations is before Parliament having received prior Cabinet approval.

Proposal
The VF Act must provide clearer guidelines firstly on developing village rules that are compliant with the Constitution, and secondly on the scope within which the traditional powers of the village councils may be exercised. These must be part of the objectives of the reforms to the Village Fono Bill 2016.

6.3.1.3 Cabinet and Drafting Handbooks

The challenge of legal pluralism for the executive as discussed in Chap. 5 is the absence of express regard for customary considerations in policy development and in drafting legislation. It is essential that the state mandate state officials, through the Cabinet Handbook and the Legislative Drafting Handbook to develop policies in light of the Samoan customary environment. The Cabinet Handbook must obligate the policy developers seeking endorsement of their policies to report on how the proposed policies have been vetted against customs.[101] This approach is feasible as Samoan leaders control the operations of the state and would argue this is already the practice.

Proposal
The law process Handbooks of the state must expressly require state officials to take account of customs at policy development. Without express requirements imposed, it is easy for the western trained officers to subconsciously revert back to modern concepts and discard customary considerations.

6.3.2 *Promote Formal Education*

The state must make accessible opportunities for formal education to facilitate an understanding of state laws. This proposal is also supported by the empirical data.[102] Formal education was non-existent in the earlier days and western

---

[100]Ibid 26.

[101]Interview with GCE Respondent 1 (Samoa, 19 January 2011).

[102]Interviews in Samoa with: VM Respondent 2 (9 March 2011); SOH Respondent 7 (22 March 2011); SOH Respondent 3 (4 April 2011).

knowledge was irrelevant to Samoans[103] as expressed by some interview respondents. The gradual shift to modernisation makes formal education necessary. Formal education teaches the English language which allows Samoa to be part of the global dialogue; thus formal education must be encouraged if Samoans are to understand laws and become part of that dialogue.[104] Education is encouraged for a better informed population in the next generation.[105] There is a proposition that the differences between customs and the laws must be part of studies on the history of Samoa, preferably in the early school years,[106] and a mandatory requirement in the secondary schools.[107] The significance of both customary laws and state laws must be highlighted in formal education.[108]

The proposal to promote formal education may be achieved in consideration of current government initiatives. Improving the focus on education, learning and training outcomes is one of the key outcomes sought under Samoa's national plan, the Samoa Development Strategy 2012–2016. In its specific Education Sector Plan 2012–2016, the education sector promotes the achievement of high quality education and training to meet the national socio-economic and cultural goals of Samoa.[109] The Ministry of Education, Sports and Culture (MESC) in Samoa conducted a mid-term review of *'Strategic Policies and Plan 2006-2015'* in 2011 where specific sector areas were reprioritized. One of those prioritised is the Samoa School Fee Grants Scheme jointly funded by the Governments of New Zealand and Australia. Under this scheme, excepting private schools, access to free education at primary level for all was provided. MESC aimed to achieve universal primary education and improve learning outcomes in Samoa.[110]

A local private primary school took a step towards introducing laws and the legal system in the school's curriculum The Year 7 students of the Peace Chapel Christian School visited the Samoa Law Reform Commission on 22 March 2013.[111] This was part of a study about *'Law in the Community'* which teaches the significant role 'law' plays in the day to day life of a community. This is a rare initiative and must be encouraged. It is an excellent way for the law to reach students as young as ten years and encourage dialogue at an early age.

---

[103]Interview with MOP Respondent 5 (Samoa, 11 January 2011).

[104]Interview with SOH Respondent 9 (Samoa, 21 March 2011).

[105]Interviews in Samoa with: VM Respondent 1 (11 March 2011); VM Respondent 2 (9 March 2011).

[106]Interview with SOH Respondent 9 (Samoa, 21 March 2011).

[107]Interviews in Samoa with: MOP Respondent 5 (11 January 2011); MOP Respondent 3 (11 January 2011); MOP Respondent 1 (22 December 2010).

[108]Interview with MOP Respondent 2 (Samoa, 4 January 2011).

[109]Government of Samoa Strategy for the Development of Samoa 2012–2016, 2012, 11.

[110]Ibid 52, 53.

[111]Samoa Observer staff in Samoa Observer, 29 March 2013.

Proposal

Improved access to formal education is achievable as there are government initiatives driving this. These contribute to developing a law reform framework that corresponds to the plural environment of Samoa. There are also government plans that acknowledge the need to strengthen the village systems and create partnerships between the state and the villages.

6.3.3 National Plans

A review of the government efforts to date to work alongside with the village systems reveals three existing avenues through which partnerships are created. The first is through the Internal Affairs division.[112] The means through which the Internal Affairs Act 1995 creates partnerships is discussed in Chap. 5, it will not be referred to further. The second approach is through Samoa's current national plan and thirdly through Samoa's law and justice sector plan.

6.3.3.1 Samoa's National Plan 2012–2016

One of the stated objectives of the national plan of Samoa is to reconcile the community structures with the state system. Community development was a priority area in the Strategy for the Development of Samoa 2008–2012 (SDS), and this saw the promotion of good governance in local communities, strengthening community economic development and enhancing social development and service provision. The government closely coordinated with the village councils and in areas where there were no village councils, the church leaders were requested to intensify their involvement in the community. In both cases, particular emphasis was placed on promoting Samoan culture, strengthening the family unit as the core of village society, and addressing tensions between customary law and traditional authority structures, on the one hand, and modern law and the court system on the other. Legislation was passed which effectively brings the village authorities and the formal courts together to determine the sentence and rehabilitation terms of an offender.[113]

---

[112] A division of the Ministry of Women Social and Community Development responsible for promoting partnerships between the state and the villages.

[113] *Community Justice Act 2008* (Samoa); *Young Offenders Act 2007* (Samoa). These two Acts are discussed in the review of the Acts of Parliament that purport to recognise customs in Chap. 5.

6.3.3.2 Law and Justice Sector Plan

The second effort is through a law and justice sector plan. Upon obtaining funding from the Australian government, a 'Law and Justice Sector Plan Samoa 2008-2012' (LJSP) was formulated and led by the Office of the Attorney-General. The Law and Justice Sector comprise the lead law enforcement ministries such as the Ministry of Police and the Ministry of Justice and Courts Administration.[114] One of the primary strategies of the sector is to promote and integrate customary and community-based justice.[115] The aim of this strategy is to recognize customary and community-based justice in Samoa and integrate or harmonize it with the formal justice system.

One of the projects under the sector plan in which information on law and the legal system is taken out to the villages is called the '*Fautasi*' (literally translated 'long boat' or to 'build together' in Samoan).[116] A committee is given terms of reference to visit the villages, explain a Parliament Act and seek views on how that Act may be improved in light of customs. The committee reports its findings to the Law and Justice Sector before seeking Cabinet's approval. If Cabinet approves the committee's recommendations the same may be endorsed as a reference transferred to the SLRC to identify and propose possible amendments to the relevant laws.

Proposals
The current initiatives of government under its national plans and policies must be utilised to create partnerships between the village sector and the state system to drive law reform that is relevant and suitable for the Samoan society. The SDS and LJSP initiatives must continue and efforts must be circulated and published to create public awareness of how Samoa is responding to legal pluralism at the village level.

6.4 Village Responsibilities in Law Reform

The village sector must take charge of their responsibilities to contribute to the development of an environment for a workable law reform framework. The proposed changes are to amend the focus of village mayors' appointment criteria and for the development of written village rules that are compliant with the Constitution. These are discussed next.

---

[114]Other members include the Office of the Ombudsman, the Ministry of Women Community & Social Development (MWCSD); the Ministry of Finance (MoF) and the Public Service Commission (PSC).

[115]Office of the Attorney-General - Samoa Law and Justice Sector Plan 2008–2012, 2008.

[116]Interview with LP Respondent 4 (Samoa, 2 March 2011).

6.4.1 Change of Village Mayor Criteria

The villages must appoint more committed, active and modern thinking village mayors for the purposes of the Internal Affairs Act 1995 (Samoa). In support of this proposition the empirical data suggests a more modern criterion. Rather than appointments being reserved for special *matai* status and influenced by cultural factors, the new criteria sought are for the appointee to be youthful, active, mobile, resourceful, and have some formal education.[117] It was observed that the cultural influences on mayor appointments are not conducive to the modern times and must change.[118] To develop villagers' understanding of proposed State reforms, each village must have active village mayors who are able to encourage villagers' interest in law reform.[119]

Such a proposal can work only if it comes from the villages and not from the state. It is a sound suggestion for modern times. The earlier criteria were fitting in the earlier times when the village mayor's traditional duties were only to the village. It is difficult for the elderly *matai* to take part in lengthy law reform consultations that have no cultural aspect. The work carried out by the village mayor involves paperwork rather than the traditional verbal oratorical speeches and exchanges. The cultural criteria were relevant and applicable to Samoa in the past. These criteria are now impractical given the developments in a modern Samoa. In addition to changing the criteria, there is a further suggestion for the state to develop guidelines to expressly state the duties of the village mayors, particularly as they are paid a salary by the state.[120] This is also viable and encourages village mayor accountability to both their villages and to the state.

Developing modern criteria for the appointment of village mayors and having proper guidelines assist the village mayors meet their obligations under the IA Act. More importantly, where village mayors are able to explain the state laws to the villagers, they will be better informed increasing the chances of law reform contributions from the village.

---

[117]Interviews in Samoa with: VM Respondent 7 (10 March 2011); VM Respondent 1 (11 March 2011); VM Respondent 4 (16 March 2011); VM Respondent 5 (16 March 2011); GCE Respondent 7 to Lalotoa Mulitalo, 19 April 2011.

[118]Interview with SOH Respondent 7 (Samoa, 22 March 2011).

[119]Interview with VM Respondent 5 (Samoa, 16 March 2011).

[120]Email from GCE Respondent 7 to Lalotoa Mulitalo, 19 April 2011. Village mayor guidelines are supported by the court in *Lufilufi v Hunt* (Unreported, Supreme Court of Samoa, Vaai, Nelson JJ, 26 April 2011).

6.4.2 Develop Constitutionally Compliant Village Rules

It is suggested that another way of responding to pluralism in law reform is for the villages to develop rules that are in line with the Constitution. This is one of the proposed amendments in the Village Fono Bill 2016 (Samoa) referred to earlier.

Such an initiative must come from the villages, and this is supported by the empirical data.[121] The village council must first appreciate that this change is required to eradicate the imbalance between the law and customs.[122] At the time of interviews it was noted that some villages had commenced actions towards this initiative,[123] particularly those villages in which village council decisions have been held by the court to be unconstitutional.[124] However, one must not hasten to make significant changes to the villages as one interview respondent cautioned.[125] He quoted a common Samoan proverb, e *le aoga ona gau mataina le laau mata* (it is unrealistic to bend a green stick) as this may further widen rather than bridge the gap between the villages and the state. Time must be allowed for changes to take place; this is necessary if law reform is to be sustainable in a customary environment.

Other studies towards workable legal pluralist approaches support the need for the village sector to take some responsibilities.[126] For Samoa, this proposal is now becoming a reality and this should be encouraged. The first village in Samoa, Afega, has launched a booklet of village rules which reportedly includes village policies and penalties.[127] The rules were developed by the village with the assistance of the Office of the Attorney-General and relevant state authorities which carried out checks for constitutional compliance.[128] Where the village rules are developed by the village rather than imposed by the state, the village autonomy is maintained and empowered. In return the village willingly seeks the state's assistance to vet their rules for constitutional compliance. This is a practice of good governance promoting collaborative partnerships which must be encouraged.

Proposals

To respond to legal pluralism through village initiatives, the villages must be willing to review and amend the criteria for more active village mayors who are able to create interest and village participation in law reform. Developing village

---

[121]Interview with VM Respondent 2 (Samoa, 9 March 2011).

[122]Interview with MOJ Respondent 5 (Samoa, 1 April 2011).

[123]Interview with LP Respondent 4 (Samoa, 2 March 2011).

[124]Interviews in Samoa with: VM Respondent 2 (9 March 2011); SOH Respondent 5 (20 July 2011).

[125]Interview with MOJ Respondent 5 (Samoa, 1 April 2013).

[126]Grenfell (2006), pp. 305, 337. Writing on legal pluralism in East Timor, Grenfell noted that where the state system is encouraged to recognise customary laws, customary settings must also make some effort in the attempt at reconciliation and harmonisation.

[127]Reported in the local newspaper, Tupufia, 31 March 2013.

[128]Ibid.

6.5 Managing Funding Constraints

Funding and resource constraints are global issues not just in the law reform sector but across sectors in developing countries. Law reform receives minimum attention and a small portion of the annual state budget.[129] There are no easy responses to resource constraints other than to enlist the support of the state. This book suggests two ways through which costs may be minimised and managed in the context of Samoa. Although it was noted in Chap. 5 that customary protocols add to law reform costs, there are ways in which the customary structures may be engaged to reduce costs of village consultations. The second way is to perhaps manage costs through prioritising and justifying costs for customary related reforms.

6.5.1 Involving Customary Structures in Law Reform Consultation

Involving customary and village structures in law reform consultation and awareness projects minimises costs. This was supported by the empirical data. The village mayors and village councils[130] and the church leaders[131] must take part in the preparation of interactive law reform consultations.[132] The central church offices must also be involved in disseminating information, seeking views of the church members and collecting those views for the State[133] to ensure wider circulation and to promote law reform initiatives.[134]

This suggestion is workable and must be encouraged according to the empirical data. The villages and churches are cooperative and even seek to be involved in the preparatory work for public consultations. As discussed in Chap. 1, the village is structured in organisations consisting of the village council, women's committees and men's groups. Each organisation holds several meetings within a month to discuss village developments. The church members who are almost always also members of the village organisations, apart from congregating at church services on

---

[129]Interview with GEC Respondent 2 (Samoa, 11 March 2011).

[130]Interview with LP Respondent 5 (Samoa, 14 March 2011).

[131]Interview with SOH Respondent 4 (Samoa, 11 July 2011).

[132]Interviews in Samoa with: LP Respondent 4 (2 March 2011); LP Respondent 2 (21 February 2011).

[133]Interview with SOH Respondent 5 (20 July 2011).

[134]Interview with LP Respondent 4 (Samoa, 2 March 2011).

Sunday, also meet periodically to discuss church activities and the spiritual development of its members.

In the absence of available social media and modern forms of communication in the village, dissemination of information is by word of mouth. Paperwork such as information papers and issue papers may be disseminated at the village organisation meetings. In addition, the objectives and background to law reform inquiries may be explained and presented to the village organisations by a few officers and not necessarily the full consultation team of the State. The village must be given a time frame to discuss the issues papers in their meetings and develop their own responses without the influence of the state, before those responses are collected by the state at a later agreed date, for review and any public consultation.

Involving the village and church structures reduces the time and expenses on public advertisement, disseminating the relevant papers, travel and accommodation costs and several public consultations. If the village community is given the requisite information and allowed to develop village responses in their own time and space, the state may need only one public consultation or may even find the above approach sufficient for the purposes of consultation.

Law reform projects that are inclusive of village organisations also serve a second very important purpose. They create a sense of ownership of laws on the part of the villagers.[135] This encourages partnerships that work towards accommodating both systems in Samoa.[136] The benefits of involving the customary structures in law reform inquiries flow two ways and thus, such an approach must be taken advantage of.

6.5.2 Prioritising and Justifying Costs for Customary Reforms

The second way relates more to budget management policies is to prioritise reforms that impact on customs and provide convincing arguments why they should receive funding. The costs for those inquiries must be identified at an early stage and convincing evidence (and research) must be presented to Cabinet (or other funding agents) to justify how the costs will promote Samoan customs and protect its traditional structures.

The empirical data suggests that for reforms that impact significantly on the customs of Samoa, funding is justified to meet public consultation expenses.[137] For example, reforms relating to kinship, marriage, children and customary landholding; simply because of their nature require more consultations, and thus costs, than

---

[135] Interview with MOP Respondent 3 (Samoa, 11 January 2011).
[136] Interview with LP Respondent 2 (Samoa, 21 February 2011).
[137] Interview with LP Respondent 3 (Samoa, 4 March 2011).

other law reform projects.[138] There are some inquiries which may not directly impact on customs[139] for example reforms on tax, insurance, international trade and policies. The relevant stakeholders are usually based in the urban area, in which case limited or no cultural protocols are required.[140]

Prioritising customary related law reform inquiries and identifying the expenses can be determined by the legal and the support staff of the SLRC. The report to Cabinet (or to another possible source) seeking funding must contain well supported arguments on how the costs are justified to advance and support inquiries impacting on customs. Arguably such inquiries require consultations with as much of the population as possible.

Proposals
An all-inclusive process involving the communities in public consultation and allowing them time and space to develop their own responses to law reform inquiries reduces costs and creates a sense of 'ownership of laws'. Guidelines on the use and dissemination of information are necessary to avoid any misinterpretation of the proposed reforms. The costs for reforms directly affecting customary laws must be prioritised as such inquiries will affect the majority of the population and its customary basis.

6.6 Local Jurisprudence: Customary Law as the Basis of Common Law

A further response to the challenges of legal pluralism advocated in this book is the development of a local Samoan jurisprudence. In an independent country like Samoa, where 96% of the people are indigenous Samoans practising customary law, customs must be the primary basis upon which common law is founded.[141]

All jurisdictions have their own jurisprudence, but in Samoa where there are pull and push factors against customs and laws, developing a Samoan jurisprudence is significant to the complexities of pluralism. This jurisprudence must recognise the relevance and importance of customs in the legal system of Samoa. This is supported by the literature; the rules and principles of common law must rest on customs, and the common law is best understood and developed when it is regarded as a system of customary law.[142] As discussed in Chap. 2, a local jurisprudence

---

[138] Powles (2005), p. 411.
[139] Interview with LP Respondent 3 (Samoa, 4 March 2011).
[140] Interview with GEC Respondent 2 (Samoa, 11 March 2011).
[141] Interviews in Samoa with: GCE Respondent 1 (19 January 2011); MOP Respondent 1 (22 December 2010).
[142] Aleck, 7:137.

must be backed by doctrine and philosophy[143]; unfortunately the lack of resources and commitment by the legal professions are barriers to the development of the Pacific Islands' local jurisprudences.[144]

A local jurisprudence is viable given the following local developments. A judicial workshop involving both the formal court judiciary and the LTC judges has taken place and funding is sought for follow up sessions. This workshop provided the opportunity for judges to share thoughts on the application of the Constitution and state law in the formal courts and the customary laws in the LTC. The Ministry of Justice in 2012 launched a legal database containing court judgments and Acts of Parliament.[145] The court decisions in *Taamale* and *Olomalu*[146] (discussed in Chap. 5) and *Samoa Public Trustee v Collins*[147] remain the leading cases on the relevance of customs in the modern state system. The Land and Titles Court of Samoa now requires parties to undergo a compulsory customary arbitration proceeding, and ADR practices and training are encouraged by the judiciary. The decisions of the Land and Titles Court are available to the public in electronic form.[148] The legal profession's 2014 Act requires the society to promote customs in the legal system. The staff of the SLRC and the state drafters have participated in training sessions, and plan to continue staff training on the Samoan oratory and language.

In relation to Parliament, as discussed above, there has been recent capacity building training for members of Parliament. The executive initiatives aim at strengthening village councils through legislative changes and periodic seminars for the village mayors. The Village Fono Act is undergoing major reviews to reaffirm the powers of the village councils, and to allow new powers to make village bylaws to promote the autonomy of the villages under the authority of the village councils. The customary laws of Samoa have survived many odds from the colonial times. It will remain a feature of Samoa's legal system into the unforeseeable future and therefore has to be addressed rather than ignored.

Proposal
The above factors are not significant developments but are preliminary steps towards building a Samoan jurisprudence. It is proposed that these current features

---

[143]Weisbrot (1988), pp. 1–5.

[144]Corrin and Paterson (2011), p. 9.

[145]Samoa Legal Information Institute (SamLII) www.samlii.org.

[146]*Taamale v Attorney-General* (Unreported, Court of Appeal of Samoa, Cooke, P, Casey and Bisson JJA, 18 August 1995) and *Olomalu v The Attorney-General* (1980–1993) WSLR 256 respectively.

[147]Reported in [1961] WSNZSC 1.

[148]This was made possible under an Australian funded 'Digitisation of Land and Titles Court Records Project' launched by the Ministry of Justice, Samoa in 2012. By June 2012, a total of 5,659 LTC court files had been scanned and the judiciary, court officers and the public had begun accessing the scanned files. See Samoa Law and Justice Sector Six Monthly Report 1 January – 30 June 2012, 2012. http://www.ausaid.gov.au/countries/pacific/samoa/Documents/law-justice-jan-june-2012.pdf.

be enhanced and encouraged further to allow for a Samoan common law rooted in the values underlying both customs and individual rights.[149] In the event of a conflict, individual rights may be considered to be aligned with customs. Although customs cannot be the basis of Samoa's legal system, it must be the basis upon which the Samoan common law is built.[150] The Samoan jurisprudence will be informed by a combination of the traditional and modern features of laws and legal systems having developed over time[151] assisted by a committed judiciary, a vigilant law society and the government to fund the necessary resources.[152]

6.7 Legislative Drafters and Draft Laws

The work of legislative drafters significantly impacts on the content of the laws in the statute books of Samoa. In the absence of qualified policy developers in Samoa and other Pacific Islands, the final draft law in form and in content is influenced largely by legislative drafters.

The following discussions suggest some ways to address the challenges for legislative drafters in a plural society. The empirical interviews and survey of Pacific drafters propose drafting practices suitable for Samoa. The viability of those proposals will be explored.

6.7.1 Pacific Specific Drafting and Law Reform Training

In response to the legal pluralism challenges faced by legislative drafters, a Pacific Islands specific training must be developed for Pacific drafters. Most of the current training is state based and offers no assistance on the challenges raised in Chap. 5 such as how to portray customs in the English language, or to draft in the English language to reflect a Samoan context. These challenges are not specific to Samoa but are experienced also by other Pacific Islands drafters.[153]

---

[149]These recommendations are supported by those in New Zealand's Law Commission report on accommodating customs and human rights in the Pacific. New Zealand Law Commission Study Paper 17, 2006, 242.

[150]Aleck, above n 142, 143. Aleck argues further that custom is the primary legitimate basis upon which the rules and principles of common law must rest, and that the common law tradition itself is best understood, employed and developed when it is regarded fundamentally as a system of customary law.

[151]Narokobi (1989), p. 15.

[152]Narokobi (1986), p. 226.

[153]Survey PL Drafter 8.

The proposal for professional training[154] specific for drafters in a plural society falls in line with the literature that encourages legal training to be more relevant to the customary circumstances of the Pacific Islands.[155] The state must promote drafting capacity that can draft laws applicable to the plural environment of the Pacific Islands.[156]

Legislative training must target drafting issues in plural Pacific societies and discourage the mainstream drafting from a state perspective. Legislative drafting training must address relevance to Pacific environments. Guidelines must be developed for drafters to maintain a conscious regard for customs in drafting laws. Such guidelines must form part of legislative drafting handbooks that guide legislative drafting such as Samoa's Legislative Drafting Handbook.

In addition, law reform training[157] must also target the customary circumstances of Samoa. There must be additional dialogue on how overseas law reform inquiry methods, legal policy formulation and law reform processes may be modified for relevance. It is pertinent that such training relates to the local realities of the Pacific Islands if it is to assist with law reform in the Pacific region.

6.7.2 Drafting in the Samoan Language, Legislative References, Context

Several suggestions were raised towards the practice of legislative drafting in Samoa by the empirical data. Firstly, laws must be drafted in the Samoan language as this depicts the Samoan meaning and nuances more accurately.[158] Secondly, in drafting provisions relating to customary matters, legislative sentences must not use specific language but instead use legislative references only.[159] Thirdly, in recognition of customary structures, drafters must recognise cultural structures in laws where they are workable, effective and appropriate. The customary system and the state system should not be considered separately but as part of one society in legislative drafting. Drafting instructions from the Ministry may require provisions that allow the state and the village councils to work together under a proposed law.

---

[154]For example, the workshops run by the Commonwealth Secretariat in collaboration with the Pacific Islands Forum Secretariat. Past workshops include 'Recognizing the need for skilled legislative drafters' (November 2006, Auckland NZ); the 'Pacific Legislative Drafters Forum' (26–28 June 2007, Vanuatu) and the 'Pacific Legislative Drafters Forum' (23–25 July 2012, Suva Fiji). The 2017 forum is held in Tonga 23–25 August 2017.

[155]Corrin (2006), pp. 171–186, 185.

[156]Nand (2008) http://wikieducator.org/images/3/37/PID_309.pdf.

[157]This includes workshops conducted by the Australian Law Reform Commission Agencies Conference (ALRAC) for the Pacific Islanders and other developing jurisdictions. See Weisbrot (2008).

[158]Interview with GCE Respondent 1 (Samoa, 19 January 2011).

[159]Interview with SOH Respondent 1 (Samoa, 8 April 2011).

6.7 Legislative Drafters and Draft Laws

In such cases, provisions can be drafted into legislation, empowering the state and the village councils to draw up village rules or bylaws to be administered by the village council. This is one of the recommendations made by the SLRC and which now forms part of the amendments in the Village Fono Bill 2016.

Although there is some unsubstantiated belief that the Samoan language is insufficient in literature and in grammar to develop legal terms,[160] the first proposal is possible given the following. The majority of legislative drafters are currently indigenous Samoans. The Samoan drafters and officials developing draft laws would be the first source and authority in the Samoan language. New Samoan expressions may be developed over time similar to the experiences of other jurisdictions where bi-lingual drafting is now the norm.[161] Drafters should be bold to draft in Samoan and take time to improve on those Samoan drafts. With regards to written sources, one source of Samoan words already commonly used in Samoan legislation is the set of glossaries of the Translation and Interpretation Division of the Office of the Clerk of the Legislative Assembly, Samoa.[162] This Division has over the years developed their own glossaries of Samoan words to translate the English version of draft Bills into the Samoan text. A second possible source of Samoan expressions which most Samoans are familiar with is 'O le Tusi Paia' or 'The Holy Bible in Samoan'. This has been revised over the years[163] since the first missionaries arrived in Samoa in 1830.[164] Samoa is predominantly a Christian country[165] and 'O le Tusi Paia' is commonly used and is generally readily accessible in most if not all families in Samoa. A third possible authority of Samoan words is the recently set up Samoan Language Commission,[166] established to lead the re-building and strengthening of the Samoan language. There are also helpful Samoan Dictionaries[167] which could be referred to where needed.

To promote the use of the Samoan language in Samoa's laws, laws must be first drafted in the Samoan language. The drafting of laws primarily in the Samoan language has not been attempted ever before, although there are discussions on its feasibility. A pilot study to test this must be undertaken as the Samoan language would more effectively portray Samoan customs in text. Drafting Bills first in the

---

[160]Interview with SOH Respondent 3 (Samoa, 4 April 2011).

[161]Yen (2010), pp. 65–69 http://www.calc.ngo/sites/default/files/paper/Yen_Apr2010.pdf.

[162]Office of the Clerk of the Legislative Assembly Corporate Plan 2013–2015, 27 http://www.palemene.ws/new/wp-content/uploads/Document/OCLA_Strategic_Corporate_Plan_21_Mar_2013.pdf.

[163]Revised editions include, 'O le Tusi Paia, O le Feagaiga Tuai ma le Feagaiga Fou' *The Bible Society in the South Pacific*, 1969.

[164]World Council of Churches, *Congregation Christian Church in Samoa*, https://www.oikoumene.org/en/member-churches/congregational-christian-church-in-samoa.

[165]Samoa Bureau of Statistics Population and Housing Census Analytical Report, 2011, 25.

[166]*Samoan Language Commission Act 2014* (Samoa). The Act declares the Samoan language an official language for Samoa. It establishes a Samoan Language Commission to carry out consultation on the 'Samoan language'.

[167]Pratt (2015), Semisi (2010).

Samoan language may encourage Members of Parliament to debate on the Samoan version of draft Bills. As alluded to in Chap. 5, currently, all parliamentary proceedings are in the Samoan language, but reference is made to the English version. Under the Acts Interpretation Act (2011) Samoa,[168] the English and Samoan versions of Acts are equally authoritative. In the event of an inconsistency the English version prevails, unless the original draft of the Act was in the Samoan language. Developing the first draft Bill in the Samoan language would therefore allow arguments in favour of the Samoan version, and require the courts to consider that perhaps the intention of the Samoan Parliament was best portrayed in the Samoan language.

The second proposal is already a reality in Samoa as observed by legislative drafters and academic scholars in Samoa.[169] As observed by the empirical data, to date, it is not customs that have been incorporated in legislation but only selected aspects of customary law.[170] Drafting customary principles and practices into laws rather than the specifics of customs is supported and achievable and there are existing examples of such in statutory provisions.[171] This practice is also within the scope of the Constitution.

The third proposal is in line with Ntumy's suggestion to broaden the jurisdiction of customary laws where they are recognised in written laws,[172] using examples such as the incorporation of customary groups to conduct business and requiring their use of ethical principles. Empowering village councils to make bylaws and thereby becoming part of the administration of the law system of Samoa has been successfully implemented in a number of pieces of legislation as discussed earlier.

6.7.3 Review of Draft Laws for Customary Compliance

A further response to drafting difficulties proposed by the empirical data is to require all draft laws to undergo a customary analysis[173] in addition to the gender and constitutional vetting. This is supported by the empirical data.[174] The proposal

---

[168] Section 11.

[169] Email from LP Respondent 6 to Lalotoa Mulitalo, Tuesday 21 June 2011.

[170] Interview with SOH Respondent 3 (Samoa, 4 April 2011).

[171] For example, the term 'village service requirements' is not defined in the Electoral Act 1963 (s 5(3)). This is appropriate as each Samoan village will have different interpretations, influenced by their village protocols.

[172] Ntumy (1995), p. 12.

[173] Interviews in Samoa with: GCE Respondent 1 (19 January 2011); LP Respondent 3 (4 March 2011).

[174] Interviews in Samoa with: MOP Respondent 1 (22 December 2010); MOP Respondent 2 (4 January 2011); MOP Respondent 4 (7 January 2011); MOP Respondent 6 (24 December 2010); MOP Respondent 3 (11 January 2011); MOP Respondent 5 (11 January 2011).

is necessary if customs are to be reflected in the formal laws of Samoa.[175] The empirical data is supported by the Pacific drafters who shared similar views in that laws must be reviewed against traditional concepts,[176] and the cultural and social makeup of the local realities.[177] Draft laws that impact on customs must be reviewed against the input of traditional leaders particularly on reforms that impact on customary land, conservation and environment issues.[178] In a similar manner, New Zealand requires new or amended legislation to comply with the principles of the Treaty of Waitangi 1840, which recognises Maori ownership of their lands, forests, fisheries and other possessions.[179]

Ideally, reviews must be carried out by properly constituted bodies. The New Zealand Legislation Advisory Committee Guidelines[180] can be used as a model in developing Guidelines that are relevant to Samoa. The New Zealand guidelines require answers to questions such as: is there a possibility of conflict between customs and the legislation? Are there any customary rights and interests affected by the legislation recognised at common law? The review team for Samoa's draft laws must have knowledge in both customary matters and state laws. To avoid having to establish a new setup and incur more costs, it is proposed that the Advisory Board of the SLRC (for customary expertise) and the drafters of the staff of the Attorney-General (legal input) constitute the body tasked with the review of draft laws of Samoa for customary compliance.

Proposals

It is proposed that the Pacific Islands create an environment in which Pacific specific legislative drafting training is available to new and future drafters. In addition, local trainers must work in collaboration with overseas trainers to make the current available training more relevant to the local environment, in particular on drafting laws that impact on customs. Drafting legislation in the local language first is encouraged to replace the traditional practices of drafting draft Bills in the English language first. When incorporating customs in laws, this must be through legislative references rather than a codification of customs. Where policy instructions allow, customary institutions may be included as part of the overall administrators of a law to broaden the application of customary laws. Finally, it is proposed that the Advisory Board and the Legislative drafting team of the Office of the Attorney-General be tasked with the review of draft laws for customary compliance.

---

[175]Interviews in Samoa with: LP Respondent 3 (4 March 2011); LP Respondent 1 (15 March 2011); LP Respondent 4 (2 March 2011); Email from LP Respondent 6 to Lalotoa Mulitalo, 21 June 2011.

[176]Survey PL Drafter 8 (Fiji, 25 July 2012).

[177]Survey PL Drafter 1 (Fiji, 25 July 2012); Survey PL Drafter 10 (Fiji, 25 July 2012).

[178]Survey PL Drafter 11 (Fiji, 25 July 2012).

[179]Ministry of Justice of New Zealand, Legislation Advisory Committee Guidelines, 2001 http://www2.justice.govt.nz/lac/doc/LAC_Guidelines_Index.pdf 6.

[180]Ibid.

6.8 Summary of Responses to Legal Pluralism

From the above discussion, this book proposes the following overall summary of how specific legal pluralism challenges may be addressed. To ensure access to justice, the state must create public awareness of state laws and individual rights in the villages. The state must remove or reduce the cost of laws and make court decisions accessible to the public in both official languages, the Samoan and English languages. This is the first step towards minimising the conflicts between customary laws and state laws.

Judicial training is required in four areas. The first is in to address the unenforceability of the decisions of the courts in the villages. The second is to identify when customs may be applicable and relevant in court proceedings. Thirdly is to develop expertise on alternative dispute resolution and to encourage ADR over adjudication and further, and the judges of the LTC must undertake training on individual rights and the Constitution. A judicial clause must be inserted in the Constitution to empower all courts to consider customs in court proceedings. Professional ethics and court procedures must be developed with reference to Samoa's customary environment, not only to encourage a better understanding of the legal structures of Samoa but also to remind the formal courts that they operate in a customary environment, and as such their decisions must be made accordingly.

Professional training for Parliamentarians on law making must include training on developing laws in a customary environment. Handbooks providing guidelines on a member's duties to the village and constituencies; relaxing the onerous Standing Orders for introducing a private members bill; and making legislative drafters and legal services available to Members are strongly supported.

Professional training is required for the legal profession, to encourage the maintenance of the rule of law to promote Samoan custom and traditions. Samoan language and cultural protocols training is necessary for the SLRC legal staff and all lawyers involved in developing law reform. Finally, the SLRC staff must also attend conferences and engage themselves in training on quality research to inform law reform projects.

It is proposed that the State set up a Committee to consider collecting and recording Samoa's customary practices (adopting Namibia's definition of 'self-stating' of customary laws), to guide the work of the state legal system. Unless there is such a document, customs continue to be largely ignored. The project must allow for periodic reviews and updates.

The state must continue with legislative amendments to the Village Fono Act to as much as possible; produce an acceptable definition of the customary powers of the village councils and the scope of the traditional penalties they may impose. Formal education must be driven by the State for a more educated population to facilitate understanding of laws and the legal system. Current village and State partnerships must be strengthened and encouraged further to drive law reform that is relevant and suitable for the Samoan society.

To strengthen the partnerships between the State and the villages, the villages may consider appointing village mayors on more modern criteria. A cultural and modern village mayor is more likely to engage the villages in law reform. Further, the villages must be encouraged and assisted in developing village rules or bylaws in line with the Constitution.

Involving the village organisations in law reform consultations has several benefits. It can reduce costs of consultation and ensure wider village participation. More importantly, village involvement allows the communities to have 'ownership of laws', having contributed to and participated in the law reform process.

There are two ways in which to manage budget constraints. First is to engage the assistance of the villages and second, reforms directly affecting custom must be flagged to be given preference funding as opposed to reforms that do not. This is justifiable as customary reforms affect the majority of the population whereas others impact on only a portion.

It is possible to develop a local jurisprudence for Samoa; however, the success of getting this off the ground depends entirely on a committed judiciary and active legal profession. It is proposed that in developing a local Samoan jurisprudence, the judiciary builds a Samoan common law rooted in the values underlying both customs and individual rights. In the event of a conflict, individual rights may be considered to be aligned with customs.

Finally, the practice of legislative drafting, like all other legal fields, must apply drafting styles capable of developing laws suitable to a plural society. Professional training must target the specific needs of Pacific drafters. Drafting laws in the Samoan language as a first draft is encouraged to develop the Samoan language in legislation. Parliament must make more use of the Samoan version of Bills in parliamentary debate. It is also recommended that where customs are to be reflected in legislation, the method of incorporation by references be adopted rather than a codification of customary laws. Policies that include the customary structures as part of the administrators of a reform must be encouraged. Finally, it is proposed that the Advisory Board of the SLRC and the legislative drafting team of the Office of the Attorney-General be tasked with the review of draft laws for customary compliance. The final chapter proposes a suitable law reform process for Samoa, drawn from the above findings.

References

Amosa MLTU (1999 & 2002) Fausaga o lauga Samoa: Vaega 1 & 2. National University of Samoa

Atonio M (1992) Palefuiono. Tofa Enterprises

Bowler S (2010) Private members' bill in the UK Parliament: is there an electoral connection? J Legis Stud 16(4):476–494

Care JC, Haller L (2004) In harmony or out of tune? Is advocates immunity an appropriate principle in common law countries? J South Pac Law 8(2)

Commonwealth Secretariat (2005) Law reform agencies: their role and effectiveness. Paper by the Commonwealth Secretariat, Accra, Ghana

Corrin J, Paterson D (2011) Introduction to South Pacific law, 3rd edn. Palgrave Macmillan, p 9

Corrin J (2006) Finding the right balance in plural systems: training lawyers in the South Pacific. J Commonw Law Legal Educ 4(2):171–186, 185

Davies E (2005) The role of private members' bills'. Political Q 28(1):32–39

Efi TATTTTT (2008) Talanoaga ma Ga'opo'a. Government Printery Samoa 12
Epiphany A (1991) Codification of customary law: a mission impossible? In: Osinbajo Y, Kalu AU (eds) Towards a restatement of customary law. Federal Ministry of Justice Lagos, p 289
Government of Samoa (2012) Strategy for the development of Samoa 2012–2016, 11
Grenfell L (2006) Legal pluralism and the rule of law in Timor Leste. Leiden J Int Law 19(305):337
Hinz MO (2011) Traditional authorities, custodians of customary law development? In: Fenrich J, Galizzi P, Higgins TE (eds) The future of African customary law. Cambridge, pp 153, 155
Kirby M (2003) The ALRC: a winning formula. Remarks at the rededication of the Michael Kirby Library of the ALRC
Le Tagaloa AF (1997) O le Faasinomaga. Lamepa Press, Alafua
Marsh H, Marsh D (2002) Tories in the killing fields? The fate of private members' bills in the 1997 Parliament. J Legis Stud 8(1):91–112
Mgbako C, Baehr KS (2011) Engaging legal dualism, paralegal organizations and customary law in Sierra Leone and Liberia. In: Fenrich J, Galizzi P, Higgins TE (eds) The future of African customary law. Cambridge, p 186
Ministry of Education, Sports and Culture Samoa (1997) Samoa Ne'i Galo: Lest we forget, vols 1–7. Commercial Printers Limited, Samoa
Narokobi B (1986) In search of a Melanesian jurisprudence. In: Sack P, Minchin E (eds) Legal pluralism, proceedings of the Canberra Law Workshop VII. Australian National University, p 226
Narokobi B (1989) The black islands, Melanesia – Melanesia jurisprudence. In: Crocombe R, May J, Roache P (eds) Lo bilong yumi yet - law and custom in Vanuatu. Melanesian Institute for Pastoral Socio-Economic Service and the University of the South Pacific
New Zealand Law Commission (2006) Converging currents: custom and human rights in the pacific, study paper, 17, p 242
Ntumy M (1995) The dreams of a Melanesian jurisprudence. In: Aleck J, Jackson R (eds) Customs at the crossroads. UPNG Law Faculty, p 12
Ochich GO (2011) The withering province of customary law in Kenya: a case of design or indifference. In: Fenrich J, Galizzi P, Higgins TE (eds) The future of African customary law. Cambridge, 153, 126
Office of the Attorney-General Samoa (2008) Samoa Law and Justice Sector Plan 2008–2012
Powles G (2005) The challenge of law reform in Pacific Islands states. In: Opeskin B, Weisbrot D (eds) The promise of law reform. Federation Press, p 411
Pratt G (2015) A Samoan Dictionary: English and Samoan, and Samoan and English: with a Short Grammar of the Samoan Dialect. United States
Salman K (2006) Codification and restatement of customary law in Africa; the journey so far. In: Borokini AA (ed) Kogi reading in law. Stebak Books & Publishers, Akure
Samoa Bureau of Statistics (2011) Population and Housing Census Analytical Report 25
Samoa Law Reform Commission (2012) Village Fono Act 1990 Report No. 09/12
Samoa Observer Staff (2012a) 1 million less dogs in Samoa. Samoa Observer 30 July
Samoa Observer Staff (2012b) A first for Parliament. Samoa Observer 30 November
Samoa Observer Staff (2013) Primary pupils question the law. Samoa Observer 29 March
Schultz E (2008) Alaga'upu Fa'aSamoa, Samoan proverbial expressions, 3rd edn. Pasifika Press, NZ
Semisi MP (2010) Tusi'upu Samoa: the Samoan Dictionary of Papalii Dr Semisi. Little Island Press, Auck, NZ
Sharma A (2006) Customary law and received law in the Federated States of Micronesia. J South Pac Law 10(1)
Supreme Court of Queensland (2005) Equal treatment benchbook. Supreme Court of Queensland Library, Brisbane, p 105
Tamanaha BZ (1989–1990) A proposal for the development of a system of indigenous jurisprudence in the Federated States of Micronesia. Hastings Int Comp Law Rev 13:72

Tavae TT (2005) Fa'afaigofieina fa'alupega o Samoa. Pasifika Education Centre
Tupufia L (2013) Afega launches book of bylaws. Samoa Observer (Samoa) 31 March
Tuvale T, Faletoese TE, Kirisome (1981) O le tusi o faalupega (Booklet of Genealogies). Malua Printing Press, Apia
Twining W (1963) The restatement of African customary law: a comment. J Mod Am Stud 1(2):221
Weisbrot D (1988) Papua New Guinea's indigenous jurisprudence and the legacy of colonialism. Univ Hawaii Law Rev 10(1)
Weisbrot D (2008) Opportunities for regional cooperation in law reform. Paper presented at the Australasian Law Reform Agencies Conference, Vanuatu, 11 September
Zorn JC (1990) The Federated States of Micronesia. In: Ntumy M (ed) South Pacific Islands legal systems. University of Hawaii Press, p 470
Zorn JC, Care JC (2002) Everything old is new again: The Underlying Law Act of Papua New Guinea. LAWASIA J:61–91

Legislation

Canine Control Act 2013 (Samoa)
Community Justice Act 2008 (Samoa)
Constitution of the Independent State of Samoa 1962 (Samoa)
Constitution of the Republic of Vanuatu 1980 (Vanuatu)
Customary Land Tribunal Act (Vanuatu) ch 271
Customs Recognition Act 2000 (Solomon Islands)
District Court Act 1969 (Samoa)
Electoral Act 1963 (Samoa)
Fisheries Act 1988 (Samoa)
Internal Affairs Act 1995 (Samoa)
Judicature Ordinance 1961 (Samoa)
Land and Titles Amendment Act (No 14) (Samoa)
Land and Titles Court Act 1981 (Samoa)
Lawyers and Legal Practice Act 2014 (Samoa)
Legislative Assembly Powers and Privileges Ordinance 1960 (Samoa)
Parliamentary Pension Scheme Act 1998 (Samoa)
Parliamentary Under-Secretaries Act 1988 (Samoa)
Pohnpei Constitution (Pohnpei, Federated State of Micronesia)
Standing Orders of the Parliament of Samoa 2006 (Samoa)
Samoan Language Commission Act 2014 (Samoa)
Underlying Law Act 2000 (Papua New Guinea)
Village Fono Act 1990 (Samoa)
Waste Management Act 2010 (Samoa)
Water Resources Management Act 2008 (Samoa)
Young Offenders Act 2007 (Samoa)

Case Law

Alfons v FSM 5 FSM Intrm.402 (App. 1992)
Lufilufi v Hunt (Unreported, Supreme Court of Samoa, Vaai, Nelson JJ, 26 April 2011)

Mauga v Leituala (Unreported, Court of Appeal of Samoa, Cooke, P, Casey and Bisson JJA, 4 March 2005)
Olomalu v The Attorney-General (1980-1993) WSLR 256
Samoa Public Trustee v Collins [1961] WSNZSC 1
Taamale v Attorney-General (Unreported, Court of Appeal of Samoa, Cooke, P, Casey and Bisson JJA, 18 August 1995)

Online Databases

Ministry of Justice of New Zealand (2001) Legislation Advisory Committee Guidelines. Legislation Advisory Committee http://www2.justice.govt.nz/lac/doc/LAC_Guidelines_Index.pdf 6

Nand N (2008) Legislative drafting, distance education and its contribution to good governance in the Pacific. Paper for the Fifth Pan-Commonwealth Forum on Open Learning, July London, 13-17 July http://wikieducator.org/images/3/37/PID_309.pdf

New South Wales Office of Parliamentary Counsel (2011) Manual for the drafting of non-government legislation 10th ed. http://www.pco.nsw.gov.au/corporate/man-ngd.pdf

Office of the Clerk of the House of Representatives, New Zealand (2011) Effective House Membership, A Guide for Members of Parliament 15, 16 http://www.parliament.nz

Office of the Clerk of the Legislative Assembly (2013-2015) Corporate Plan 27 http://www.palemene.ws/new/wp-content/uploads/Document/OCLA_Strategic_Corporate_Plan_21_Mar_2013.pdf

Pacific Judicial Development Programme (2003) Land and Titles Court Benchbook Samoa http://www.fedcourt.gov.au/__data/assets/pdf_file/0018/18711/The-Land-and-Titles-Court-2003-English.pdf

Pacific Judicial Development Programme (2009) District Court Bench Book, Samoa http://www.paclii.org/pjdp/files/2011/07/District-Court-of-Samoa-Benchbook-2009.pdf

Pacific Judicial Development Programme (2011) Kiribati Code of Judicial Conduct cl 4.2 http://www.paclii.org/pjdp/

Pacific Judicial Development Programme (2011) Codes of Judicial Conduct Completion Report. http://www.paclii.org/pjdp/

Pacific Judicial Development Programme (2012) Programme Overview. http://www.paclii.org/pjdp/

Parliament of Samoa official website http://www.parliament.gov.ws/

Pillans K (2011) Final Report, Codes of Judicial Conduct in the Pacific, Pacific Judicial Development Programme, Appendix 2 http://www.fedcourt.gov.au/__data/assets/pdf_file/0006/18699/CoJC-Completion-Report-2011.pdf

Samoa Law and Justice Sector (2012) Six Monthly Report 1 January – 30 June 2012. http://www.ausaid.gov.au/countries/pacific/samoa/Documents/law-justice-jan-june-2012.pdf

Samoa Legal Information Institute (SamLII) official website www.samlii.org

Samoa Law Reform Commission (2016) List of Conference/Seminars/Workshops and Trainings attended by SLRC http://www.samoalawreform.gov.ws

The Bible Society in the South Pacific (1969) O le Tusi Paia, O le Feagaiga Tuai ma le Feagaiga Fou. World Council of Churches, Congregation Christian Church in Samoa https://www.oikoumene.org/en/member-churches/congregational-christian-church-in-samoa

United Nations Rule of Law (2002) The Bangalore Principles of Judicial Conduct. http://www.unrol.org/doc.aspx?d=2328

Yen T (2010) Bi-lingual drafting in Hong Kong. CALC - The Loophole 65-69 http://www.calc.ngo/sites/default/files/paper/Yen_Apr2010.pdf

Chapter 7
A Suitable Law Reform Framework for Pluralist Countries

Contents

7.1	Introduction		170
7.2	A Suitable Law Reform Process for Samoa		171
	7.2.1	Before the Terms of Reference (TOR)	171
		7.2.1.1 Step 1	171
	7.2.2	After a TOR Is Received by the SLRC	171
		7.2.2.1 Step 2: Research and Consultation	171
		7.2.2.2 Step 3: Issues Paper	173
		7.2.2.3 Step 4: Research and Consultation	173
		7.2.2.4 Step 5: Final Report with Recommendations	174
		7.2.2.5 Step 6: Report Tabled in Parliament	174
	7.2.3	The Draft Bill Process	175
		7.2.3.1 Legislative Drafting	175
		7.2.3.2 Vetting for Customary Compliance	175
		7.2.3.3 Passage Through Parliament	175
	7.2.4	Law Reform Process of Law Reform Agents	176
		7.2.4.1 Commissions of Inquiry, Ombudsman, NGOs	176
7.3	Legislative Reforms and Guides		176
	7.3.1	Local Jurisprudence	177
	7.3.2	Judicial Clause and Guides	177
		7.3.2.1 Constitutional Amendment	177
		7.3.2.2 Code of Judicial Conduct	178
		7.3.2.3 Court Benchbooks	178
	7.3.3	Reference Guide to Customary Practices	178
	7.3.4	Parliament Guides and Procedures	179
		7.3.4.1 Guide for Members of Parliament	179
		7.3.4.2 Standing Orders of Parliament	179
		7.3.4.3 State Handbooks	179
	7.3.5	Statutory Obligation to Consider Customs	180
7.4	Conclusions		181
	7.4.1	Systematic Studies on Law Reform	181
	7.4.2	The Challenges of Legal Pluralism for Law Reform in Samoa	181
	7.4.3	Taking Advantage of Pluralism	182
	7.4.4	Emerging Trends	183
		7.4.4.1 A Winning Model?	183
		7.4.4.2 Incorporation by Reference	183
		7.4.4.3 State Initiatives that Accommodate Pluralism	184

7.5 Future Research 184
    7.5.1 Constitutional Review 184
    7.5.2 Local Jurisprudence 185
    7.5.3 Pacific Island Specific Research 185
    7.5.4 Samoa's Constitutional Compliant Village Rules 185
    7.5.5 Follow up Research on Legal Pluralism and Law Reform in Samoa 186
    7.5.6 Pacific Research Methodologies 187
    7.5.7 Professional Training that Addresses Customs 187
References 188

7.1 Introduction

A suitable law reform process for Samoa must reflect the cultural context and the local realities of Samoa.[1] The unique features of each Pacific society determine the law reform process that is suitable for their needs. The most effective way to secure public acceptance of new laws or any change in laws is to gain the public's respect for the process.[2] A fitting law reform process requires a holistic effort from Parliament, the judiciary, the institutional law reform, law reform agents, the State and state agents, the legal profession, the village councils and traditional structures and the general public of Samoa. As the State is accountable for the country's development as a whole, it must lead the required changes through the relevant constitutional offices, state ministries and agencies.

The holistic approach proposed in Sect. 7.2 of the chapter is discussed under four sections. Section 7.2.1 looks at what the Samoa Law Reform Commission (SLRC) must meet before a law reform terms of reference is received by the Commission. The SLRC currently operates a 6 step framework for every law reform terms of reference received.[3] Section 7.2.2 explores and recommends the incorporation of specific actions and considerations that best accommodate customs into the same six step process. After Parliament endorses that a draft Bill be drafted from the recommendations of the Commission, Sect. 7.2.3 inspects the draft Bill process and its passage through Parliament. Section 7.2.4 ends Sect. 7.2 by exploring how other law reform agents discussed in Chap. 5 may take account of legal pluralism in their respective processes. Sect. 7.3 offers practical ways through which the above proposals may be achieved, suggesting draft provisions for Judicial Codes and State Handbooks. Sect. 7.4 provides conclusions and Sect. 7.5 suggests areas for further research to continue discourse into achieving a balanced consideration of both the customary laws and the state laws in the process of law reform in the South Pacific.

---

[1] Paterson et al. (2008).
[2] Powles (2005), p. 420.
[3] Samoa Law Reform Commission official website.

7.2 A Suitable Law Reform Process for Samoa

7.2.1 Before the Terms of Reference (TOR)

7.2.1.1 Step 1

The following are suggestions on activities to be undertaken before a TOR is received by the SLRC. The importance of an informed and educated public cannot be over emphasised. Ongoing public awareness of state laws is vital for progressive reforms. Community programmes must run parallel with state efforts to develop reforms that take account of customs. This collaborative approach increases opportunities to develop an understanding of law reform. Community awareness of state laws and individual rights entrenched in the Constitution is crucial for a whole of society approach to law reform. Parliamentary laws and court decisions must be more readily available to the public than they currently are, in the Samoan language. The state ministry responsible for villages (Internal Affairs) and the Ombudsman (under its human rights functions) are some of the state offices best placed to drive awareness programmes.

When a Ministry decides legislation is necessary to give effect to state policies, it must look at the Cabinet Handbook on the requirements for proposed law, for guidance. This Handbook must require the Ministry to formulate their policies with a conscious regard to custom. Not all reforms impact directly on traditional structures and customary practices, such as those relating to foreign relations and taxation. The documentation forming part of the proposal to Cabinet to endorse legislation that impacts on customs must contain firstly an explanation on the policies to be translated into legislation, and secondly how these policies have addressed customary considerations. As discussed in Chap. 5, the SLRC receives all TORs from Cabinet. After Cabinet endorses a proposal for review, it issues Terms of Reference to the SLRC to undertake law reform.

7.2.2 After a TOR Is Received by the SLRC

7.2.2.1 Step 2: Research and Consultation

7.2.2.1.1 Doctrinal Research

Having received a TOR, the Commission embarks on researching the subject matter/s of the project and prepares the material for public consultations. In addition to the conventional doctrinal research typical for law reform inquiries,[4] the SLRC must base its recommendations on research on local primary material. It is useful to

---

[4] For example, as discussed in some of the scholarly work referred to in Partington (2005), p. 136.

develop databases for example of all Supreme Court and Court of Appeal judgments in which the courts dealt with customary issues, a second database on all decisions of the Land and Titles Court where matters were the subject of judicial review proceedings in the formal courts, and a third database for all legislation of Samoa, with a sub-database for legislation that impacts on customary practices. There should be ongoing analysis of firstly cases as they are decided and added into the relevant database, and secondly analysis of legislation as it is passed, particularly those that purport to protect customs. The discussions on the 17 Acts of Parliament analysed in Chap. 5 provide a useful analysis to include in this database. A well-equipped library and reliable internet facilities are vital for both doctrinal legal research and socio-legal research particularly to access the research and legal websites of other Commonwealth countries.

7.2.2.1.2 Socio-Legal Research

To take account of Samoa's customary basis, the Samoa Law Reform Commission's socio-legal research should include historical analyses of the social and political context of Samoa.[5] This includes the study of the history, the ideologies and philosophies of Samoa as a society, the *faamatai*, village governance, rules of succession and genealogical links of villages and districts. The Samoan texts referred to in Chap. 6 would prove useful with this contextual information. As alluded to in Chap. 6, the SLRC should be involved in research and presentations at local conferences in partnership with the local university, to develop useful and relevant local literature to inform law reform issues papers and inquiries.

In the preliminary consultations, the SLRC must approach the relevant stakeholders and interest groups seeking views on the subject of the inquiry. At this early stage in the process, it is important to identify *matais* (who can be from other state Ministries such as the Ministry of Women, Social and Community Development, the Internal Affairs Division) who can lead the consultation in the villages. The involvement of relevant village councils and village organisations such as the youth group, the women's committees, and the church leaders should be considered at this stage.

The analysis of preliminary consultation should determine how the law reform inquiry impacts on customs, what areas of customs, and the level of consultation that may be required. As lack of funding is a reality, the SLRC must be strategic in seeking funding for customary related inquiries. For example, the SLRC may prioritise such reforms and provide sufficient evidence that the inquiry impacts on the core values of customs and therefore the funding sought is justified for an inquiry that is in the national interest as well as in the interests of justice.

---

[5]Ibid.

7.2.2.2 Step 3: Issues Paper

Laws and information on laws must be made available in both the Samoan and English languages. A notice informing the public on where the Issues Papers are available for collection may be published in the Samoa Observer[6] in both the English and Samoan languages. This is to cater for those who do not have access to the internet.

The Issues Paper stage must be fully utilized to raise potential issues arising firstly from placing or finding the inquiry in the context of the *fa'a Samoa*, and secondly where resulting reforms impact directly or indirectly on customs. This is the opportunity to raise questions and provide feedback on how customs and any possible reforms can be resolved, and these can be further consulted upon in Step 4.

7.2.2.3 Step 4: Research and Consultation

The doctrinal and socio-legal research considerations in Step 2 are applicable here. In addition to the above research, where the Commission considers that customary practices or rules should be incorporated in legislation, they may consider as part of their recommendations to Cabinet and Parliament, suitable approaches to the recognition of customs.[7] The preferred approaches include the 'specific or general forms of incorporation by reference' which avoids the need for precise definitions of customary laws. There are current examples of legislative and constitutional provisions to this effect found in other Pacific Islands. Other approaches include the translation of customary rules into formal laws to give them equivalent effect; and accommodating traditional or customary ways in legislation. For reasons discussed in Chaps. 2 and 4, the codification of customary laws is not recommended for Samoa.

As discussed in Chap. 6, the importance of involving the customary institutions in law reform consultation. The assistance of the village council, other village organisations and church leaders must be sought before this consultation. Arrangements can be made with the village councils on how they (village councils) may assist in disseminating issues papers and any other relevant documentation which will be referred to. All consultation documents must be in the Samoan language. Time must be given for the villagers to consider the issues raised by the inquiry and to formulate responses before the actual consultation. At the consultations a *matai* identified in step 2 must lead the consultation in a participatory *Talanoa* manner in the Samoan language to encourage active participation and public views. The SLRC must be able to relay the law reform objectives and issues in the Samoan language.

---

[6]The Samoa Observer is the most widely circulated local newspaper as discussed in Chap. 3.
[7]Australian Law Reform Commission Report (1986), p. 122.

A possible arrangement to take advantage of the stable village setting and the monthly meetings of the village organisations is for the Issues Papers to be disseminated by the village council to its village organisations. A time frame may be given for the village to discuss issues in the issues paper (either collectively under the village council guidance) or within individual village organisations. Each organisation may record its own responses in a report to be collected later by the SLRC. Similar arrangements may be used as preliminary steps before a wide scale consultation. In a tight frame inquiry, this can still be practised and the village's assistance may be sought to provide their views within a shorter period of time. Involving the village organisations in consultation may reduce costs, ensure more village participation and create a sense of ownership of laws.

7.2.2.4 Step 5: Final Report with Recommendations

In addition to the normal requisites of a Final Report, as proposed in Chap. 6, it must include a Customs Impact Report, if the policies and proposed laws have some customary implications. This report must inform the Parliament of any customary related issues raised in the Issues Paper and how those issues have been addressed. The final report must be available to the public, particularly those who were involved in consultation, in English and Samoan versions. This is in line with discussions in Chap. 6 where laws and law reform material in the Samoan language is promoted. Where the members of the public consulted consent to it,[8] their contributions should be acknowledged, and a reference made to how their input has been considered and used in the final report and recommendations. To maintain good relationships with the village respondents who participated in the reforms, it is good practice for the relevant state officers to send them written acknowledgments, which may also serve to inform of the next steps in the law reform process should the respondents wish to follow up on the reforms. This is an ethical practice,[9] which may sustain good relationships up to and beyond the implementation stage where inquiries result in legislation.

7.2.2.5 Step 6: Report Tabled in Parliament

A Final Report which recommends reforms that impact on customs must be tabled with the relevant supporting documentation, such as the Customs Impact Report, the record of the consultation output giving support to the recommendations and

---

[8]Consent must be sought as some consultation respondents may wish to remain anonymous particularly if the reform enquiries relate to controversial issues.

[9]As discussed in Chap. 3, one of the ethical principles of *Talanoa* is to maintain good relationships, this also applies to law reform consultations. It is important to maintain good relationships from the first meeting with those consulted to the end of the consultations and beyond, even after the completion of a law reform project.

any supporting literature found in Step 2. The SLRC officers must be prepared to be called in by any Parliamentary Committee that reviews the Report to make submissions or to explain the contents of the Report. The officers must be prepared to make cultural addresses at the opening and closing of the parliamentary committee sessions, and to make submissions in both the Samoan and English language.

7.2.3 The Draft Bill Process

7.2.3.1 Legislative Drafting

Following Cabinet and Parliament approval of the SLRC Final Report and the Customs Impact Report, the next step is to engage legislative drafters. In drafting legislation based on the SLRC's recommendations, the legislative drafter must also be informed of and utilise the Customs Impact Report. The drafter must ensure that legislative provisions do not contradict customary practices in addition to conventional best practices in legislative drafting. Where there are policy instructions that are likely to contradict customs at implementation, the SLRC may be consulted for a clarification of their recommendations and both parties work towards the best way the policies can be reflected in draft laws.

7.2.3.2 Vetting for Customary Compliance

As suggested in Chap. 6, before a Bill is submitted for Cabinet endorsement, it must undergo a customary compliance review, in addition to the procedural vetting for constitutional compliance and gender neutrality.[10] This should be carried out by selected members of the SLRC Advisory Board (for customary expertise) and the drafters of the staff of the Attorney-General (legal input). This is intended to make both the legal expertise (lawyers) and customary expertise (*matai* in the Advisory Committee) available for a balanced review of the reform.

7.2.3.3 Passage Through Parliament

When a Bill (including those from law reform inquiries) is tabled, the professional training proposed for members of Parliament discussed in Chap. 6 is relevant and comes into practice at this stage. As proposed there, it is important that professional training is available for Parliamentarians to enhance capacity to develop policy and pass laws relevant to the plural characteristics of Samoa. Select Committees must

---

[10] A point also strenuously argued Interview Respondent GCE Respondent 1 (Samoa, 19 January 2011).

encourage public consultations to be carried out in the Samoan language on a Samoan version of a Bill and in a Samoan conversation like manner such as in *Talanoa*.

The law reform process proposed above allows for a consistent, continuous and conscious consideration of customs at each step of the process of law reform. In the context of Samoa, such a process is necessary to ensure that reforms developed by Samoa's line ministries, the SLRC, the Samoan public (through public consultation), drafters, cabinet and Parliament give adequate regard to legal pluralism from policy development to parliamentary enacted laws.

7.2.4 Law Reform Process of Law Reform Agents

7.2.4.1 Commissions of Inquiry, Ombudsman, NGOs

Commissions of Inquiry (COI) are convenient for urgent inquiries in the national interest. As alluded to in Chap. 5, the Cabinet appears to favour COIs in law reform inquiries of a customary nature as opposed to the SLRC. However, COI's are costly exercises and in a small developing country, COI's are unaffordable. On this basis, the SLRC's capacity must be developed to investigate urgent inquiries and projects of a customary nature. If the law reform process proposed above is made available to the SLRC, it will increase the SLRC's capability to comply with its statutory objectives to promote customs and usages. More importantly, it will command faith and respect (of the SLRC and law reform) from the Samoan public. The office of the Ombudsman must have as part of the staff a lawyer to give legal advice and assistance in meeting its law reform functions under the empowering Act discussed in Chap. 5. The NGOs must employ or engage legal assistants to advise on the implications of State reforms before the NGOs take action as considered in Chap. 6. Opposition and support of a reform is then based on sound legal argument and may save costs to civil societies.

7.3 Legislative Reforms and Guides

The proposed law reform process can be strengthened by amendments and modifications made to the existing written laws and policies that currently govern duties and procedures of law reform institutions and agents. This section will be discussed in the following order, developing a local jurisprudence, strengthening the court system, parliamentary guides, State handbooks, and imposing a statutory obligation to take account of customs in the relevant laws.

7.3.1 Local Jurisprudence

Chapter 6 discussed some developments in Samoa's legal system that may be taken advantage of in building a Samoan jurisprudence. That chapter also sets out the requirements for a Samoan jurisprudence; it will not be explored further here other than to reiterate a few important factors. A local jurisprudence must be built on a common law system that is based upon customary laws.[11] Although customs cannot be the basis of Samoa's legal system, it can be the basis upon which Samoan common law is built.[12] All institutions of the legal system must acknowledge this goal and take responsibilities to achieve that goal.[13] They must also be empowered to achieve their individual objectives towards achieving that goal. One way of empowering the legal system is to strengthen the relevant sources of authority and rules of procedure. The next discussions provide some recommendations on how this may be achieved.

7.3.2 Judicial Clause and Guides

7.3.2.1 Constitutional Amendment

As discussed in Chap. 5, the formal courts lack jurisdiction on customary issues. Chapter 6 recommended that judges be given more opportunity to apply customs where appropriate, and reference was made to other Pacific Islands whose laws require the judiciary to take account of customs in court proceedings. As alluded to in Chap. 6, Samoa's Constitution should be amended to empower the courts to take account of Samoan customs in court proceedings, and to give due regard to the preamble of the Constitution. This can be achieved by inserting the following after article 81 of the Samoa's Constitution.

> 81A. *Judicial Guidance* – Subject to the provisions of this Constitution, customs must be taken into account in all courts of Samoa.

This advances the recognition of customs in court decisions and encourages the recognition of customs and usages as 'law' as a result of court judgments under Article 111 of the *Constitution of Samoa 1962* (Samoa). Other judicial guides such as codes and benchbooks must be developed in line with this provision.

---

[11] Supported in the New Zealand Law Commission Report (2006), p. 242.
[12] Aleck (1995), p. 137, 143.
[13] Narokobi (1989), p. 15.

7.3.2.2 Code of Judicial Conduct

Chapter 6 also proposed that the Code of Judicial Conduct scheduled to be developed for Samoa under the Pacific Judicial Development Programme should include references to ethics that are entrenched in Samoan customs. Samoa should adopt in this Code provisions similar to the Kiribati's Code of Judicial Conduct such as the following,

> Whatever a magistrate does he must do properly, according to the law and with respect for the customs and traditions of the people.[14]

7.3.2.3 Court Benchbooks

As suggested in Chap. 6, some features of the benchbook of the Supreme Court of Queensland[15] should be adopted in the Samoan benchbooks. It should include references to the customary society of Samoa, its village systems and village organisations, the use of two languages and specific socio-cultural factors. These inform not only the judiciary but also the users of the courts of Samoa. More importantly, it will facilitate a Samoan consciousness in the courtroom that this is the Samoan courts in operation and the judiciary, lawyers and litigants alike must apply the laws in the context of Samoa.

7.3.3 Reference Guide to Customary Practices

Chapter 6 explored the possibility of a judicial device in the form of a reference guide containing a record of agreed customary practices commonly used and applied in Samoa. This guide shall not have legislative status and must be subject to periodic review. As also stated in Chap. 6, the main objective is to have a guide for the use of the judiciary, the Parliament and the legal profession (SLRC staff and the legislative drafters). This proposal requires further research and studies, however there must be a physical form of a reference guide to customs, lest the importance of customary laws is only paid lip service without commitment and action.

---

[14] Pacific Judicial Development Programme, (2011) cl 4.2.
[15] Supreme Court of Queensland (2005).

7.3.4 Parliament Guides and Procedures

7.3.4.1 Guide for Members of Parliament

A possible model as discussed in Chap. 6 is 'A Guide for Members of Parliament' of New Zealand containing provisions on how individual members contribute to parliamentary functions.[16] This may be an express requirement in the 'Samoa Parliamentary Practice and Procedure Manual'. This Manual should have provisions requiring a member to continue village services to their villages[17] and constituencies such as explaining the laws to the villages and seeking input on tabled Bills during village meetings.[18] In addition, to require Parliament to consider customs in policy development, the said Manual should adopt a clause in line with the following,

> As far as is practicable and where it is not contrary to the Constitution, the Acts of Parliament must promote Samoan customs and traditions, enhance the social, cultural, economic and commercial development of Samoa and meet the needs of the government and the community.

7.3.4.2 Standing Orders of Parliament

As discussed in Chap. 6, the Legislative Assembly should facilitate the use of Private Members Bills (PMB) by relaxing the procedures for PMBs under the Standing Orders of Parliament.[19] Laws and policies initiated from within the villages should be encouraged and legislative drafting services should be made available to members to encourage the use of PMBs.

7.3.4.3 State Handbooks

7.3.4.3.1 Cabinet Handbook

The 2011 Cabinet Handbook must have express requirements for customs to be considered at the start and during the whole process of policy development. In that handbook, under the requirements headed 'Proposals Requiring Legislation',[20] the following should be inserted where appropriate,

---

[16] Office of the Clerk of the House of Representatives (New Zealand), 2011, 15, 16.

[17] This is a candidacy requirement under the electoral laws; see *Electoral Act 1963* (Samoa) s 5.

[18] Shields (1991). An existing Pacific Island source to consider is Vanuatu's Parliamentary Handbook, although there is no published material available on the strengths and weaknesses of this Handbook to date.

[19] *Standing Orders of Parliament 2006* (Samoa) O 115.

[20] Ministry of the Prime Minister and Cabinet (Samoa) (2011), pp. 33–34.

A Ministry or government agency seeking legislation must provide a Customs Impact Report as part of its proposal for legislation. This report must set out how the proposed legislation may impact on Samoa's custom and usages, if at all and how the Ministry or agency has addressed or proposes to address this.

7.3.4.3.2 Legislative Drafting Handbook of Samoa

To ensure that draft laws have regard to customs, this handbook must have provisions to this effect as part of its objectives. This can be done by inserting the following clause immediately after the heading '4.0 Preparations for Legislative Reform,'[21]

> As far as is practicable and where it is not contrary to the Constitution, all laws drafted for Samoa must promote Samoan customs and traditions, and enhance the social, cultural economic and commercial development of Samoa.

7.3.5 Statutory Obligation to Consider Customs

For a future Act of Parliament that empowers or imposes a law reform function, that law should have a provision requiring that body to promote Samoan customs and traditions in developing reforms. Such a provision is already part of the *Samoa Law Reform Commission Act 2008* (Samoa) and the *Lawyers and Legal Practice Act 2014* (Samoa).

The above recommendations are formulated to be realistic and implementable in the current environment of Samoa. Theoretical, costly and out of context proposals are unhelpful in developing suitable responses to the challenges of legal pluralism. The proposals require political support and a commitment from all areas of the legal system. The suggestions provide a path to achieving a balanced consideration of the customary legal system in the processes of the state legal system. Time, effort and funding must be put towards realistic proposals such as offered above designed specifically to cater for the local environment.[22]

---

[21] Office of the Attorney-General (Samoa) (2014), p. 13.

[22] Interview with SOH Respondent 5 (Samoa, 20 July 2011).

7.4 Conclusions

7.4.1 Systematic Studies on Law Reform

Existing scholarship suggests that there is a need for systematic studies on law reform in the South Pacific. The two overlapping legal frameworks 'legal pluralism' and 'law reform' have largely been investigated separately. This book is a response to the call for research on law reform. The study investigates law reform and legal pluralism together, arguing that the customary and state laws divide may be reduced by requiring those institutions, offices and officials with law reform functions to take account of custom in that law reform process. To obtain data from a Pacific perspective, a Pacific specific interview method *'Talanoa'* was employed for interviews carried out with Samoan respondents in Samoa, as discussed in Chap. 3. Other documentary data relied upon was obtained from the local government authorities, Parliament and local newspaper. The findings and outcomes of this study are therefore informed by the people and local authorities of the country of study.

7.4.2 The Challenges of Legal Pluralism for Law Reform in Samoa

The challenges of legal pluralism for law reform derive from both the customary system and the state system. Chapter 4 found the following as hindrances to law reform in Samoa. There is the presence of two conflicting legal philosophies in Samoa; the public has aspirations for customary laws to be the basis of Samoa's legal system and there is overwhelming support for customs to form part of Samoa's formal laws. Chapter 5 however found that customs are not entrenched nor given a priority in the law reform framework of the state. Rather, the current rules and processes promote state driven laws upholding individual rights while customary considerations are ignored. A number of factors attribute to this, the first being that there are insufficient systems in place to assist those with a law reform capacity[23] to give consideration to and promote customs in formal laws. Secondly, the constitutional provisions give little scope for the courts to apply customs; and further, the law making process rules in the Cabinet Handbook and the Legislative Drafting Handbook do not expressly require a mandatory consideration of customs in policy development or draft laws.

Chapter 6 explored suggested responses to the challenges raised in Chaps. 4 and 5. In essence, the gap between the village and the state must be removed. This can

---

[23] The Samoa Law Reform Commission, the judiciary, members of Parliament, the state ministries, the legal profession and other law reform agents such as the Ombudsman and NGOs discussed in this book.

be achieved by raising public awareness on state laws through community programmes. Professional training and seminars for all institutions and agents performing law reform functions must promote the recognition and application of customs in formal laws. Chapter 7 puts forward a recommended holistic approach involving both the customary and the state systems. The findings of Chaps. 4–6 are reviewed and synthesised to suggest specific recommendations on how the SLRC may best accommodate customs in its six step law reform process. An approach to law making must take account of both legal systems. Addressing pluralism through the process of law making is one way of responding to efforts to accommodate two co-existing and sometimes conflicting, legal systems.

7.4.3 Taking Advantage of Pluralism

As discussed in Chap. 4, generally the State cannot effectively carry out its policies and undertake effective law reform without the support of the traditional structures. In turn, the customary system is relying more on the State for full participation in the modern political, economic and legal systems. This interdependency is a positive force to be utilised and controlled[24] as reflected and encouraged in the law reform framework put forward above. Rather than viewing customs as a hindrance to law reform and development, the traditional village institutions can be effectively engaged to facilitate law reform and development. The strengths and limitations of each system allow them to be supplementary and accommodating in given circumstances.

Samoa's law reform process must be a pluralist approach, taking advantage of its local characteristics. There are two over-arching legal systems that need to be reconciled, as opposed to other societies which grapple with more complex issues of legal pluralism. Samoa is also a small society in land size and population, which practises two main languages. Although village rules differ in each of the 300 villages, the underlying values of the *faamatai*, which forms the basis of each village is understood by all Samoans. Perhaps this is the main feature that Samoa must fully take advantage of; it is united in its *faamatai*. As a customary basis, the *faamatai* complements the limitations of the state legal system and receives respect for it. This system keeps state domination and legal positivism at bay. The holistic law reform framework and the recommendations proposed in Sect. 7.2 are feasible with the support of the *faamatai* as most (if not all) holding the relevant positions of authority are *matai*. Samoa must take advantage of these customary features to develop a justice system suitable for the population.

As the Samoan society evolves and customary law changes along with time, the law reform process may develop towards a singular approach when the local

---

[24] Sack (1986), p. 14.

structures require, but only when society is ready to accommodate[25] an approach different from that proposed in this book. However, for now, both legal systems must be respected, acknowledged and filtered into state policies and laws.

7.4.4 Emerging Trends

7.4.4.1 A Winning Model?

In Chap. 5 it was suggested that combining both *matais* and legal expertise in a body responsible for law reform might be an ideal approach to take account of both legal systems. The newly established Customary Land Advisory Commission also discussed in Chap. 5 is an example of Samoa's recent attempt at creating such a body.[26] The Commission will be constituted by *matai* and staff (likely to be lawyers) to discharge the legal functions of the Commission. Time will tell how this new Commission will fare. However, from Samoa's experiences with the work of COIs (that it requires legal expertise) and the work of the SLRC (that it requires customary expertise) as discussed in Chap. 5, this may well be an ideal formula.

7.4.4.2 Incorporation by Reference

An overall analysis of Samoa's 277 Acts of Parliament to 2016[27] highlights two factors. The first feature identified is that recognition is mainly through 'incorporation by reference' (discussed in Chap. 2) rather that specifying the actual customs. Second and as indicated in Chap. 5, there is an increasing number of Acts that expressly require the application[28] and protection[29] of custom and customary practices.[30]

---

[25]Society changes were envisaged by the Court of Appeal in *Olomalu v The Attorney-General* (1980–1993) WSLR 256. In upholding *matai* suffrage on the basis that Samoa is based on the traditional *matai* system, the court stated that Samoa will accept modern concepts of democracy when it is ready to. Eight years later in 1990, Samoa replaced *matai* suffrage with universal suffrage. Change is inevitable, when change takes place must be largely influenced by society. Similar principles apply to a law reform process that is suitable for Samoa. Its features will change along with time, with gradual changes to meet the demands of society.

[26]*Customary Land Advisory Commission 2013* (Samoa).

[27]Pacific Islands Legal Information Institute (PacLII) official website.

[28]*Young Offenders Act 2007* (Samoa); *Community Justice Act 2008* (Samoa); *Samoa Law Reform Commission Act 2008* (Samoa); *Electoral Amendment Act 2005 (No. 3)* (Samoa); *Electoral Amendment Act 2009 No. 21* (Samoa).

[29]*Water Resources Management Act 2008* (Samoa).

[30]For example, the *Lawyers and Legal Practice Act 2014* (Samoa); the *Samoan Language Commission Act 2014* (Samoa); the *Customary Land Advisory Commission Act 2013* (Samoa); *Prisons and Corrections Act 2013* (Samoa).

The above analysis signifies a new trend in law making in Samoa. There is a consciousness of customs and a boldness to test the feasibility of customs in legislation that was absent before the 2000s. Employing the 'incorporation by reference' approach is an application of caution and deference to the evolving nature of customs. The lack of provisions on specific rules of customs allows the relevant authorities to apply both state written provisions and unwritten customs to meet the purposes of the Acts. In essence, the lack of specificity permits situations where legal pluralism is best applied, where the two legal systems are relied upon and applied as the circumstances of the affected parties permit. From the empirical data, there is assurance from the government of the day that the recognition of customs in laws is a conscious party objective that will be continuously pursued.[31] This emerging trend of law making is positive for the advancement of laws that are about and for Samoans.

7.4.4.3 State Initiatives that Accommodate Pluralism

The national and sector plans discussed in Chap. 6 indicate substantial support from the current government for the application and recognition of customs in government policies. This is indicated by the development of strategies to integrate or harmonise customary and community-based justice in Samoa with the formal justice system.[32] The country's national plans discussed in Chap. 6 prioritise objectives that strengthen community economic development and good governance in villages and local communities. The continuation of such initiatives facilitates a positive application of legal pluralism in Samoa. In the process of investigating, gathering and analysing the material for this book, six opportunities for future research and a suggested focus on future legal training were identified. These are discussed briefly in Sect. 7.5 below.

7.5 Future Research

7.5.1 *Constitutional Review*

Evidence suggests that Samoa is serious about giving recognition to customary laws in Parliament laws; perhaps it is time for a full review of the Constitution of Samoa. This review must have well developed objectives and proper defined goals. Meaningful and extensively conducted research must inform this review. Given that indigenous Samoans control Samoa's developments and is a dominant race running

---

[31] Interview with SOH Respondent 2 (Samoa, 8 March 2011).
[32] For example, as indicated in the first Samoa Law and Justice Sector Plan (2008) Office of the Attorney-General (Samoa) (2008).

the affairs of its own country, this is in the best interest of both the leaders and the general population of Samoa. A Constitution that caters for the needs of all times must be the goal. In these modern times, Samoa's Constitution and people have matured to the stage where, Parliament must demand that the customary values and principles are considered in all steps of law making.

7.5.2 Local Jurisprudence

It is suggested that research be undertaken on the feasibility of a local jurisprudence based on the customary laws of Samoa. This research must be developed through a systematic approach backed by doctrine and philosophy.[33] Further it may be a combination of classical and contemporary ideas whatever their sources or origins.[34] Several studies have identified various challenges to developing a regional or a local jurisprudence in the Pacific Islands.[35] This is therefore not a new proposal, but one that is crucial for the development of plural societies of the Pacific.

7.5.3 Pacific Island Specific Research

The findings and conclusions of this book may be transferrable to other Pacific Islands with similar historical backgrounds and customary characteristics. However, individual Pacific Island research is encouraged to find challenges and responses specific to each Pacific Island.[36] The diversity in traditions and cultures, populations, the variety of languages, international influences, economical basis and political aspirations makes individual studies more plausible.[37] It is suggested that these individual studies be treated as ground work to the development of a regional law reform commission, as recommended by the literature in Chap. 2.

7.5.4 Samoa's Constitutional Compliant Village Rules

Further research might explore the success of Samoa's constitutionally compliant village rules discussed in Chap. 6. There have been studies on the village courts of

---

[33] Ntumy (1995), p. 17.
[34] Narokobi, above n 13.
[35] Weisbrot (1988), p. 9.
[36] Pacific Islands are best studied individually according to McLachlan (1988), p. 336.
[37] Powles, above n 2, 419.

Papua New Guinea,[38] the island courts of Vanuatu[39] and local courts of the Solomon Islands.[40] No similar studies have been undertaken on a Samoan village council's dispute resolution mechanisms and decision making in Samoa. The significant differences between Papua New Guinea's village courts,[41] Vanuatu's island courts,[42] Solomon Islands' local courts[43] and the village councils of Samoa is that those three are courts operate as formal structures, with procedures and jurisdiction (civil and criminal) established by legislation. The *Village Fono Act 1990* (Samoa) does not bind the village councils to similar legislative requirements. Samoan villages develop their own rules setting out governance and dispute resolution mechanisms; as such, these rules have a better chance of success as they are depicted by the villages and command the respect of its subjects. Whether this will be realised may be the basis of future research, as Samoa continues to explore and encourage law making frameworks that are initiated by the village within the scope of the Constitution. This research may extend to whether village rules (or bylaws) may possibly be the strongest ally in the development of pluralist frameworks that are not only pluralist in nature but are also constitutionally compliant.

7.5.5 Follow up Research on Legal Pluralism and Law Reform in Samoa

There must be ongoing systematic and periodic research on law reform in the Pacific Islands. Future legal pluralism research may target one or all of the following areas. For Samoa, the first is to assess progress in legal pluralism and law reform against the findings, conclusions and recommendations in this book, inclusive of the success or the main obstacles in application. This may extend to examining whether institutional law reform (the SLRC) does facilitate development and in what form. Secondly, future research may explore whether Samoa has advanced to the post modernism level of legal pluralism, which involves supra state and intrastate interaction as described in Chap. 2 (literature), and if so, how this impacts on law reform in a plural environment. Post-modern pluralism does not currently apply to Samoa and is outside of the scope of this book. Thirdly, religion plays a significant role in social order and village governance. Religion is outside the focus of this book to allow for a manageable research topic. However, future research may include religious structures as the third influential system alongside the customary

---

[38]Zorn (1990), 2(2).
[39]Jowitt (1999), 3(3).
[40]Evans et al. (2011), p. 13.
[41]*Village Courts Act 1989* (Papua New Guinea).
[42]*Island Courts Act* (Vanuatu) ch 167.
[43]*Local Courts Act* (Solomon Islands) ch 19.

7.5.6 Pacific Research Methodologies

There are recent developments in the search for Pacific specific research methodologies in New Zealand and elsewhere. As indicated in Chap. 3, the Pacific research methods are informed by a relational ontology, epistemology and axiology. This book draws from and builds upon the *Talanoa* interview method. More research needs to be undertaken towards the advancement of Pacific specific research methodologies. More specifically, future research is suggested on how Pacific specific research methods can be effectively employed in legal research on the Pacific Islands, in particular where the research impacts on the customs and usages of the Pacific peoples.

7.5.7 Professional Training that Addresses Customs

Finally, diverting from suggestions for research to future training, this book suggests that all future legal professional training should address customary laws, and for legal trainers to identify first where customary laws are placed in the context of that Pacific training. No doubt the professional legal training made available to the Pacific Islands by partner organisations and affiliations are valuable to the legal systems of the Pacific Islands. However, it is time for Pacific Islanders to be more committed to, on their own initiative and in joint forces with overseas trainers, create training environments that target issues at the core of Pacific Islands' struggles. Such issues include developing suitable systems that accommodate both the customary legal systems and the state legal system in each Pacific Island. Identifying the challenges and finding possible responses to the central issues must be pursued in all fields of the legal profession. Legal training with a focus on Pacific local contexts as discussed in Chap. 2 is strongly advocated here. The study of customary laws as core courses in Pacific regional universities,[44] in New Zealand universities and elsewhere is encouraged.

---

[44]For example the customary law courses being taught at the University of Papua New Guinea and the University of the South Pacific Law School, Emalus Campus, see University of Papua New Guinea, 'Law School Courses – Faculty – Academic Staff' http://www.pngbuai.com/300socialsciences/340-law-schools/upng-law-school-courses-0412a.html.

Further research to contextualise courses, primarily land law and family law to take account of the local realities further is necessary. These are the two areas which have significant impact on the Pacific realities. For example, in Samoa, 'family' is the primary institution, and genealogies connect families and the village chiefly systems to customary land. There are linkages between families, between villages and districts, and this makes the family and lands the core essentials to defining the identity of an individual. It is hoped this will be a reality in the near future. Support is vital for the update of and the continued availability of research databases such as the Pacific Islands Legal Information Institute (PacLII). Professional legal training with a pluralist focus is essential to developing justice systems that are more relevant to the Pacific Islands. This way, no matter the varying strengths of currents, the Pacific Islands would still be able to navigate the double hulled *'alia* forward, and beyond.

References

Aleck J (1995) Beyond recognition: contemporary jurisprudence in the Pacific Islands and the common law tradition. Queensl Univ Technol Law J 7:137, 143
Australian Law Reform Commission (1986) Recognition of aboriginal customary laws. ALRC Rep 31:122
Evans D, Goddard M, Paterson D (2011) The hybrid courts of Melanesia, comparative analysis of village courts of Papua New Guinea, island courts of Vanuatu and local courts of Solomon Islands. Justice and Development Working Papers, World Bank's Justice Reform Practice Group 13
Jowitt A (1999) Island courts in Vanuatu. J S Pac Law, Working Paper 3(3)
McLachlan C (1988) State recognition of customary law in the South Pacific. PhD Thesis, University of London, p 336
Ministry of the Prime Minister and Cabinet (Samoa) (2011) Cabinet Handbook, pp 33–34
Narokobi B (1989) The black islands, Melanesia – Melanesia Jurisprudence. In: Crocombe R, May J, Roache P (eds) Lo bilong yumi yet - law and custom in Vanuatu. Melanesian Institute for Pastoral Socio-Economic Service and the University of the South Pacific, p 15
New Zealand Law Commission (2006) Converging currents: custom and human rights in the Pacific. Study Paper 17:242
Ntumy MA (1995) The dream of a Melanesian jurisprudence. In: Aleck J, Rannells J (eds) Custom at the crossroads. University of Papua New Guinea, p 17
Office of the Attorney-General (Samoa) (2014) Legislative Drafting Handbook, p 13
Partington M (2005) Law reform in Pacific Island states. In: Opeskin B, Weisbrot D (eds) The promise of law reform. Confederation Press, p 136
Paterson D, Tom'tavala Y, Jowitt A (2008) Legal traditions and systems in the Pacific: an overview of challenges and opportunities for legislative reform. Paper for the Legislative Reform and the Convention on the Rights of the Child (CRC) in the Pacific: Sub-Regional Meeting 25–28 August Vanuatu
Powles G (2005) Law reform in Pacific Island states. In: Opeskin B, Weisbrot D (eds) The promise of law reform. Confederation Press, p 420
Sack PG (1986) Legal pluralism: introductory comments. In: Sack P, Minchin E (eds) Legal pluralism, Proceedings of the Canberra Law Workshop VII. Pink Panther, ANU Canberra, p 14
Samoa Law and Justice Sector, Office of the Attorney-General (Samoa) (2008) Samoa Law and Justice Sector Plan 2008–2012

Shields M (1991) Republic of Vanuatu parliamentary handbook. UK Department for International Development
Supreme Court of Queensland (2005) Equal treatment benchbook. Supreme Court of Queensland Library, Brisbane
Weisbrot D (1988) Papua New Guinea's indigenous jurisprudence and the legacy of colonialism. Univ Hawaii Law Rev 10:2
Zorn JG (1990) Customary law in the Papua New Guinea village courts. Contemp Pac 2(2)

Legislation

Community Justice Act 2008 (Samoa)
Customary Land Advisory Commission Act 2013 (Samoa)
Electoral Act 1963 (Samoa)
Electoral Amendment Act 2005 No.3 (Samoa)
Electoral Amendment Act 2009 No.21 (Samoa)
Island Courts Act (Vanuatu) ch 167
Lawyers and Legal Practice Act 2014 (Samoa)
Local Courts Act (Solomon Islands) ch 19
Prisons and Corrections Act 2013 (Samoa)
Samoan Language Commission Act 2014 (Samoa)
Samoa Law Reform Commission Act 2008 (Samoa)
Standing Orders of Parliament 2006 (Samoa) O 115
Village Courts Act 1989 (Papua New Guinea)
Water Resources Management Act 2008 (Samoa)
Young Offenders Act 2007 (Samoa)

Case Law

Olomalu v The Attorney-General (1980–1993) WSLR 256

Online Databases

Office of the Clerk of the House of Representatives (New Zealand) (2011) Effective House Membership, A Guide for Members of Parliament 15, 16 http://www.parliament.nz
Pacific Islands Legal Information Institute (PacLII), Consolidated Acts of Samoa 2015 (1 September (2016) http://www.paclii.org/ws/legis/consol_act/
Pacific Judicial Development Programme (2011) Kiribati Code of Judicial Conduct cl 4.2. http://www.paclii.org/pjdp/
Samoa Law Reform Commission official website (2016) The Law Reform Process. http://www.samoalawreform.gov.ws/?page_id=165
University of Papua New Guinea, 'Law School Courses – Faculty – Academic Staff' http://www.pngbuai.com/300socialsciences/340-law-schools/upng-law-school-courses-0412a.html

Appendices

Appendix A: List of Interview Participants

Interview categories	Participant	Interview date
Village Council 1 (Focus Group)	VC1 Focus Group (MT, FK, TTF, LS, LV)	1 March 2011
Village Council 2 (VC2 x 5 *matai*)	VC2 Participant 1	15 March 2011
	VC2 Participant 2	10 March 2011
	VC2 Participant 3	7 March 2011
	VC2 Participant 4	10 March 2011
	VC2 Participant 5	15 March 2011
Village Mayors *(Sui o le Nuu)* (VM x 9)	VM Participant 1	11 March 2011
	VM Participant 2	9 March 2011
	VM Participant 3	8 March 2011
	VM Participant 4	16 March 2011
	VM Participant 5	16 March 2011
	VM Participant 6	9 March 2011
	VM Participant 7	10 March 2011
	VM Participant 8	16 March 2011
	VM Participant 9	7 March 2011
Government Women Representatives *(Sui o le Malo)* (GWR x 2)	GWR Participant 1	21 March 2011
	GWR Participant 2	21 march 2011

(continued)

Interview categories	Participant	Interview date
Significant Office Holders (SOH x 9)	SOH Participant 1	8 April 2011
	SOH Participant 2	8 March 2011
	SOH Participant 3	4 April 2011
	SOH Participant 4	11 July 2011
	SOH Participant 5	20 July 2011
	SOH Participant 6	12 April 2011
	SOH Participant 7	22 March 2011
	SOH Participant 8	Email of 7 May 2012
	SOH Participant 9	21 March 2011
Members of Parliament (MOP x 6)	MOP Participant 1	22 December 2010
	MOP Participant 2	4 January 2011
	MOP Participant 3	11 January 2011
	MOP Participant 4	7 January 2011
	MOP Participant 5	11 January 2011
	MOP Participant 6	24 December 2010
Members of the Judiciary (MOJ x 7)	MOJ Participant 1	28 March 2011
	MOJ Participant 2	13 July 2011
	MOJ Participant 3	7 March 2011
	MOJ Participant 4	5 April 2011
	MOJ Participant 5	1 April 2011
	MOJ Participant 6	4 April 2011
	MOJ Participant 7	4 April 2011
Government Chief Executives (GCE x 7)	GCE Participant 1	19 January 2011
	GCE Participant 2	11 March 2011
	GCE Participant 3	12 April 2011
	GCE Participant 4	18 January 2011
	GCE Participant 5	18 January 2011
	GCE Participant 6	22 December 2010
	GCE Participant 7	Emails of 15 April 2011
Legal Profession (LP x 6)	LP Participant 1	15 March 2011
	PL Participant 2	21 February 2011
	LP Participant 3	4 March 2011
	LP Participant 4	2 March 2011
	LP Participant 5	14 March 2011
	LP Participant 6	Email of 21 June 2011

Appendix B: Commissions of Inquiry and Legislative Reforms

	COI into the Electoral Act (2001)	COI into the Electoral Act (2006)	COI into Matters relating to the Alii and Faipule and the Formal Courts (2007)	COI into Freedom of Religion (2010)	COI into Matai (Chiefly) Titles 2010
No. of recommendations	22	25	15	6	4
No. of recommendations for legislative changes	17	20	12	2	1
No. or legislative changes made	13	16	4	Both under legislative review	1
No. of legislative changes not made	4	4	8	3	0
Recommendations not related to legislative change	5	5 (Constitution)	3	1	3

Reports:
1. Samoa, Commission of Inquiry into the Electoral Act, *Report* (2001).
2. Samoa, Commission of Inquiry into the Electoral Act, *Report* (2006).
3. Samoa, Commission of Inquiry into Matters Relating to the Divergence Between the Decision Making Authority of the *Alii and Faipule* and the Formal Courts, *Report* (2007).
4. Samoa, Commission of Inquiry into *Matai* Titles, *Report* (2010).
5. Samoa, Commission of Inquiry into the Freedom of Religion, *Report* (2010).

Appendix C: Law Reform Commissions Statutory Functions

Section 1
Australia, NZ, Canada: Law Reform Commission Legislation – Functions

Australia, NZ, LRC Statutory Functions	NZ LC Act 1985 (s5)	Canada LC Act 1996 (s3)	Australia LRC Act 1996 (s21)	Victoria LRC Act 2000 (s5)	Qld LRC Act 1968 (s10)	NSW LRC Act 1967 (s10)
Examine and review for systematic development and consistency in reforms	✓	✓	✓	✓	✓	✓
Develop new approaches to reforms & new concepts in the development of law	✓	✓	✓	✓	✓	✓
Repeal obsolete laws, defects & anomalies		✓	✓		✓	✓
Simplify law expression & content	✓		✓		✓	
Advise on the reviews by government departments	✓				✓	
Develop productive networks	✓	✓				
Recommendations to take account of indigenous and multicultural society	✓					
Power to sponsor, undertake, initiate research, publish & disseminate studies, support seminars & conferences	✓			✓		
Consolidate, codify, revise laws						✓
Simplify, modernise to bring it into accord with current conditions						✓

Section 2
Pacific Islands: Law Reform Commission Legislation – Functions

Pacific Is LRC functions	PNG LRC Act 1975, s9	Fiji LRC Act Cap 26 s5	Vanuatu LC Act Cap 115, s7	Sol Is LRC Act 1994, s5	Tonga LC Act 2007, s29	Cook Is Act 2007, s5	Samoa LRC Act 2008, s6
Examine, study and review for systematic and consistency in reforms	✓		✓	✓		✓	✓
Develop new approaches to reforms & new concepts in the development of law	✓	✓		✓	✓	✓	✓
Codify, revise, consolidate laws		✓		✓	✓		

(continued)

Section 2
Pacific Islands: Law Reform Commission Legislation – Functions

Function							
Reduce separate enactments, simplify law expressions & content	✓	✓		✓	✓	✓	
Repeal obsolete laws & eliminate anomalies	✓	✓	✓	✓	✓		
Simplify, improve and modernise the law		✓		✓	✓		
Recommend restatement, codification, amendment & reform of customary laws	✓			✓			
To take into account local customs; to reflect in the law the distinctive concepts of customs, and to reconcile those concepts;			✓				✓
Develop new approaches and concepts responsive to the changing needs of the small societies & individuals within the country	✓		✓	✓		✓	✓
Promote customs & traditions; enhance the social, cultural, economic and commercial development						✓	✓

Appendix D: Samoa Law Reform Commission: Law Reform Process[1]

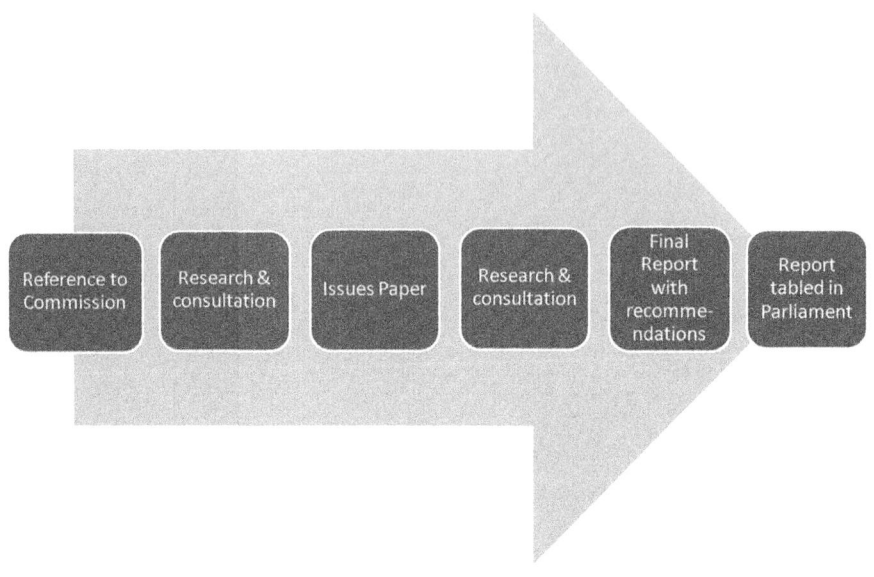

Appendix E: Respondents: Pacific Islands Legislative Drafters Survey

Pacific Island Representatives	Survey Pacific Legislative Drafter
Vanuatu	Survey PL Drafter 1
Kiribati	Survey PL Drafter 2
Solomon Islands	Survey PL Drafter 3
Federated States of Micronesia	Survey PL Drafter 4
Papua New Guinea	Survey PL Drafter 5
Nauru	Survey PL Drafter 6
Palau	Survey PL Drafter 7
Cook Islands	Survey PL Drafter 8
Niue	Survey PL Drafter 9
Republic of Marshall Islands	Survey PL Drafter 10
Samoa	Survey PL Drafter 11

---

[1] Samoa Law Reform Commission website, Samoa Law Reform Commission, *The Law Reform Process*, http://www.samoalawreform.gov.ws/?page_id=165.

Printed by Printforce, the Netherlands